T0124627

• 2ND EDITION •

SINGAPORE

A VERY SHORT HISTORY

FROM TEMASEK TO TOMORROW

ALVIN TAN

TALISMAN

First published in 2020
This second edition published in 2022

Talisman Publishing Pte Ltd
talisman@apdsing.com

www.talismanpublishing.com

ISBN 978-981-18-4090-6

Cover Design Stephy Chee, Wong Sze Wey
Studio Manager Janice Ng
Publisher Ian Pringle

"This is a general history of Singapore written in a light and breezy style with clear, crisp and short sentences. Alvin Tan offers intelligent, and often quirky, insights into well-known, but also lesser known, and sometimes hidden, parts of the Singapore past. The reader is captivated as a passing caravan of larger than life characters goes by as each page is turned. Tan offers easy to understand explanations of the Singapore past from whether Singapore was founded in 1299, 1390, or even 1819, right up to giving us insights into Singapore's contemporary 'poisonous shrimp' and 'porcupine' national defence policies."

— **Associate Professor Kevin Blackburn,** National Institute of Education, Nanyang Technological University

"This little book sparkles. It is concise and succinct, yet rich and analytical; pithy and clear, yet scholarly and intelligent. It is a masterly little history of Singapore that reads more like a mystery thriller than a serious chronicle of the past, which it is. We need more histories like this."

— **Professor Kevin YL Tan,** Historian & Legal Scholar, Former President of Singapore Heritage Society

"This book stands out among the books published on the Bicentennial of Raffles' arrival on this island for the verve and especially the passion it is written in. It tells a familiar story of Singapore in an engaging style. A compelling read."

— **Kwa Chong Guan,** Co-author of *Seven Hundred Years; A History of Singapore*

CONTENTS

Preface

Alvin Tan

When I was twelve, for reasons that remain unknown to me still, my mother bought me a copy of H.F. Pearson's *Singapore: A Popular History*. That was my initiation into a life-long interest into Singapore history as well as long-form historical writing. Pearson's concise and vivid prose left its imprint in me – a history book need not have long sentences, sound solemn and serious, and worst of all, be boring. So, when Kevin Tan, my old friend and mentor, passed to me a copy of *The Shortest History of Germany*, something in my mind clicked. This book was also concise and vivid; it even used diagrams to explain the key concepts and historical developments. Handing me the book in a flourish, Kevin said, 'You should write a book like this on Singapore.' It was an irresistible challenge — to write a very short history of Singapore covering 700 years, in 60,000 words or less, to cap off the Bicentennial year. This book is the result of that challenge.

In studying Singapore history, most readers (whatever their age), are often confronted with certain historical tropes that are supposedly self-explanatory but are not. And if they are explained, these explanations often fail to take into account the larger historical forces at play and their contexts. Singapore's 'strategic location' is a case in point. Beyond the obvious (such as its geographical location), what exactly does this really mean? Who were the people who considered Singapore 'strategic'? And why was Singapore 'strategic' at one stage of its history, but not another? Surely it was not just geography. Similarly, Singapore's growth, development and progress is assumed to be linear and even inevitable. But it was not. Lurking in the shadows of history's curtains were events that could easily put an end to everything that was happening but ultimately didn't. This book goes beyond these tropes to uncover the complexity and richness of Singapore's history.

Spanning a period of 700 years, this account places Singapore's history in the context of the region and the world. It opens with a look into Singapore's early modern history and its rise as a regional trading port that made itself useful and relevant to the demands of specific moments in history. This usefulness and relevance was re-established and further augmented by British, whose arrival in 1819 plugged Singapore into their global empire. Up till 1942, before the Japanese invasion upended everything, Singapore grew steadily in its multiple roles as the capital city of British Malaya, a staple port that served the imperial economy and a defence node responsible for the defence of British interests in the Far East. Subsequently, from 1945 to 1963, the frenzied contest over Singapore's political future was constantly underlined by one concern – how would Singapore survive without a hinterland? And it was this concern that led to Singapore's merger with the Federation of Malaya in 1963, an unhappy experience that ended with Singapore's independence on 9 August 1965. Post-1965, the island nation was gripped by the need to survive – to do so, it made the world its hinterland. Singapore engineered conditions that made it relevant and useful to the needs of the global economy. It is a story of how a country and its people became conditioned to be agile and nimble to seize whatever opportunities presented themselves, and ameliorated or neutralised threats to their survival. The price of Singapore's global role is hyper-vigilance. It has to be for there is nothing permanent or certain or inevitable about a small nation-state's success.

This Bicentennial year has seen the publication of many books, big and small, to commemorate the occasion. I hope this little book – possibly the shortest single-volume of Singapore's history since Pearson's (which was published in 1961) – will add to this corpus of work by providing a concise and easy-to-grasp account that complements and extends existing historical narratives. And while I have striven to be comprehensive, I don't pretend to be exhaustive. I hope the reader will enjoy this book as much as I enjoyed writing it.

FOREWORD

Kwok Kian-Woon

Singapore: A Very Short History is a little gem of a book, which I hope will play a role in the public understanding of Singapore history in the longer term. Alvin Tan had set himself a rather ambitious and audacious goal: to write "a concise and easy-to-grasp account that complements and extends existing historical narratives". This is a challenging task, requiring any author to possess both a masterly grasp of the history of Singapore and an engaging writing style. Readers can judge for themselves how far the author has succeeded in achieving his goal. For me, this book passes the acid test of a detective novel: one wants to read the entire book from cover to cover and, in reading a chapter, one is anticipating what comes next and wondering how the various pieces of the jig-saw puzzle would fall into place.

A satisfying novel is one in which readers are not led impassively to its conclusion; instead, they are constantly piqued by twists and turns, picking up clues, formulating their own questions, forming their own opinions on this or that character – it helps that the good guys and bad guys are complex characters – and speculating on plausible and probable outcomes. Readers immerse and invest themselves – they have a stake – in the unfolding story.

There is one crucial difference, though: historical writing can be enhanced by the skills of a good storyteller, but the story that is told is not fiction, not made up by the historian. A good historian (or scholar or scientist) must be like a conscientious detective, who does all the hard work in establishing and assembling all the relevant facts – including 'inconvenient' facts – from various sources scrupulously and honestly.

In reading *Singapore: A Very Short History*, my mind is drawn to another little book, one of the most important books on the discipline of history: Marc Bloch's *The Historian's Craft*, incompletely written by the French historian before he died in 1944 and published posthumously in 1949, followed by the English translation in 1953. Bloch wrote the book, based on notes and memory, under tragic circumstances in Vichy France: he was awaiting execution for his role as a leader of the anti-Nazi resistance. This is not the place to delve into the many precious lessons offered by Bloch. It may suffice for me to highlight his idea of the historian's "primary duty of the patient quest for truth".

Bloch's words were written many decades before what we now call the "post-truth era". If "post-truth politics" has become a reality today, then all the more there must never be anything like a "post-truth history". This entails learning from the craft of cross-examining multiple sources and posing significant humanistic questions as the basis for historical interpretation, without resorting to quick ideological judgement. Such labour cannot be undertaken – and its fruits shared – only within the highly specialised world of academia, but more widely as part of what has been called "public history", extending historical discourse into the public sphere.

The craftsmanship of the historian is amply evident in this book, as is the concern with reaching out to the reading public. Here I would like to note the "voice" of the author in his narration of the history of Singapore. Beyond his preface, the word "I" completely disappears, and the word "we" hardly appears as a reference to Singaporeans, as much as he himself is a Singaporean. In writing this book, Alvin Tan was conscious that the author should recede into the background and that the history – the past that still speaks – has to be in the foreground. Hence his voice is dispassionate, and this also encourages readers to suspend their own judgement so as to appreciate the complexities of each historical period. The historian does not "let the facts speak for themselves". In interpreting the circumstances faced – and choices made – by historical actors across time, he found it necessary to play the role of an "outsider", keeping a critical distance and yet having an empathy for the "insiders".

Such a balanced historical approach must surely be a potent antidote to the post-truth era, which also coincides with the age of digital transformation, and with it the constant overload of bits and bytes of information streaming incessantly into our electronic devices, shortening our attention span. This is why I dearly wish that this "very short history" will not prove to be overly long for some readers.

A "sense of history" allied with "the patient quest for truth" is even more important today than ever. If indeed Singaporeans had neglected this in our restless race into the future, and if state-led efforts in propagating a single national narrative are met with scepticism, if not cynicism, it is vital for us to cultivate a rich sense of "the history of the present" and "the present as history" as we enter an even more complex era of technological and social change, and not least under the shadow of climate change.

Historical literacy is just as important as digital literacy and climate literacy in our education and public life. And this book provides a most welcoming entry point.

Kwok Kian-Woon is Professor of Sociology at the Nanyang Technological University, Singapore, where he has served as a founding member of the School of Humanities and Social Sciences, and the first Head of Sociology, Senate Chair, and Associate Provost of Student Life. His research areas include the study of social memory, mental health, the Chinese overseas, and Asian modernity. He has been actively involved in civil society and the public sector in Singapore, especially in the arts and heritage.

CHAPTER ONE

Fate & Fleeting Fortunes

c. 13th Century – early 19th Century

And Our Story Begins

'What does the future have in store for Singapore?' With this question towards the end of his memoirs, Lee Kuan Yew contemplated Singapore's future. 'City-states do not have good survival records. ... Will Singapore the independent city-state disappear? The island of Singapore will not, but the sovereign nation it has become, able to make its way and play its role in the world, could vanish.' The answer lies in the history of Singapore's last seven hundred years. In these seven hundred years, kings and princes came and went, colonisers and occupiers planted their flags and left, settlements rose and sometimes faded into oblivion. But the island was always here, waiting for the moment when history would once again intervene and make it useful, relevant and important.

Singapore, a diamond-shaped island measuring 720 square kilometres today, sits at the southern tip of the Malay Peninsula, one degree north of the Equator. To the island's south is the Singapore Straits, a vital maritime channel that connects the Straits of Melaka, one of the busiest waterways in the world, with the South China Sea. It is endowed with a deep and sheltered harbour that can accommodate large ocean-going vessels. This is the sum of Singapore's geographical advantage. Whoever controlled Singapore would derive strategic value from it. It could be a stopover, a port of call, a marketplace, an exchange or a naval base. From these roles, it could project power in various guises – the power to safeguard and protect or the power to coerce and threaten. It is this power that makes these roles possible. But it all hinged on one thing – what was the need of the moment? Did anyone need Singapore?

Riding The Monsoons

For the trader in the Age of Sail, all that mattered was the wind. That propelled their ships. If there was no wind, no one was going anywhere. For traders in India, Southeast Asia and China, this wind referred to the monsoons. The monsoons, as their Arabic name *mausim* suggests, were seasonal and switched directions with such regularity that it was possible to time voyages to coincide with them. Every year, around May and June, traders would set off from ports in Arabia and India to ride the southwest monsoon across the Bay of Bengal to reach ports in the northern end of the Straits of Melaka, and then sail onwards to the Chinese ports of Guangzhou and Quanzhou. In November and December, the reverse took place as traders set off from Chinese ports to ride the northeast monsoon to destinations in Southeast Asia, India and beyond.

The regularity of the monsoons made travel within the 'single ocean' that spanned the Indian Ocean, the Straits of Melaka and the South China Sea a predictable enterprise. These voyages also gained one or two knots to their speed as ocean currents moved in tandem with the seasonal monsoon. To ride the monsoon was not entirely without risk for these rain-bearing winds could reach gale force during peak season. A stopover located in Southeast Asia, somewhere in the heart of this 'single ocean' would be great. While Singapore stood at the crossroads of Southeast Asia and this 'single ocean', so too did other ports. What made Singapore stand out?

Temasek: The Fleeting Fortunes Of A Sea Town

Sri Vijaya was Southeast Asia's undisputed maritime power from the 7th to the 14th century. Its principal ports at Palembang and Jambi, which flourished as entrepots, were well-served with commodities from its hinterland and its feeder ports. Its naval fleet, made up of *Orang Laut*, was on hand to 'persuade' traders to call at these ports. So long as Sri Vijaya's power held, so too did this state of affairs. The trader had neither choice nor incentive to call elsewhere. This pre-eminence started to fade from about the 11th century and in 1275 the inevitable happened – its capital Jambi was sacked, and Sri Vijaya became a vassal of Singasari of Java. Now utterly ruined, its networks broke up. A power and economic vacuum emerged in maritime Southeast Asia at a time when increased trade meant more economic opportunities. This triggered the establishment of a clutch of new port cities in the 13th and 14th centuries. These were not grand entrepots like Palembang or Jambi, and they specialised in niche products from their immediate hinterland. One of these was Temasek which emerged around 1299 –the first recorded settlement on the island of Singapore.

While the exact events and reasons behind its sudden emergence remain contested, Temasek's relevance and usefulness to the economic demands of its time is clear. It began as a collection centre for products from its hinterland in South Johor and the seas around it. Chinese traders were drawn by Temasek's ready supply of hornbill casques, lakawood, sea cucumbers and turtle shells. Hornbill casques, a substitute for ivory, were particularly prized by the Chinese. The Chinese also wanted good quality lakawood to use as incense wood – Temasek was one of two ports in the Melaka Straits that supplied this. Temasek thus acted as an export gateway to the Chinese market.

Whatever came into Temasek was bought and sold or exported to other parts of the region and beyond to markets in China or the Indian Ocean littoral. Chinese traders brought highly prized and sought-after goods like fine ceramics from the Jingdezhen kilns. These were then re-exported to their regional markets. The same Chinese traders also found Temasek's location useful and accessible. They could get what they wanted in Temasek. And they could buy products from other places here without the extra costs or risks that a voyage across the Indian Ocean meant. Plugged into the international maritime trade and also to its regional markets and sources for its goods, Temasek soon became a regional port of note. This was the first iteration of the role that the island would reprise over the centuries.

But the settlement only lasted about seventy years or a century at most. Just as external forces beyond its control triggered Temasek's rapid rise, these forces also triggered its decline. Climate change, in the form of the Little Ice Age, brought drought and famine to Yuan China. In 1368, as the Mongols of Yuan China withdrew to the steppes, the Ming Dynasty took its place. In a major policy reversal, the Ming Court decreed that all trade would be carried out under its centralised direction. It would decide who China could trade with and where it traded. Private trade carried out by individuals was banned. In one stroke, Singapura's livelihood was obliterated. It no longer had access to goods the region wanted, and it had no market for the goods its former buyers wanted. Singapura's relevance and usefulness as a port city and a regional gateway connecting regional markets with the Chinese market waned as quickly as it emerged.

Temasek was further crippled by the rise of Melaka in the early 15th century. In the 1420s, the new upstart port-city assiduously sought the patronage of the Ming Court as an overlord to fend off Siamese aggression. In return, the Ming Court recognised Melaka as a vassal. With this, Melaka became the Ming Court's port of choice for its trade with the region and beyond. This was fatal to Temasek as the raison d'etre for its entire existence was thoroughly undercut. Over time, as trade dwindled, so too did Temasek's population and economic activity. They decamped to Melaka, which had displaced Temasek in its role as a regional trading port.

As a prosperous trading port located on a small island, Temasek attracted the predatory attentions of the regional powers and was vulnerable to attacks. In 1365, the Majapahit invaded. By the 15th century, the island became a vassal of Sukhothai. It had to surrender its revenue to its Siamese overlord. Even this did not last as Temasek's revenue dwindled and it was eventually ceded to Melaka. The island's autonomous existence ended with this, and it became part of a larger other politically. Only in 1965 did it become an independent nation-state in its own right.

Slipping Into Obscurity: Singapore (1400s – Late 1700s)

From 1400 onwards, Temasek thus survived in a much-diminished state as an outpost of the Melaka Sultanate. If geography is destiny, then why did the island, with its superb strategic location, slip into obscurity for some two hundred years prior to its re-discovery by Stamford Raffles?

Even after the Melaka Sultanate displaced it as a regional emporium, the Melakan sultans held on to the island for as long as it could since the Sultans traced their lineage and legitimacy back to it. It became a fief of Seri Bija Diraja, an official who served as the *laksamana*, the commander of its naval and military forces. Given its location, it can be surmised that the island served as the Sultanate's naval outpost. Even though the island no longer played a major role in regional trade, it was retained for its symbolic importance and strategic location.

Even after the Portuguese conquest of Melaka in 1511, the settlement persisted. The titular successor to Melaka, the Johor Sultanate, maintained a *shahbandar*, who performed the roles of a consul and a harbour master in Singapore. In this capacity, he oversaw all trade in the Kallang River estuary and managed relations with foreigners.

However, from 1500 to 1650, Singapore was razed to the ground more than once. The first blow has been attributed to the Portuguese sometime in the early 16th century in its attempt to extinguish any attempt at re-establishing the Melaka Sultanate. The second blow has been attributed to the Acehnese, a rising regional power in the early 17th century. With each blow however, rebuilding always followed. In their reports, contemporary observers such as Saint Francis Xavier and Jacques de Courtre mentioned the presence of a town and port in Singapore. And though Singapore never regained its pre-Melakan glory, its relevance and usefulness endured to some degree.

So, why did the Portuguese and the Dutch not establish themselves at Singapore? Both powers were certainly aware of Singapore's superior location and strategic potential. Yet, they chose to focus on their settlements in Melaka and in Java respectively. Whatever plans the Portuguese and Dutch had, and no matter how comprehensive and detailed these were, they were never translated into reality. There were simply better alternatives elsewhere that suited their strategic needs.

Jacques de Coutre, who was based in Melaka and Manila from 1593 to 1603, submitted one such plan to the Iberian crown around 1625. To contain the Dutch threat, de Coutre proposed building a fort on the western end of what is today Sentosa. Interestingly, the fort was to be located at the site where the British later built Fort Siloso in 1874. From here the Portuguese could command and control the Straits of Singapore. He also proposed other fortifications in eastern Singapore and on Pulau Tekong Besar and even urged the king to claim sovereignty over the island. These plans never materialised.

In 1609, the Dutch proposed to build a fort and a garrison in Johor but were rebuffed by their allies, the Johor Sultanate. But things changed, with the rise of Aceh. In 1614, the Johor Sultanate had a change of mind – a fort was needed after all. This triggered a flurry of activity. Suitable islands in the Straits of Singapore were identified, reconnoitred and surveyed. A report was filed. It recommended that a fort be built on Karimun and a colony be set up in Johor. However, these elaborate plans never materialised as the Dutch lacked the financial resources to fund the venture. In any case, they shifted their attention to developing Batavia in Java.

What ultimately doomed Singapore to obscurity was the gradual decline in the strategic value and importance of the Straits of Melaka to the Dutch from the 17th century. They focused on developing Batavia and diverted regional shipping routes away from the Straits of Melaka and through the Sunda Straits. Melaka, finally conquered by the Dutch in 1641, was left disused. All that was left in Singapore was a village of *Orang Laut* and Malays. Even the Sultan of Johor regarded the island lightly. In 1703, the Sultan offered Singapore as a gift to an English trader, one Alexander Hamilton, who demurred. Hamilton had no use for the island at all.

Between History & Myth

In 1969, on the 150th anniversary of the founding of Singapore, it was declared that 'modern Singapore began in 1819'. With this emphatic pronouncement, Singapore's past was divided into two. *History* began after 1819. All that happened before that was at best 'of antiquarian interest only' or otherwise irrelevant in helping to understand the present. Fifty years later, on the 200th anniversary of Singapore's founding, this pronouncement no longer holds. Singapore's pre-1819 history now plays an important role in driving the national narrative that trumpets Singapore as a global city and an island city-state. This is made possible by a growing corpus of supporting evidence comprising colonial accounts, historical texts and archaeological findings. Though gaps exist, a coherent if not compelling story about early modern Singapore can be woven from it.

The Portuguese accounts, written in the 16th century, just after their conquest of Melaka, attribute the founding of Temasek in 1390 or 1391 to Parameswara, a renegade prince from Palembang. Parameswara had, eight days after arriving on the island, murdered the reigning raja and usurped the throne. Six years later, he fled the island after a Siamese expedition was sent to exact revenge for his heinous act. Shortly after this, he founded the port of Melaka – this was the opening act of the Melakan Sultanate. The intention behind these accounts was to record the memories of Melaka's founding and development, from the viewpoint of its inhabitants, soon after the city capitulated to the Portuguese in 1511.

Part history and part legend, the *Sejarah Melayu* (The Malay Annals), however, present an alternative interpretation by attributing the founding of Singapura to Sri Tri Buana (or Sang Nila Utama), a Sri Vijayan prince from Palembang. Having landed at Temasek, he spotted something that caught his breath. 'It had a red body and a black head; its breast was white; it was strong and active in build'. Sri Tri Buana had spotted a lion and the rest as we know it, is history. Singapura, the Lion City, was founded. After Sri Tri Buana, four kings ruled Singapura. During the reign of the last king, Iskandar Shah, tragedy struck. Iskandar Shah accused one of his concubines of adultery and ordered her to be stripped naked in public. Seething with rage and looking for vengeance, her father, who was one of Iskandar's courtiers, betrayed the kingdom and literally opened its gates to Majapahit invaders. Iskandar Shah fled north for his life, first to Muar, and then onward to Melaka, where he founded a port city in 1400. The *Sejarah Melayu* therefore bridges the historical time and space between Sri Vijaya and the Melaka Sultanate. In this sense, the *Sejarah* Melayu, couched in metaphor and symbolism, is a mythologised past and not a literal historical text.

Can myth co-exist with historical facts? Broadly speaking, the *Sejarah Melayu* and the Portuguese sources agree on the following: Singapura was founded by a prince from Palembang; it flourished as a port city and it slipped into decline towards the end of the 14th century. Both attribute the founding of Singapura to one man, whether he is represented as Sri Tri Buana (or Sang Nila Utama) or Parameswara. Similarly, one man, be it Iskandar Shah (a descendant of Sri Tri Buana) or Parameswara, was responsible for the founding of Melaka. Both sources therefore agree on one critical issue – Singapura was founded in response to the trade that was flourishing across the region in the 14th century.

Not all sources however were concerned with the founding myth. The *Daoyi Zhilue*, published in 1349, provides useful information about the Malay world, its settlements and the goods it traded in. Written by a Chinese trader, Wang Da Yuan, it paints a useful and informative picture about Singapore. Wang makes two entries about Singapore. In the first, he records his observation of *Lung-Ya-Men* or Dragon-teeth Straits, which corresponds with Tanjong Berlayer, the western approach to today's Keppel Harbour. In the second, he describes a settlement at *Pan-Tsu* which is Fort Canning Hill. He also reports on the goods imported and exported from these two places. Other than the *Daoyi Zhilue*, the official history of the Yuan Dynasty also makes reference to Singapore – in 1318, a mission was despatched to three places in the region in search of tamed elephants and Singapore was one of them. In this way, the Chinese records corroborate the Portuguese accounts and the *Sejarah Melayu* about Temasek's existence as a regional trading port.

Furthermore, archaeological excavations in Singapore since 1984 have yielded extensive artefacts to establish that by 1330, an autonomous port city known as Temasek did exist. This city engaged in regional trade and its political, social and economic structures and hierarchies were well developed. Not only do these findings validate Portuguese and Chinese sources, they also give the *Sejarah Melayu* a veneer of legitimacy as a mythologised historical source.

Never Just A Sleepy Fishing Village

Five hundred years before the British planted the Union Jack here in Singapore, its history began, triggered by the convergence of geography and larger historical forces. Geography is immutable but what can and did change in the centuries before 1819 were the priorities and interests of others in relation to Singapore. And at various points during this period, Singapore simply did not fit their priorities and interests because Singapore was neither useful nor relevant to them. Singapore faded and became a backwater, but it persisted, it endured, either because it was symbolically important, as it was to the Melaka and Johor sultans, or because it had the potential to be useful and relevant, as it was to the Portuguese and the Dutch. To pronounce that modern Singapore history began in 1819 is to dismiss and negate all that happened before 1819 as irrelevant, even useless. As the record shows, sleepy and obscure as Singapore apparently was, it was never quite forgotten. In the late 18th century, global historical forces were once again on the move and gathering momentum. It was a matter of time before the island would once again return to the spotlight of those who found it interesting, and at the same time, needed what it offered.

CHAPTER TWO

Decisive Moments

1819–1826

A Story Of Two Addictions: Tea & Opium

In 1757, East India Company (EIC) forces under the command of Robert Clive defeated the Nawab of Bengal and his French allies in India at the Battle of Plassey. With this victory, the EIC began its expansion into India and this brought rich pickings. From 1765, the EIC acquired the rights to collect revenue in Bengal. This became an important source of capital for investment in the cultivation, delivery and distribution of a vital cash crop – opium. A narcotic, opium was in great demand in the growing and increasingly addicted market in China from the 1770s. Selling opium to China reduced the outflow of silver from the EIC's coffers. It also provided the EIC with the means to pay for its highly valuable and profitable export from China – tea. With the collapse of the Dutch East India Company (VOC) in 1792, the EIC completely dominated the India-China trade in the exchange of a highly addictive narcotic paste for a mildly stimulating drink. In other words, they traded opium for tea. In 1796, the Qing government banned the import of opium. But nothing deterred the EIC – through the country traders, opium continued to be trafficked, smuggled and sold to China. And tea continued to be shipped out from China and the EIC continued to profit from this lucrative trade. Whether it was opium or tea, this trade was all channelled through the Straits of Melaka.

All trade sailing through the Straits of Melaka had to navigate through the Straits of Singapore. This dictate of maritime geography became complicated from 1784. Having ousted the Bugis that year, the Dutch reduced Johor-Riau to a vassal state. They now had a chokehold over this vital shipping artery. The British were worried. There was no port anywhere in that vicinity to resupply and service British ships, and this at a time when British trade in the Malay Archipelago was growing as a result of Britain's victory in the 4th Anglo-Dutch War. Much of this trade was in the hands of 'country traders', essentially private traders operating independently of the EIC, who could now sail freely in these seas. Many of these traders called at Malay ports that were not under Dutch control. From these ports, they acquired much of the pepper and tin that supplemented the EIC's opium trade with China. This was no small-scale barter trade. From 1784 to 1819, the EIC enjoyed a positive trade balance with China only because of the contribution of these country traders. This trade also signalled a shift in trading patterns – neither the VOC (up till its demise) or the EIC were the dominant players in this arena any longer. A trading network that connected the east coast of India with ports along the Straits of Melaka had emerged. It was clear to the British that a port of call was urgently needed.

In response to the need of the moment, Penang (or Prince of Wales Island as it was then known) was secured as a British base in 1786. Penang failed as it was too far to the north of the Straits of Melaka to exert any influence on activity at the Straits' southern end. A more suitably placed location was needed. In British eyes, Riau was an ideal place for a base. Singapore was not on their short list.

The outbreak of the Napoleonic Wars in Europe put all these concerns on hold. In 1795, the British occupied Melaka as trustees for the Dutch under the terms of the Kew Letters. In 1811, Java came under British administration. Trade grew substantially during this period as the British had acquired a de facto empire in the region. By 1814, as the war drew to a close, this state of affairs ceased to exist. On 13 August 1814, the British and the Dutch concluded the London Convention. Driven by the need to keep the Dutch as a buffer and deterrent against the French, the British government agreed to return all Dutch possessions in the region. They assumed that in its weakened state and with the EIC dominating the lucrative India-China trade, the Dutch posed no economic threat at all. An empire in the East was not needed, much less a port of call. This was a terrible mistake as the British effectively ceded control of the region to the Dutch.

The Dutch showed that they were neither economically enervated nor suffering from a paucity of political ambition in the region. They moved quickly, first recovering Palembang and Banca in December 1816. The Moluccas were next in 1817. They signed treaties with rulers in Banjermassin, Sambas and Pontianak that allowing them to establish monopolies and later getting their traditional rulers to surrender their sovereignty. By 1818, they had cornered Borneo. The entire Malay Archipelago and its two approaches, the Straits of Melaka and the Sunda Straits, were under their control once more.

Initially, some British officials refused to surrender their posts. Thomas Stamford Raffles himself petulantly held onto Lampang and, in May 1818, even raised the Union Jack there to prove a point. Similarly, he refused to give up Padang. Though symbolic, these actions did little to stem the systematic and deliberate Dutch takeover of the region.

More practically, actions were taken to protect British trade. John Bannerman, the Lieutenant-Governor of Penang, sent emissaries to sign treaties with the rulers of Siak, Johor-Riau and Pontianak in Borneo. In Johor-Riau, William Farquhar managed to secure most favoured nation privileges in the ports of Johor, Riau, Lingga and Pahang. This rear-guard action smacked of desperation and, in the end, proved futile. In late 1818, as the Dutch returned to Melaka, they despatched Admiral C J Wolterbeek to Johor-Riau to renew the treaty of 1784. The reigning Sultan acquiesced and Johor-Riau became a vassal of Holland once again. Bannerman's rearguard action was nullified by the Wolterbeek mission.

Somewhat belatedly, the men on the spot, men like Lord Hastings, Stamford Raffles and William Farquhar, realised that this was a crisis. The British had to have a base in the region and fast.

The Game's Afoot

To the three men, the British position in the Malay Archipelago in 1818 must have looked precarious and perilous. All Britain had to protect its interests in the region were Penang, which was poorly located, and Bengkulu, which was facing the Indian Ocean rather than the Straits of Melaka.

Born in 1781, Thomas Stamford Bingley Raffles joined the EIC at age fourteen. An auto-didact, he was fascinated with the Malay world. His first foray into the region was in 1805 when he was appointed as Assistant Secretary in the Penang presidency. In 1811, he was appointed Lieutenant-Governor of Java which, like Melaka, had come into British trusteeship under the terms of the Kew Letters.

In 1815, he was recalled from Java and in 1817, he was knighted in recognition of his two-volume historical work, *The History of Java*. His intellectual reputation was further enhanced with his election as a Fellow of the Royal Society, which earned him the right to the letters 'F.R.S' after his name.

In 1818, Raffles returned to the region as Lieutenant-Governor of Bengkulu. From there, he soberly observed the pace and extent of Dutch expansion in the region. The Dutch, he warned, 'possess the only passes through which ships must sail into the Archipelago, the Straits of Sunda and Malacca'. The British situation was grim for they did not have 'an inch of ground to stand upon between the Cape of Good Hope and China, nor a single friendly port at which they can water and obtain refreshment.'

Though Raffles' warnings were largely unheeded in London, Lord Hastings, the Governor-General of India, was more receptive. Born in 1754, Francis Rawdon Hastings, the 1st Marquess of Hastings, was a Major-General who held command in both the American War of Independence and the Napoleonic Wars. In 1812, with his prospects in politics dimming, Hastings took up the post of Governor-General and Commander-in-Chief in India. He was keenly aware of how the Dutch had expanded aggressively and rapidly throughout the region and the threat that this posed to the EIC's valuable trade between India and China.

Although Hastings previously censured Raffles over his reported maladministration in Java, his impression of Raffles had improved by the time they met again in October 1818. It helped that Raffles had friends in high places – Princess Charlotte and her husband, Prince Leopold, were but two of the luminaries with whom Raffles hobnobbed. It also helped that Raffles was admired and recognised as a serious scholar of history and botany. Above all, Hastings was impressed with Raffles' deep knowledge of the region.

Hastings was not enamoured of Raffles' plans to expand British influence in Sumatra to counter the Dutch in the region. In Hastings' mind, the most direct and effective way to challenge Dutch expansion and the threat they posed to the India-China trade was to set up a base at the southern end of the Straits of Melaka. Hastings had decided – all that was left to do was to inform Raffles who was permitted to carry out a tightly limited operation. Hastings authorised Raffles to secure the Straits of Melaka. Raffles was to do this by establishing two bases, one in Aceh and another at the southern end of the Straits of Melaka, no further than Johor and Riau. He was sternly warned not to come into any form of conflict with the Dutch. Hastings was right to be cautious – the Dutch were their allies, after all, in Europe. These instructions were formally issued on 28 November 1818.

On 7 December 1818, Raffles set sail from Calcutta with Hastings' words of assurance in his mind – 'Sir Stamford, you may depend on me'. Partnering him was an old friend, Major William Farquhar. Farquhar, a Scotsman, was born in 1778 and joined the Madras Engineers in 1791. In 1795, he took part in the capture of Melaka and met Raffles for the first time in 1807. He assisted Raffles and also fought in the war to capture Java in 1811. Having served thirty years here in the region, he was no stranger to its people and its politics. More crucially, he had contacts with the Malay chiefs and insights into the intrigues of Johor-Riau politics that proved to be critical in the founding of Singapore.

Like Raffles, Farquhar was wary and suspicious about Dutch actions in the region. As early as October 1816, he proposed to the Penang Government to set up a base at the mouth of the Straits of Singapore. In these aspects, Farquhar and Raffles were alike. To them, the Dutch presence was inimical to British interests and they had to be stopped. Raffles, riven by ambition and urgency, sought to allay the fears of his superiors in India whilst exploiting his instructions to the hilt and taking chances like a seasoned gambler. Farquhar, with his knowledge of the region and its politics, set the stage for the British to set up a base south of the Straits of Melaka. Their partnership was to be a resounding success.

Finding Singapore

On 29 December 1818, Raffles arrived in Penang. A sense of urgency suffused the air as Raffles received news that the Dutch had renewed their 1784 treaty with Johor-Riau. To reinforce their position, they had fortified Johor-Riau 'with a large naval and military force'. Raffles hastened to report this development to Hastings and reiterated the urgent need to press ahead with the mission. He warned that the Dutch actions were merely opening moves of a 'more extensive policy not yet divulged', surmising that the Dutch 'must secretly be aided by some other power'. More significantly, Raffles informed Hastings that he was 'fully satisfied of the value and importance of the Island of Singapore which commands Johor – there is a most excellent Harbour which is even more defensible and more conveniently situated for the protection of our China Trade and for commanding the Straits than (Riau).' To allay Hastings' fear and to assure him that he was obeying his orders, Raffles reported that Singapore 'has been deserted for Centuries and long before the Dutch power existed in these Seas'. Like a once errant child who has since been forgiven, Raffles sought to convince Hastings that he would 'cautiously avoid all collision with the Dutch'. For the first time, Singapore emerged as a serious contender for a British base.

Although outwardly supportive of this mission, Bannerman made it known privately on 1 January 1819 to Hastings that it was a fool's errand that was sure to provoke the Dutch, who had amassed a large naval and military force in the region. But Bannerman, as Lieutenant-Governor of Penang, would have hated to see any rival port challenge or even surpass his own. It is telling that he recommended that if Raffles persisted (and succeeded) in this mission, then the new settlement should be placed under the Penang government.

Farquhar sailed southwards in the brig *Ganges* on 18 January 1819 to rendezvous with two British survey vessels, the *Discovery* and the *Investigator* at Karimun. He continued his journey to survey Singapore, then sailed to Riau to set the stage to enable the establishment of a British settlement in Singapore. Raffles of course had to have a part in this great adventure. In defiance of Bannerman's orders, he slipped out of Penang in the small hours of 18 January 1819 to catch up with Farquhar.

On 26 January 1819, Farquhar and Raffles linked up off Karimun. Other than Farquhar, no one in the party was enthused by the islands as they could not locate a suitable anchorage. There was a bright spot though. Over dinner, Daniel Ross, who captained the *Discovery* and served as Raffles' hydrographer, mentioned that there was a suitable site in Singapore that called for further investigation. There was no time to lose. The little squadron of eight ships set off early on 28 January 1819 and at 4 p.m., dropped anchor off St. John's Island in the Straits of Singapore.

Founding Singapore

Upon sighting the British ships, Temenggong Abdu'r Rahman sent word via Orang Laut messengers that there were no Dutch on the island. The next day, the Temenggong made known his concern to Raffles and Farquhar – he wanted a resolution of the succession dispute in Johor-Riau in Tengku Hussein's favour. The heir apparent to the throne, Tengku Hussein, was away in the royal capital of Pekan in Pahang getting married when Sultan Mahmud Shah passed away in 1811. Court factions took advantage of his absence to install his younger brother, Tengku Abdu'r Rahman, on the throne. Hussein was cast into political wilderness at Pulau Penyengat, where he languished in poverty without a throne and a realm. Now, eight years later, this was set to change.

For Raffles and Farquhar, this dispute provided them with the perfect opportunity to intervene. By recognising Tengku Hussein as the rightful Sultan of Singapore, they would in return be able to secure the British position in Singapore and establish a base. The shrewd Temenggong was clear about what the British brought to the table. He trusted Farquhar as their relationship went back more than a decade. To him, the British were no different from the Dutch – they were mere levers to be used to secure recognition for Tengku Hussein. And neither the Temenggong nor Tengku Hussein were trying to overthrow Hussein's brother, Sultan Abdu'r Rahman, in Riau – they were only seeking a title and recognition that would enable Hussein to set up his own realm in Singapore.

On 30 January 1819, the Temenggong signed a Preliminary Agreement with Raffles and Farquhar – the EIC was given the right to set up a factory (trading post) on the island in exchange for an annual payment of 3000 Spanish dollars to the Temenggong. Tengku Hussein arrived in Singapore on 1 February 1819 and concurred with this agreement. Following this, the Singapore Treaty was signed on 6 February 1819 with the newly installed Sultan Hussein Shah. This treaty confirmed the Preliminary Agreement and provided for an annual payment of 5000 Spanish dollars to the Sultan, in addition to the payment promised to Temenggong earlier. The Union Jack was hoisted at the end of the signing and ceremonial salutes were fired by British artillery and the Temenggong's own gun battery.

For Raffles, as it was for both Sri Tri Buana and Parameswara, Singapore was ideal. Its geographical advantages and strategic value were beyond doubt. Its natural endowments – a sheltered and deep harbour, plentiful drinking water and firm, level ground northeast of the river – meant that the urgent and harried search had come to an end. The founding of Singapore, as he observed then on 19 February 1819 in Penang, 'breaks the spell and they (the Dutch) are no longer the exclusive sovereigns of the eastern seas.'

Raffles' optimism belied the immense vulnerability of the infant British settlement. It was practically undefended – on Singapore, there were a hundred Indian sepoys, their European officers and a gunboat. This was all that stood against the entire military might of the Dutch in the region comprising an immense naval force and 15000 European troops. To make things worse, Singapore's legal status was questionable at best. The recognition of Tengku Hussein as Sultan of Singapore was a sleight of hand, giving only the barest cover of legitimacy.

On hearing the news of Singapore's founding, Bannerman's responses exposed his inability to see past self-interest. When it was rumoured that the Dutch were planning to use military force to drive the British out of Singapore, he advised Farquhar to quit the place and avoid a clash he was bound to lose. And, in turn, he informed the Dutch that Raffles had acted beyond the remit of his instructions. The Dutch were enraged but the Dutch Governor-General of the Netherlands Indies, Godert van der Capellen, expected Calcutta to disown Raffles' actions. They therefore left Singapore alone, fully expecting the matter to be resolved quickly.

Raffles was extremely fortunate in this political game. In Calcutta, Hastings, saw value in what Raffles had done and stood with him. He ticked Bannerman off and ordered him to help Singapore in any way possible. Bannerman did so most unhappily, but 200 troops and money were sent to Farquhar. As these events played out between Raffles, Calcutta, Penang, London and the Dutch, Farquhar stood firm in Singapore. This took courage on his part. By August 1819, when news of Singapore's founding finally reached London, its geographical advantages and strategic value convinced the British government that Raffles had pulled off a spectacular coup. The dominant Dutch position in the region and the threat this posed to British interests was effectively neutralised. Raffles' insubordination was quietly overlooked.

Singapore's legal status vis-à-vis the Dutch was ultimately settled with the signing of the Anglo-Dutch Treaty on 17 March 1824. The treaty drew lines that partitioned the region into two spheres of influence and established Britain's control over Singapore and the Malay Peninsula. In return, the British ceded Bengkulu and all its possessions in Sumatra to the Dutch. To this day, these lines form the maritime boundary between Singapore and Indonesia. In signing this treaty, the Dutch in effect recognised that it was no longer the leading seaborne empire and naval power in the world. The British had inherited this mantle and Pax Britannica would dominate the world for the next century or so.

Securing Singapore

Having signed the Singapore Treaty, Raffles left Farquhar with a handful of instructions before leaving Singapore on 7 February 1819. Having gone to such great lengths to eke out a toehold in the region, Farquhar had one job – to ensure that Singapore did not fail. Farquhar was in a difficult position. To accomplish this mission, he had to tread the thin line between ensuring Singapore's survival and fulfilling Raffles' instructions and vision. Raffles' presence in Singapore from 1819 to 1823 was sporadic. After leaving in February 1819, he made two more visits, a four-week sojourn in May 1819 and another in October 1822 which stretched for eight months. Left mostly on his own, Farquhar tried to make Singapore work. Poor communications with Raffles in Bengkulu during this period did not help.

Raffles' initial instructions to Farquhar were scant. Skeletal as they were, his instructions reflected the raison d'etre behind Singapore's founding. Singapore needed to succeed and to succeed, it needed trade. To attract traders, he pronounced Singapore a free port – there would be neither taxes on trade nor port charges. To provide security, he ordered defences to be put up and to generate trading activity, he lured traders from Melaka to come to the infant settlement. He also instructed Farquhar to 'post a responsible European on St. John's Island to inform passing ships about the new settlement'.

In May 1819, Raffles returned to Singapore and left more directives. This time, he focused on the layout of the settlement. Land was reserved on the left bank of the Singapore River and the plain (which is the Padang today) for government and military use. He designated specific quarters for specific ethnic groups. To the east of the government district was the European quarter. The right bank of the river was assigned to the Chinese. To connect the Chinese quarter with the rest of the settlement, a bridge had to be built. Law and order was left to the community and their respective *kapitans*, who had to keep the peace and resolve disputes. This allowed the British to adopt a hands-off policy towards the different ethnic groups that persisted well into the late 19th century.

To further cement the British presence, Raffles signed another agreement with Sultan Hussein and the Temenggong to establish and recognise the settlement's boundaries. The settlement was bound by Tanjong Malang in the west and Tanjong Katong in the east, which was about four kilometres in length. Its inland boundary was determined by the distance of a cannon shot fired inland. Having done all these, Raffles left Singapore for Bengkulu. He would only return three years later in October 1822.

Raffles' departure marked the beginning of frontier-town Singapore. As Resident and Commandant of the infant colony, Farquhar faced many challenges. But he was also a pragmatic man who was clear about his objectives – to consolidate Singapore's position as a British settlement and to grow Singapore's trade. He was acutely aware that the British had no legal rights over the island. And he knew that the Dutch were capable of turfing them out if they wanted to. In these circumstances, Farquhar was absolutely right to prioritise Singapore's survival and growth. It would be more difficult for the Dutch to dislodge them once Singapore began drawing traders and hosting a bustling trade. Everything else really could wait.

Farquhar faced an unenviable reality. He had to work with a tight budget which he could not supplement because Singapore was a free port and no revenues could be derived from trade. He could not sell land to raise revenue as it was not his to sell. He was also understaffed. In 1820, Calcutta removed the position of Assistant Resident and reduced his staff to just one clerk. Eventually, in 1822, Farquhar was forced to hire and pay for two clerks out of his own pocket. Although Raffles imposed austerity on Singapore, he did not apply this to Bengkulu. Singapore's annual expenditure on wages was reportedly equal to what Bengkulu spent in a single month.

To fix this revenue shortfall, Farquhar undertook a series of targeted measures. He introduced small port clearance fees in May

1820 to pay for the Master Attendant's staff. Later, in September 1820, he introduced the practice of tax farming. Monopoly rights were auctioned off – these covered opium sales, alcohol sales and gambling. In other words, sin was taxed. Aware that he had to boost confidence in the settlement, Farquhar put this revenue to good use through a public works programme.

Very often, as the man on the spot, Farquhar was the mediator between the people he governed and his superior, Raffles, who was ensconced in Bengkulu. One of these instances arose as a consequence of Farquhar's public works programme, which succeeded as a confidence building measure. Convinced that the British were here for good, the merchants soon clamoured for land to build warehouses for their goods. Farquhar found himself in a fix – he could not sell or grant land to anyone as he had no legal right to do so. The land was still the property of Sultan Hussein Shah. Furthermore, the merchants did not want to use Raffles' designated commercial district as they could not land their goods on the swampy ground there. Alexander Guthrie, a leading merchant, even threatened to quit the island if he was not given a better site. Since he did not have the remit to decide, he sought Raffles' views on the matter in April 1821. Raffles only replied eleven months later in March 1822, when he expressly forbade any permanent building. Faced with his superior's unhelpful missive and the merchants' logical and practical demands, Farquhar decided to grant land to the merchants and allowed them to build their brick warehouses on the north bank of the Singapore River. But Farquhar was scrupulous – these grants were made with a caveat that they might later have to move.

Farquhar's scrupulous adherence to the Singapore Treaty was another source of tension. To him, the British were tenants in Singapore, and they had acquired the rights to set up a trading post and little else. He recognised that, as sovereign, Sultan Hussein Shah retained the right to expect customary dues and to administer laws. Farquhar chose to respect these rights and thus erred on the side of caution. In May 1820, as a workaround, an allowance was paid to Sultan Hussein Shah and the Temenggong in lieu of the customary dues. In June 1820, he referred their request to tax the Chinese who were returning to China for good to Raffles for his guidance. He did not hear from him for eight months.

Despite all these constraints, Singapore succeeded as a trading port. It offered a unique proposition as the only free port in the region. This drew traders who saw Singapore as an attractive alternative to the Dutch ports. And it caused them to reorient their trading routes and networks to converge at Singapore. Within six weeks of Singapore's founding, a sizeable number of ships comprising small craft, a Siamese junk and two European merchant ships were anchored in the harbour. Melakan merchants also flocked to Singapore, partly because of Farquhar's reputation as the former Resident of Melaka. Though these were but small beginnings, they were the first steps in reconnecting Singapore with its dormant trading networks and re-establishing its relevance.

Farquhar proved to be a remarkably practical and sensible administrator who was respected and well-liked. Whatever problems arose, big or small, Farquhar attended to them with patience and ingenuity. When it was reported to him that a rat infestation was causing the population great discomfort, he introduced a rats-for-cash policy. This was a resounding success – rats were brought in by the thousands and the infestation ended. A later infestation, this time of centipedes, was dealt with similarly with great success. It certainly did not hurt that he was well-liked and enjoyed a good reputation amongst the population. He was known to be fair in his rulings and demonstrated much consideration and kindness to the people, of whom he was genuinely fond.

Was Farquhar intentionally insubordinate towards Raffles and intentionally defiant of his orders? Certainly not. For one, communications were poor, and he would sometimes not hear from Raffles for months. Oftentimes, his requests and referrals to Raffles were left unattended and unanswered. Ironically, this logjam was created by Raffles, who wanted to be informed of all matters big and small. But whether Farquhar liked it or not, the problems he faced were his to own and being the man on the spot, he had to rely on his own judgment and resourcefulness to solve them.

So where was Raffles, during these three years when Farquhar was left on his own to develop the island? Pacing around like a caged tiger in Bengkulu, he was busy pursuing his ambitions and coveting a position that would enable him to administer all of the EIC's possessions in the region. Singapore was, for him, a sideshow until all these other pursuits came to naught. Meanwhile, Singapore was growing rapidly but he paid little attention to it until 1822, when he decided to visit Singapore just before he retired.

'My Almost Only Child'

Arriving in October 1822, Raffles saw a bustling and vibrant settlement, a far cry from what he had left behind in 1819. But a feud was brewing between the two old friends. Raffles hated the way Farquhar ran Singapore. He disagreed with how Farquhar dealt with the Sultan and the Temenggong, both of whom he saw as obstacles to his vision for Singapore. He was livid to find that Farquhar legalised gambling and tolerated slavery – both of which were abhorrent in his puritanical eyes. The settlement looked haphazard and untidy because of the way Farquhar had distributed and allocated land. To him, Farquhar was old-fashioned and lacking in vision. Worse, with his decisions, Farquhar had corrupted Raffles' romantic vision of a great, enlightened and moral commercial settlement that was destined to be the intellectual and cultural heart of the region. It was ironic that these harsh views came from a man who was blind to his own negligence and tardiness in dealing with Singapore's issues while he was busy stoking the flames of his burning ambition.

Finding the physical appearance of the town to be an eyesore, Raffles moved quickly to remedy it. Although commonly referred to as the Raffles Town Plan, the *Plan of the Town of Singapore* was prepared by Lieutenant Phillip Jackson of the Bengal Artillery. It was subsequently published in London in 1828.

The plan used a grid layout and reflected the presence of natural features such as the Singapore River. Zones were marked out for specific activities. All commercial activity was centered around the south bank of the river. To do this, an expensive reclamation project paid for with money carefully saved from Farquhar's frugal administration, was carried out. A hill was levelled to form Commercial Square, and swampland filled in to become Boat Quay. Land on the north bank was reserved for the government. Rochor, eastwards of town, was where wealthy Europeans and Asians would reside.

The colonial policy of divide and rule to manage the various ethnic groups that had begun settling in Singapore was manifested in the plan. The Chinese were allocated land west of Commercial Square and the Indians land further up the river. The Malays, Bugis and Arabs were given land adjoining the Sultan's compound in Kampong Glam. There would be long straight roads meeting at right angles. Shophouses would be built with masonry and tiled roofs, neat uniform facades and be linked by continuous walkways, the ubiquitous five-foot ways.

To address issues regarding Singapore's free port status, land distribution and the administration of law and order, Raffles made several important decisions. He extended Singapore's free port status in perpetuity, utterly convinced that this was what made Singapore successful. To regulate development, land in Singapore would be registered and sold by auction on a freehold basis. Lastly, English law was adopted and applied to all, except for specific issues pertaining to the 'native inhabitants', namely religious practice, marriage and inheritance.

As expectedly, he moved quickly to rein in Sultan Hussein Shah and the Temenggong. On 7 June 1823, he signed a new treaty with them. This removed the customary dues that they insisted were their entitlement and which annoyed Raffles no end. In effect, they surrendered their rights to exact these dues. In return, the government provided them with monthly payments. Critically, the treaty stipulated that 'all land within the island of Singapore, and islands immediately adjacent' was allocated to be 'at the entire disposal of the British government'. This was the first step towards the eventual cessation of Singapore to the British.

Raffles' Enlightenment ideals and bold vision shone through in the reforms he wrought. He set up a justice system of twelve European magistrates. Slavery was banned in May 1823 and existing debt slaves were to be freed in five years. He also set out regulations to address debt bondage and the semi-slave status of Chinese immigrants; these were however difficult to enforce. Just before he left Singapore in June 1823, a 48-acre experimental Botanic Garden was planted at the foothills of Government Hill. He also laid the foundation stone of the Singapore Institution, leaving instructions on how the school should be set up.

The Feud

Though kept rather busy, Raffles still found time to pillory Farquhar, his erstwhile trusted ally. This feud was largely petty and personal. In April 1820, Captain William Flint, Raffles' brother-in-law, was appointed Master Attendant and Marine Storekeeper. But the nepotism cut both ways, for the man Flint had displaced in these jobs was Francis Bernard, Farquhar's son-in-law. Raffles had promised Flint the job and Bernard was replaced. Flint was insufferable as Master Attendant. He set himself up with a sizeable staff while Farquhar was making do with just one clerk. Arrogant and greedy, he pocketed the profit from the rental of marine vessels for both official and private use. Raffles did himself no favours by indulging Flint and the latter's interminable grouses about Farquhar's supposed put-downs and hurtful behaviour.

In 1822, when Raffles returned to Singapore, he picked his side. He chose to stay with Flint and undermined Farquhar by enlarging Flint's remit to cover the collection of port charges. These duties of course came with their own allowances. Rather vindictively, he humiliated Farquhar by divesting some of the latter's duties to junior staff. George Bonham, merely a twenty-year old writer, was put in charge of land sales and revenue collection.

Of course, Raffles had his own bone to pick with Farquhar, whom he accused of indulging in private trading, even though Farquhar had openly disclosed this to Raffles. Things got worse. Having moved Bernard to the police department, Farquhar took umbrage with Raffles about the pay cut suffered by Bernard. Pettily, Raffles reported Farquhar to the Governor-General in Calcutta for not showing up in military uniform. In this accusation was an oblique slur – Farquhar had gone native by taking a 'native' wife, fathering mixed-race children and wearing a sarong when off duty. In January 1823, he acted to remove Farquhar completely. Writing to Calcutta, he charged that Farquhar was incompetent and in April 1823 summarily dismissed him as Resident and assumed the post himself.

What irked Raffles so much that it drove him to treat an old friend so humiliatingly and so shabbily? It is commonly known that the feud was about how Raffles' romantic and soaring visions for Singapore clashed with Farquhar's practical outlook in developing Singapore. Having been mostly absent after Singapore's founding, Raffles was seized by these grand visions again in 1822, when he set eyes on the bustling settlement that Farquhar had nursed from infancy, after Raffles' other ambitions had crumbled.

For Farquhar, governing Singapore and the day-to-day realities kept such grand visions in check. He was constantly reminded that Singapore's precarious existence was kept alive only with the tacit acquiescence of the Dutch, the Sultan and the Temenggong. Any move by one of these three actors could have extinguished the settlement.

But a large part of the feud was personal and driven by vendetta, slights and putdowns. Raffles wanted Farquhar gone and to do so, he pulled out all the stops to discredit Farquhar's work, question his competence and ruin his reputation. In November 1823, writing to Nathaniel Wallich, Raffles revealed that he 'found it necessary to prosecute (his) course with vigour and effect'. Raffles was ruthless when it came to Farquhar. Like the Sultan and the Temenggong, he was an obstacle to his vision that had to be expurgated.

Farquhar, much loved by the population, stayed on in Singapore till December 1823. He received a resounding and warm send-off from the people of Singapore who turned out in droves to see him off. It took two hours for Farquhar to say his goodbyes, such was the depth of regard and affection they had for him. This was unsurprising for without Farquhar's steady nursing of the settlement and his fortitude in what was at best a difficult situation, Singapore's survival would have been in doubt. To realise his ideals, Raffles was unsentimental, ruthless and crass in handling his friendship with Farquhar. And ironically, Raffles 'was stooping to his lowest in hounding and ousting the unfortunate Farquhar' just as he was setting out his grand vision for Singapore.

Sense And Sensibility

John Crawfurd, Farquhar's replacement as Resident, has been described as a 'somewhat austere and forbidding character'. A Scotsman, he was in many ways a realist and perhaps even more pragmatic than Farquhar. Two achievements characterised his Residency. First, he secured Singapore for the British, irrevocably. Second, he disregarded and jettisoned Raffles' ideas that he felt were impractical or unrealistic. In sum, Crawfurd brought to Singapore a healthy dose of sense and sensibility after the rancour over the Raffles-Farquhar feud.

Shortly after assuming the Residency, Crawfurd wrote to Calcutta in January 1824 for permission to resolve the issue of Singapore's sovereignty. Both the 1819 Singapore Treaty and Raffles' 1823 Treaty were inadequate. They did not provide the British with sovereign rights over Singapore. To him, Sultan Hussein Shah and the Temenggong were, with their stand on slavery and demands for more compensation, roadblocks in the way of British administration. Calcutta concurred and gave Crawfurd the go-ahead.

On 2 August 1824, Sultan Hussein Shah and Temenggong caved in to financial pressure from Crawfurd and signed the Treaty of Friendship and Alliance with the EIC. Crawfurd agreed to pay their allowances in perpetuity, together with an additional sum of 20,000 Spanish dollars and the cancellation of their debts. In return, they would cede the island of Singapore, the seas, straits and islands within ten geographical miles, to the EIC and its heirs in perpetuity. To take possession and mark the successful conclusion of the treaty, Crawfurd sailed around the island on the HMS *Malabar*, a jaunt that took ten days. A final flourish was executed with a 21-gun salute on Pulau Ubin. Taken together with the Anglo Dutch Treaty of March 1824, Singapore's legal status was finally secure. Neither the Dutch, nor Sultan Hussein Shah, nor the Temenggong, had any valid claim. The British were now sovereign in Singapore.

Much like Farquhar, Crawfurd was a realist and, as Resident, he focused on the practical and necessary. He maintained Singapore's status as a free port. Understanding that Raffles' rough and ready judicial system was in essence illegal, he pushed for Singapore to be given its own Charter of Justice and for proper courts to be established. He pursued the suppression of slavery. In September 1824, he freed twenty-seven female slaves who had escaped from the Sultan's compound.

Crawfurd ran a lean and tight administration. As expenses were low, he abolished port charges, further burnishing Singapore's position as a free port. Unlike Raffles, Crawfurd lacked Raffles' puritanical zeal towards opium and gambling which he tolerated and taxed. To raise revenue, he taxed these twin vices and also sold licences for pawnbroking and the manufacture and sale of gunpowder. By 1825, Singapore's tax revenue tripled to $75,000. Up until the early 20th century, opium consistently accounted for one-third to two-thirds of Singapore's tax revenue. Gambling was the other major contributor. All these made up for Singapore's revenue shortfall. By 1826, Singapore's revenue exceeded Penang's. Crawfurd also implemented Raffles' 1822 Town Plan with fidelity – bridges were built, streets widened, street signs and lighting put up to conform to Raffles' standards of 'beauty, regularity and cleanliness'. In late 1823, the Sepoy Lines, a military cantonment, was established on the outskirts of town. Singapore town was slowly taking on an ordered and settled appearance.

In August 1826, Crawfurd relinquished his office, having acquitted himself well as a Resident. Though not as loved or as popular as Farquhar, Crawfurd left his mark on Singapore by shrewdly and sensibly picking and implementing the more practical parts of Raffles' plans. More critically, Crawfurd had moved very quickly to secure sovereign rights over Singapore for the British, putting to death once and for all, the legal limbo in which Singapore existed.

Crawfurd never visited Singapore again but, together with William Henry Read, a merchant from A.L Johnston & Co., he remained an advocate for the colony all his life. In the twilight of his life in 1868, Crawfurd became the first president of the Straits Settlements Association, a London-based advocacy group focused on Singapore's interests. Dour and brusque though he might have been, Crawfurd's no-nonsense brand of administration was exactly what Singapore needed.

Reconnecting With The Region

Declaring Singapore a free port was the most important and consequential of Raffles' early instructions. But it was not just a free port in the sense that trade was not taxed. It was literally *free* because John Crawfurd had abolished port charges and fees. It was also the only free port in the region at that time. Traders and businesses in Singapore enjoyed substantial cost savings because of this. A laissez-faire trade policy also meant that all traders, regardless of nationality, were free to trade in Singapore. Together, these two policies generated the economic activity that powered the colony's growth and expansion in the years to come.

Three trading networks converged on Singapore, drawn undoubtedly by its free port and open trading policies. The China trade, the Malay Archipelago trade and the India trade all came together in Singapore. In the Age of Sail, the monsoons were all that mattered. It was so during the time of Temasek in the 14th century and it remained so during this period in the early 19th century. Singapore's position made it a convenient stopover point in the middle of the India-China trade route. And while everyone was here waiting for the winds to change, why not do some business?

The China trade drew both country traders and Chinese traders in their junks. Singapore saw its first junk from China in February

1821 and the first China-bound merchant ship arrived in July of the same year. This was significant. Before this, the Chinese junk trade was compelled to call at Batavia because of the Dutch monopoly. The arrival of Chinese junks meant that this monopoly was being undercut by free port Singapore. Singapore was also a useful place for the country traders and Chinese traders to sidestep another monopoly – that of the EIC over the China trade. This was ironic for Singapore was founded primarily to protect the EIC's trade with China.

The Bugis-dominated Malay Archipelago trade in Straits produce that existed in Riau before 1784 was now revived and centered on Singapore. In reconnecting the old trading networks in the archipelago, Sultan Hussein Shah and the Temenggong were critical in channelling the existing Riau trade, especially in gambier, to Singapore. Displaced by the Dutch from Riau, five hundred entrepreneurial Bugis arrived in Singapore in 1820. This quickly cemented Singapore's position as the heart of Bugis trade in the Malay Archipelago.

The India trade brought raw opium to Singapore where it was processed by the Chinese before it was sold to the Bugis. Penang and Melaka, Singapore's elder siblings, were also important trading partners. Singapore's 14th century role as an entrepot port was now being revived in the early 19th century. By 1821, some 3,000 vessels carrying an estimated eight million Spanish dollars' worth of import-export trade had called at Singapore.

With trade came people, and the island's population grew to 5,000 during this period, giving it a distinctly cosmopolitan flavour. In January 1824, during the Crawfurd Residency, Singapore's population grew to 11,000. The Malay community remained the largest, with the Chinese coming in second and the Bugis in third place. By 1827, its population was just touching 16,000 and with the influx of newcomers, Singapore's demographics were beginning to change.

And with people came connections and networks and, over time, rich opportunities for trade and commerce. The Chinese brought with them their trading network that spanned the Malay Archipelago as well as Bangkok and Manila. The ports of Riau, Penang and Melaka were all hosts to well-established Chinese communities of traders, farmers and miners. From Melaka came three of Singapore's earliest Chinese merchant settlers. Tan Che Sang, a Hokkien, built a warehouse in Singapore in 1819 and acted as agent for the Chinese junk trade. Choa Chong Long, also a Hokkien, was head of the

Hokkien community and the first opium revenue farmer. Tan Tock Seng became an early 'rags to riches' success – coming to Singapore as a vegetable seller in 1819, he worked his way to become a wealthy businessman and philanthropist.

Trade was facilitated by Straits Chinese middlemen and European agency houses. The former, many of whom came from Melaka, acted as middlemen or compradors between European and Asian merchants due to their ability to speak both English and Malay. Despite Singapore's uncertain status, country traders such as Alexander Johnston and Alexander Guthrie established the first European firms and agency houses from 1820 onwards. These firms bought and sold goods on concession and operated entirely on trust. As trade grew, so did their numbers – the Singapore River became replete with their warehouses on both banks.

So Who Founded Singapore?

The name Raffles is everywhere in Singapore, with scores of roads and schools and other buildings named after him. Of Farquhar, there is almost no mention and no public commemoration. John Crawfurd is luckier – Crawford Street bears his name as do Crawford Lane, Crawford Bridge and Crawford Park. Similarly, in narratives of Singapore's history, Raffles looms large as the founder of modern Singapore. To him alone is ascribed the intelligence, the ambition and vision that led to the founding of Singapore in 1819 and the early plans for the development of the colony. Farquhar is often seen as the Resident who failed to meet Raffles' expectations, went his own way, went native and was eventually dismissed by Raffles. Crawfurd's legacy is secure in the 1824 Treaty of Friendship and Alliance between the EIC, Sultan Hussein Shah and the Temenggong, which ceded all rights to Singapore and all islands within ten miles of its shores to the EIC. Otherwise, Crawfurd's presence in Singapore's history is diminutive. The reality is that all three men played distinct roles in the Singapore that they collectively founded, nursed and secured. All these roles were equally important, for without them, the fledging colony would not have survived, much less thrived.

There is however one founder that Singapore has completely forgotten: the Marquess of Hastings. It was, after all, Hastings who ordered Raffles to explore the possibility of establishing a station south of the Straits of Melaka to check Dutch expansion and protect British trade. If he had decided otherwise, the Dutch could very well have extended its control over Singapore eventually. In 1809, Abraham Couperus, the last Dutch governor of Melaka, proposed founding a 'greenfield colony' to take advantage of the shifting trade patterns in the region. A location at the southern end of the Straits of Melaka was possibly one of his considerations. If this had materialised, Singapore would have become a Dutch possession. It is thus only fitting that we remember Hastings and the enormity of the decision he made, which led to the founding of Singapore by Stamford Raffles and William Farquhar.

CHAPTER THREE

A Whole New World

1826–1900

A New Port And A Familiar Role

For most of the 19th century, Singapore reprised a familiar role as a regional entrepot but with some subtle differences. Much like Singapura, its earlier incarnation, the colony depended almost solely on trade and commerce – this was the raison d'etre behind its founding and existence. There was little manufacturing. And by the mid-1800s, having exhausted the soil, gambier and pepper planters moved their holdings up north to Johor.

Just as it was in the 14th century, Singapore's trade was still dependent on the wind. Whether they were Bugis perahus, Chinese junks or square-rigged European sailing ships, they all depended on the wind to propel them to their destinations. In this respect, its geographical location was significant. Trading networks soon converged on Singapore – traders found that all manner of business was possible. They could buy goods in Singapore and re-export them. They could also sell goods in Singapore to others who would re-export them; to do so, they would import goods. This trade was mostly regional and maritime, focusing heavily on Southeast Asia and its produce. This trading activity, multiplied many times over, made Singapore thrive as an entrepot. In 1845, the steamship called at Singapore for the first time. Even though trade depended less and less on the wind, the networks and connections here mattered and remained.

The mutually beneficial relationship between the European merchant houses and the Chinese middlemen shows how important the convergence of networks at Singapore was. Commerce flowed in two directions. In one direction, European merchants, with their capital, obtained goods from Britain and India and in turn extended them to the Chinese middlemen on credit. They in turn sold these goods to fellow Chinese businessmen or traders from the region. In the other direction, Chinese middlemen sold goods from their fellow Chinese businessmen or traders from the region to European merchants who then sold them to British and Indian markets. The Chinese middlemen were indispensable in bridging distribution networks, business contacts and production sources, all of which converged in Singapore. By 1846, this business model had been adopted by all forty-three merchant houses in Singapore. It was a model that worked for everyone.

Singapore's fiercest economic rivals, the Dutch, tried to prevent their trade from connecting at Singapore by imposing a range of surcharges, taxes and duties on goods heading from Dutch ports to Singapore. These ultimately failed because Malay and Bugis smugglers were more than willing to risk Dutch ire just to make a profit at Singapore, where their goods were in demand. The moment these restrictions were lifted in 1841, trade between the Dutch East Indies and Singapore grew. Similarly, the Anglo-Siamese Treaty of 1855 opened a new market and resulted in a rapid increase in trade volumes between Singapore and Siam.

No economy is immune from the boom and bust economic cycle and no one understood the regularity of this cycle more than the merchants. In 1864, at the nadir of the nadir of a bust cycle, D'Almeida and Sons, an established name amongst the merchant houses, collapsed. The other firms, both European and Asian, were not spared from this economic carnage.

The Crusade For Reform

Singapore's economic activity was growing both in volume and complexity, but in terms of governance and administration, it was stuck in a rut. In 1826, the EIC put Singapore, Melaka and Penang together to form the Straits Settlements. Four years later, the Straits Settlements were downgraded to become an appendage of the EIC Presidency in Bengal. In 1832, Singapore became the seat of government given its increasing prosperity and importance.

The merchants knew that Singapore's success and in turn their businesses depended on its free port status. To them, Singapore's free port status was inviolable. But they were frustrated. They chafed at the lack of representation in government. The persistent policy of non-intervention in the Malay States annoyed them as it left their upcountry investments vulnerable and unprotected.

At the same time, the merchants were a contradictory but organised group. In the name of free trade, they were against any form of taxation, fees or charges that would have enhanced Singapore's infrastructure, social services or safety. In 1829, the government's attempt to introduce a new tax on exports was defeated. Next, in 1836, an attempt to impose port charges was retracted after the merchants lobbied the EIC in London. In 1837, the Singapore Chamber of Commerce was founded to serve as a lobby group in the fight against any form of taxation. In the 1850s, they protested and lobbied against proposed taxes and charges that would have paid for the something that would have made shipping safer – the Horsburgh Lighthouse on Pedra Banca.

The Indian Mutiny of 1857 was the proverbial straw that broke the camel's back in this acrimonious relationship. Singapore was rife with rumours about the apparent restiveness of its Indian Sepoy garrison. An urgent anxiety seized the European community over the presence of Indian convict labour in Singapore and this was further worsened by news that Calcutta was planning to dump its most dangerous convicts on Singapore.

In September 1857, the merchants acted. Led by John Crawfurd, who was in England, and William Henry Read, an energetic and activist merchant from A L Johnston & Co., they petitioned for the Straits Settlements to be transferred to the Colonial Office and administered directly as a Crown Colony. They demanded a Legislative Council for the Straits Settlements and the right for them to participate in government and administration.

In their petition, they accused Calcutta of a multitude of sins. But underlying these grievances was the lack of representation for the Straits Settlements in the India government. To them, the Governor was no better than a despot as he had little awareness and no regard for local issues. Calcutta had failed to take action to protect the merchants' interests. For instance, it had not dealt with piracy, it had not provided an adequate legal system and it persisted in a policy of non-intervention in the Malay States. Worse, it intended to dump more Indian convicts in Singapore, which the merchants saw as both a danger and humiliation.

It took more than a decade to address these grievances. The British government would only accede to the petition if Singapore was self-sufficient in its revenue. Eventually, on 1 April 1867, the Straits Settlements became a Crown Colony. As a Crown Colony, it was given its own constitution in the form of an 'Order in Council'. The structure and provisions of this constitution remained fundamentally unchanged for seventy-five years until Singapore fell to the Japanese in 1942. Singapore had a Legislative Council, and later, an Executive Council. The Colony was ruled by the Governor, who was the legal representative of the Queen. All executive authority centred on him. Defence, foreign affairs, finance and internal security were firmly controlled by the British.

The merchants had succeeded, and they got their wishes for direct rule and more political participation. The frontier-town era of Singapore's growth ended with the Transfer. But colonial rule was something that everyone would take a little getting used to. Little did they know that two years after the Transfer, there would be events that would transform Singapore and make their concerns look utterly provincial, narrow and self-serving.

Singapore's Breakout Moment

On 17 November 1869, some 5,000 nautical miles away from Singapore, the Suez Canal opened for business. By cutting through the Isthmus of Suez, this waterway connected the Mediterranean Sea to the Red Sea. The journey from Europe to Asia had suddenly became a lot shorter as ships no longer had to sail round the Horn of Africa and the Cape of Good Hope. The immediate impact of the opening of the Suez Canal was seen in Singapore's trade figures in 1870. A year after the canal's opening, total trade volume had almost doubled to $71 million. It was clear that Singapore was on the verge of its breakout moment, but a few other pieces had to be in place before that came about.

Though steamship technology and shorter travelling times between Europe and Asia mattered, Singapore's breakout moment really came when it gained a hinterland in the Malay peninsula. On its own, without any factories and plantations, Singapore's growth relied solely on entrepot trade, on connecting trading networks with other trading networks. A hinterland would be the source of goods that a port city like Singapore could export to markets all over the world. How did Singapore gain its hinterland? And what did this hinterland have that transformed Singapore from a regional port into a maritime gateway of global importance?

The benefits of having a hinterland were apparent from the 1840s, when Daeng Ibrahim, the shrewd and capable son of Temenggong

Abdu'r Rahman, opened up Johor to Chinese gambier and pepper planters. These crops, which become Johor's cash crops, were exported from Singapore. In turn, Chinese investment and manpower flowed into Johor from Singapore, further fuelling its growth and expansion.

These benefits multiplied when British policy in the Malay States shifted towards intervention. Although Singapore merchants agitated ceaselessly for intervention, the British were finally prodded into action only by their fear of other foreign powers extending into the Malay States. On 20 January 1874, the British and the local Malay chiefs signed the Pangkor Treaty. Intervention meant that the British now more or less ran Perak as a colony through a British Resident. Though the Resident was supposed to advise the Sultan, his de facto remit covered everything except Malay religion and custom. The Residential system, as it was known, soon extended to Selangor, Negeri Sembilan and Pahang which eventually joined Perak, to form the Federated Malay States in 1896. In 1888, Sarawak, North Borneo and Brunei became British protectorates. By the end of the century, British Malaya was a reality.

British intervention, which was really a euphemism for colonisation, catalysed and accelerated the transformation of both Singapore and Malaya. British investments in the tin industry in Malaya now boomed. Tin ore was mined in Malaya and then transported to Singapore, where it was smelted and then exported to American factories which demanded more and more tin for its food canning needs. By 1896, tin exports had quadrupled, and it all went through Singapore. Tin had become Singapore's first staple and Singapore had become a staple port. This relationship, where the hinterland supplied the raw material and Singapore provided the processing and then exported it globally, became the backbone of the entire Malayan economy.

Next, the seeds for the cash crop, rubber, were sown when Henry Ridley, arrived in Singapore to head the Botanic Gardens in 1888. 'Mad' Ridley, as the brilliant botanist was derisively called, was a rubber evangelist who truly believed in its economic value and potential. But the rubber boom would only materialise a decade later in the early years of the 20th century. And when it did, the rubber industry rode on the economic connections forged by the tin industry, driving Singapore's economic transformation as a staple port even further.

With these developments, Singapore put its typecast role as a source of Straits produce behind it. Its future was in exporting commodities that the global economy was hungry for. By the end of the century,

Singapore's trade was six times that of the 1870s. Singapore had come a long way from its humble trade in hornbill casques, lakawood and sea cucumbers. It was now a gateway to the global economy.

The tin boom brought new opportunities for businessmen. In 1890, the Straits Trading Company built a tin smelter on the island of Pulau Brani, which was situated in the port. In the same year, the Straits Steamship Company, a joint venture between European and Chinese businessmen, was founded to supply ships with the stores they needed. The number of shipping lines in Singapore also increased rapidly, with the German Norddeutscher Lloyd Company being the dominant player by the 1880s.

The same enterprising mindset cannot be said of the Tanjong Pagar Dock Company which owned Singapore's port facilities located in Keppel Harbour. In its hands, they were shabby, outdated and congested. Despite having acquired all its rivals by 1900, it still refused to invest in modernising the port which, with its wooden wharves and inability to service big ships, was becoming a disgrace. It was not just about prestige and reputation though. The port was the sole reason for Singapore's existence and the lifeline for the Malayan economy. Clearly, something had to be done.

Strategically, Singapore became a vital coaling station along with Gibraltar, Malta, Suez, Aden and Hong Kong in a chain of logistic bases that refuelled and resupplied the vessels of the Royal Navy. For the British, the Straits of Melaka became a critical sea lane between Europe and Asia. Singapore, very conveniently for the British, was in the middle. Consequently, the role of defending Britain's interests in the Far East would eventually converge on Singapore. But for now, in the era of Pax Britannica, there was no threat or enemy and until the late 19th century, no potential ones either.

To Need Them And To Suffer Them: The British & The Chinese In Singapore

No history of Singapore is complete without the story of the Chinese immigrant who came to Singapore, worked hard, avoided vice, made good, rose from rags to riches and became a solid pillar of the community. In reality, only a few became wealthy and, in turn, respected community leaders. Some immigrants were fortunate to make enough to return home to China. For most of them, this was a distant dream – life was hard, work was exhausting and living conditions were squalid. Many never saw home again.

Up until the late 1860s, only two things mattered to the British in frontier town Singapore – first, to keep free trade going and second, to keep costs down by using indirect rule. And with regard to the Chinese, they preferred to deal with community leaders or with the Straits Chinese merchants whom they could converse with more easily. For the new Chinese immigrant arriving in Singapore, the colonial government was a bit of an abstraction, like a distant, disinterested uncle.

During this period, who did the new immigrant in Singapore come into contact with? First it depended on which *bang*, which was dialect-based, he belonged to. Beneath the *bang* umbrella were the clan associations (*huiguan*) which were based on surnames, localities, economic activities or occupations. The Ngee Ann Kongsi, set up in 1830 and the Hokkien Huay Kuan, set up in 1839 are amongst the oldest clan associations in Singapore. They assisted the new immigrant with housing, employment and also acted as a support group. It is at this point that lines between the clan associations and the secret societies (*tiandihui*) become blurred. Nominally descendants of anti-Manchu organisations, the first secret societies came with the early immigrants and boasted a membership roll of some 5,000 by the mid-1800s.

The relationship was symbiotic. The merchants relied on the secret societies to provide and control the labour force. The secret societies also defended the merchants' 'turf'. They controlled much of the planting of gambier and pepper in Singapore through appointed headmen (*kangchu*). The merchants acted as tax collectors, particularly on opium, gambling, spirits and prostitution via the tax farm – the highest bidder was given the rights to collect taxes. The merchants (and the clan associations they led or were members of) were thus tightly integrated with the activities of the secret societies. This tight web, and the social control wielded by the clan associations and secret societies, kept the Chinese community under close management.

The colonial government did not find this repugnant. After all, the bulk of government revenue came from the opium taxes. Besides, the Chinese population were seen as transient rather than permanent. They dealt with leading Chinese merchants, who then dealt with their own dialect groups. Whether some of these leaders, for example, Hoo Ah Kay, held leadership positions in the secret societies is a matter of conjecture. To sink resources into managing the Chinese was an expense the government did not need nor saw the need for.

The power to manage and organise the Chinese also gave the secret societies the power to mobilise them for gang violence. In May 1854, a ten-day riot broke out between the Hokkiens and Teochews, leading to five hundred deaths and three hundred homes destroyed. The government found itself impotent. The police force was utterly inadequate and military force had to be deployed. Still, this spate of large-scale gang violence paralysed the colony and demonstrated the serious inadequacies of indirect rule. Something had to be done before the *bang*, clan associations and secret societies became a de facto state within a state.

It was another twenty years before the colonial government acted to manage the Chinese community more directly. Mass immigration was partly responsible for this. The Chinese population grew by 30,000 annually from the mid-1800s. This also meant that the secret societies became bigger and more powerful. Also, Singapore was a Crown Colony by this time and the colonial government, compelled by the Colonial Office in London, had to act to investigate and regulate the labour situation.

Some fact-finding was in order and this was what Governor William Jervois intended when he appointed a commission in 1875. Its report, presented in 1876, was telling. It admitted that the government knew 'little or nothing of the Chinese' and concluded that 'the immense majority of them know still less of the government'. The colonial government knew that to continue with indirect rule was to court disaster.

In 1877, the colonial government moved towards direct rule by setting up a Chinese Protectorate. William Pickering was appointed as the 'Protector of Chinese'. Pickering, who spoke and read Chinese, soon stamped his authority on the coolie trade and then on the affairs of the Chinese community at large. He began by smashing the control that secret societies exerted over the coolie trade. To do so, the Legislative Council enacted the Chinese Immigrants Ordinance and the Crimping Ordinance. Even before any Chinese immigrant was allowed to come onshore, a Protectorate officer boarded the ship to inspect it. This officer gave out handbills that told them they could come to the Protectorate for help. Employment contracts, duly numbered and lodged at the Protectorate, were made mandatory. The presence of these officers and the immigration process made it clear that Singapore was run by the British and not by the secret societies.

Pickering next turned his attention to the protection and welfare of Chinese women and girls. From 1881, the Protectorate took over the administration of the Contagious Diseases Ordinance. All brothels and prostitutes had to be registered. A *Poh Leung Kok*, loosely translated as 'Office for the Protection of Virtue', was set up to protect women or girls who had been sold, lured or forced into prostitution. This applied to most of the young Chinese girls who came to Singapore in the late 1870s.

Both Pickering and Samuel Dunlop, who were joint Registrar of Societies, were however not in favour of an outright ban of the secret societies, preferring instead a gradual clampdown. They both felt that this would drive the secret societies underground where they could no longer be monitored or engaged. However, Governor Cecil Clementi Smith, who succeeded Jervois, favoured such a ban. Banning them, he reasoned, would establish the British as the supreme government of Singapore in the eyes of the Chinese. He prevailed, and in 1890, the Societies Ordinance was introduced.

The logic behind this landmark law was subtle. All societies with more than ten members must be registered and approved. Those who failed to do so were illegal and could be banned. It was not an out-and-out ban on secret societies, but no sane secret society leader would voluntarily register his outfit and give up details of its members or information about what it did. And since all of them acted rationally, their societies were all banned. Eventually, ten major secret societies were broken up and their power over the Chinese community was smashed. Though small-time gangsterism still persisted in the form of extortion and turf wars, the secret societies no longer called the shots in the Chinese community. As a last resort, the colonial government had the power to banish troublemakers from Singapore. This was a powerful deterrent.

In 1889, the government created the Chinese Advisory Board. It could now rule the Chinese community through its intermediaries and community leaders from the various *bang* appointed to the Board. In a way, engagement had begun earlier in 1869 when Hoo Ah Kay was appointed to the Legislative Council. But to sit on the Council, one had to be able to speak English. This automatically ruled out most of the leaders in the Chinese community and also privileged the Straits Chinese community. However, the Straits Chinese commanded little influence or respect amongst the Chinese masses. Still, both the Board and Chinese representation on the Legislative Council gave meaning to a sense of being 'Chinese', which was beginning to be more than just a colonial administrative classification.

As the British were making their first overtures to the Chinese community, the Qing government also decided that its overseas Chinese subjects had to be engaged. In 1876, it set up a consulate in Singapore and in 1880, appointed Tso Ping-Lung as the Chinese Consul. In 1900, Dr. Sun Yat Sen, visited Singapore for the first time to meet with the noted reformer, Kang Youwei. Kang, the exiled leader of the abortive Hundred Days' Reform Movement in China, was in Singapore at the invitation of Khoo Seok Wan, a leading Straits Chinese merchant. The contest for the loyalty of the Singapore Chinese had begun.

The Reality Of Political And Economic Displacement: The Malays In Singapore

When Sultan Hussein Shah was recognised on 28 January 1819 by the British, he harboured hopes of establishing a new *negeri* (state) in Singapore with their support and enjoying the customary privileges and dues that came with it. In his eyes, as the *raja* (king), the British presence in his *negeri* was dependent on his royal writ and they were here as tenants.

But with one stroke – the Treaty of Friendship and Alliance of 2 August 1824 – those hopes were extinguished for good. Now bereft of his realm and his customary dues, Sultan Hussein Shah was relegated to the political margins in his Istana in Kampong Glam in Singapore. His death in Melaka in 1835 saw his descendants being reduced to a genteel poverty from mid-century. Without a *raja*, Singapore's Malay community found itself lacking leadership and organisation in a time of rapid and unsettling change.

The ones who benefited most from this political ambiguity were the descendants of Temenggong Abdu'r Rahman. His resourceful and intelligent son, Daeng Ibrahim, would oversee the successful opening and development of Johor from the 1840s. In 1855, Ali, who was Sultan Hussein Shah's heir, was all but in name bought out by Temenggong Daeng Ibrahim for the sum of 5,000 Spanish dollars and an allowance of 500 Spanish dollars for himself and his heirs. In return, he ceded the full sovereignty of Johor, with the exception of Kesang in Muar. In 1886, the British crowned Temenggong Abdu'r Rahman's grandson, Abu Bakar Sultan of Johor. Sultan Hussein Shah's political bloodline had come to a sorry end.

With the Temenggong's descendants focusing their political and economic energies on Johor, Singapore Malays were bereft of leadership. The community struggled as Singapore developed rapidly as a British colony. Lacking the technical skills that the colonial economy demanded, the majority of Malays were unable to partake in the colony's rapid growth and transformation into a modern economy with global significance. They were also squeezed out of commerce and trade by Chinese and European merchants. As a result, they tended towards work as boatmen, fishermen or carpenters. Over time, they were employed as policemen, watchmen, gardeners or drivers. As European and Chinese economic domination grew, the Malays were gradually marginalised.

Malay immigrants from the archipelago assimilated easily into the community. Some became economically successful, such as the Bugis, who owned substantial property in Singapore. Some took up positions as imams, in mosques or became small-time traders. The Arabs became very successful in Singapore. With their wealth, influence and religious orientation, the Arabs became the de facto leaders of the Malay community by late 19th century.

At the same time, the Singapore Malays had to confront the reality of their numbers being diluted by the mass influx of Chinese and Indian immigrants. From 1824 to 1911, the proportion of Malays in the population fell from 60.2% to 13.8%. In contrast, the proportion of Chinese grew from 31% to 72.4%, overtaking the Malays in 1836. Such was the scale and extent of the Chinese and Indian immigration that the arrival of Malay and Arab immigrants had little impact in rebalancing the population distribution. By the mid-19th century, Singapore was a city run by Europeans and populated by a Chinese majority.

Singapore's strategic location provided significant connections for Singapore Malays. Singapore was the heart of the pilgrimage traffic to Mecca. It was also the hub for Dutch East Indies labourers from Java who were employed in the rubber plantations. Singapore also served as the cultural hub of the Malay-Muslim world in Southeast Asia with Bahasa Melayu (Malay) as its lingua franca. In sum, however, the 19th century saw the Malay community being confronted with a modernity that they were unprepared for. There were also big questions unanswered. For instance, who would and who should lead the Singapore Malays? How should the Malay way of life be protected? In sum, these questions sowed the seeds that only a nascent Malay nationalism that emerged later in the 20th century could answer.

The Indians in Singapore

The first Indians in Singapore were the sepoys of the Bengal Native Infantry and the Bazaar Contingent that came with them. The latter comprised *dhobis* (laundrymen), milkmen, tea-makers and house servants. As with the Chinese, most of these immigrants did not identify with being 'Indian'. The Indians who came to Singapore tended to cluster along the lines of ethnicity, class, religion and occupation. But unlike the Chinese however, there was the added element of caste. As their numbers were small, the community was fragmented and did not develop the social structures or organisations that provided community leadership. Also, the Indian community was more transient. By the early 20th century, the community numbered some 28,000, comprising 9% of the population. For every one hundred Indians arriving in the Malay Peninsula, there were sixty who left Singapore for India. They were a minority group with little political clout. For them, Singapore was a place to make their fortunes and then return home.

Otherwise, Indian immigrants tended towards niche sectors that supported the colonial economy. North Indian immigrants such as Sikhs took up positions in the Straits Settlements Police Force in 1879. The Chettiars, who were amongst the earliest of entrepreneurs, established the financial backbone of the colony, serving all and sundry, including European planters, Chinese businessmen and Indian traders by extending credit to them. This plugged into a larger regional network that spanned Southeast Asia and South India. Others such as Parsis, Gujaratis and Bengalis were active in commerce and trade. As colonial society developed, its demand for educated workers increased. To meet this demand, Sri Lankan Tamils and Malayalees were recruited as teachers, doctors, administrators and junior staff in the government.

Not all Indian immigrants came here as free men. The colonial policy of employing Indian convict labour in Singapore for public works projects began in 1825. By 1860, some two thousand convict labourers were deployed in Singapore and they contributed greatly to the Singapore's physical development through land clearance, bridge building and road construction. Some of our finest examples of colonial architecture such as the Saint Andrew's Cathedral, built in 1862, and the Istana, built in 1869, were the handiwork of convict labour.

CHAPTER FOUR

Decline and Fall

1900–1942

Imperial Hubris

On the night the first Japanese bombs fell on Fortress Singapore, on 8 December 1941, it was business as usual at the opulent Raffles Hotel, with well-heeled patrons enjoying its nightly dinner and dance. On 31 January 1942, two weeks before the Singapore's surrender to the Japanese, the Raffles was still advertising this nightly reveric in *The Straits Times*. Singapore island glittered in the night sky and the Japanese pilots found their targets easily. As dawn broke, it became clear that Singapore was at war. The Japanese had landed troops in Kota Bahru and they were heading south fast. Before long, the defences and defenders of Fortress Singapore would be tested and found wanting. And in a matter of seventy days, the Japanese would capture Fortress Singapore, on 15 February 1942. This was a British tragedy of hubristic proportions.

Imperial City

In 1941, Singapore was one of the British Empire's leading cities. It was the capital of the Straits Settlements and British Malaya and the bastion of British military power in the Far East. The power and might of the Union Jack radiated from Singapore. It conveyed a sense of order and stability that only the rule of law could have brought about. This was the flag that protected all who lived, worked and toiled under its sway. Singapore's handsome cityscape proudly proclaimed: British power was permanent, inviolable and unshakeable. But as the adage goes, pride comes before the fall.

Anyone visiting Singapore in 1941 would have been impressed by its many beautiful and monumental civic buildings. The Municipal

Building (later known as the City Hall) with its Corinthian columns and the classical style Supreme Court with a dome reminiscent of Saint Paul's in London fronted the Padang, the green rectangular lawn that had been an open civic space since Singapore's founding. Across from the Padang stood the Cenotaph inscribed with the words 'Our Glorious Dead' – a solemn memorial to those who left to fight in the First World War in Europe and made the ultimate sacrifice. To the east on Beach Road was the Art Deco-styled home of the Singapore Volunteer Corps and the Straits Settlements Volunteer Corps. North of the Padang, at the foothills of Fort Canning Hill, were the Central Fire Station with its distinct 'blood and bandages' façade of red and whites and the Hill Street Police Station with 927 double-leaved louvred windows that punctuated its neoclassical façade. Closer to the Singapore River and the bustling commercial hub at Raffles Place were the imposing Fullerton Building that housed the General Post Office and the Empress Place buildings that housed the offices of the colonial administration. These buildings served as powerful reminders of Singapore's importance in the British Empire and that here, free trade and rule of law reigned supreme.

Singapore's other physical structures and buildings reflected its prosperity. In 1905, a medical school was established after much pressure from the Straits Chinese. In 1926, it moved into its new premises located on the grounds of the new General Hospital and was renamed the King Edward VII College of Medicine. Two years later, and once again after much Straits Chinese pressure, Raffles College commenced classes at its leafy campus with its stately buildings built around two quadrangles in Bukit Timah, occupying the grounds of the Botanic Gardens' former Economic Garden. The founding of these institutions demonstrated how influential the Straits Chinese community was in advancing its interests, in this case, funding for tertiary education.

The Colonial Economy And Its Gateways

Beyond these symbols and structures, Singapore was nothing without its economy and the activity it generated. Any visitor to Singapore during this period would be impressed and fascinated by its variety and intensity of commercial activity. In the city were to be found businesses of all sizes: European agency houses, Chinese trading enterprises, small shops, street traders. Bales of rubber, piles of newly-harvested pineapples and tin ore sat in warehouses, canneries and smelters, waiting to be processed and then shipped out to markets all around the world. Most of the rubber would end up as tyres on American cars. The pineapple, the symbol of tropicality and sunshine, would be canned and adorn the shelves of grocers in the United Kingdom and America. Already by the 1920s, only Hawaii outstripped Singapore in the export of canned pineapples. The same can be said of other commodities such as petroleum and palm oil.

In the 20th century, Singapore's new role as a staple port became bigger than ever. It was more large scale and intense. Now, not only British Malaya but the entire region funnelled its raw produce through Singapore for shipment to destinations around the world. Singapore had neither huge rubber plantations, nor rich tin mines or oil wells of its own. Yet, Singapore provided the crucial final step that added value – raw, unprocessed commodities became useable primary products for the manufactures of the industrial world. And it all converged in Singapore because it was extensively connected with the world through its port.

Rubber became Singapore's second staple in the early 20th century, after tin. The efforts of 'Mad' Ridley finally bore fruit as Singapore planters turned to rubber after coffee failed as a cash crop. Rubber was profitable because it was in great demand – the motorcar with its promise of mobility and the automobile industry needed rubber in large quantities to make car tyres to provide a comfortable ride. Riding this tide, the rubber industry boomed, and Malayan rubber cornered half of the world's market by 1914. Most of this was exported through Singapore.

Oil was Singapore's third staple. The oil-fired ship became more popular and common during this period. Singapore's businessmen tapped into this by building bunkers and berths on Pulau Bukom for petroleum coming through the Dutch East Indies. It was then refined and exported. By 1939, more than 700,000 tons of petroleum was refined here. Once again, most of it was exported through Singapore.

A port city's lifeline is its port. The port is however more than just its ships, docks and wharves. Behind every port's warehouses, wharves, docks and coal stacks is an entire infrastructure system that connects warehouses with ships, and ships with wharves and docks. It is an interface that works seamlessly to make commerce and trade possible. Singapore's port was not just one of the strategic nodes in the British Empire that served the global markets. It was also a prestige project, a status symbol that befitted the splendour of the British Empire. To serve only an economic function was not enough, it had to be of a certain size, scale and stature to impress and overawe.

In 1903, John Anderson, the Governor, decided that the port had to be modernised. To do so, he 'calmly set in process a policy of expropriation'. In 1905, the Government bought out the Tanjong Pagar Dock Company, hitherto owner and operator of the port. The port, the seventh largest in the world, was too important and strategic to be left in private hands and to the whims of its shareholders. The public stood solidly behind John Anderson on this matter. To run the port, the Tanjong Pagar Dock Board was set up. On 1 July 1913, the Singapore Harbour Board was set up as a board under the auspices of the 1912 Straits Settlements Port Ordinance to manage and run the port of Singapore.

Under the direction of the Singapore Harbour Board, the port became a truly impressive creation, rivalled only by a handful elsewhere in the Empire and the world. It had a railway terminus and a railway line. It had approximately 11,000 feet of wharves and quays in water deep enough for large vessels to berth alongside. It had its own power station, its own workshops, slipways and heavy machinery for ship repair. There were five dry docks for ship repairs – the largest of these was the King's Dock that was 879 feet long, 100 feet wide and 34 feet deep. Together with its coal stacks, warehouses, refrigerated stores and storage tanks, Singapore's port was well equipped and more than capable of handling vast volumes of cargo that passed through it.

In 1923, the Johore Causeway opened and provided Singapore with its first land-based gateway and with it, its first direct road and rail link to the Malay States up north. A visitor could now travel upcountry via trunk road or railway to major cities such as Kuala Lumpur, Ipoh and Johore Bahru without disembarking at Kranji to ford the Straits of Johore by ferry. Similarly, goods could be transported directly from mine or plantation all the way into the port itself. 'Now the produce of the entire Peninsula drained southward into Singapore' – this was a fitting description of the inter-dependence between Singapore and its hinterland. On 2 May 1932, the elegant Tanjong Pagar Railway Station with its high-ceilinged main hall and four allegorical statues symbolising Agriculture, Commerce, Transport and Industry, opened in Singapore. The four pillars of the Malayan economy converged at Tanjong Pagar, a symbol befitting Singapore's economic role.

Singapore's final and most modern gateway, the Art Deco styled Kallang Airport, built at a cost of $9 million, opened in style on 12 June 1937. Escorted by twenty-four aircraft from the Royal Air Force and the Straits Settlements Volunteer Air Force, an Imperial Airlines Atlanta airliner carrying governor Shenton Thomas touched down on its grassy runway at 4:30 p.m. Kallang Airport (officially named the Singapore Marine and Land Airport) was, after the usual speeches, declared open. In Shenton's eyes, Kallang Airport was the very 'essence of modernity' and undoubtedly 'the finest airport in the world'. Amelia Earhart, the renowned female aviator, stopping over on 20 June 1937, described it in similarly glowing terms as 'the aviation miracle of the East'. Less than a fortnight later, Amelia Earhart disappeared while flying over the Pacific Ocean – she was never heard from again.

Designed by the Public Works Department's (PWD) chief architect Frank Dorrington Ward, Kallang Airport comprised a rectangular terminal building with a distinctive circular control tower in the middle. A traveller who arrived or departed Singapore no longer did so from the RAF airfield at Seletar, which received Singapore's first civilian aircraft in 1928. The stylish and well-appointed Kallang terminal building awaited him, and while he was there, he could send a postcard (postmarked 'Singapore') to loved ones back home, pick up a book or change some money or simply enjoy a meal while waiting for his flight. Kallang Airport was truly the jewel of the empire's aeronautical crown.

On 28 June 1937, Wearne Air Services began a regular service between Singapore, Kuala Lumpur and Penang. Deploying the de Havilland Dragon Rapide, a twin-engine biplane capable of carrying up to eight passengers, the service soon expanded to cover towns such as Taiping, Ipoh and Kota Bahru. These early air services carried mail and newspapers, bringing the world a little closer to Singapore. And although these were early days for civil aviation in Singapore, Kallang Airport's opening signalled the expansion of Singapore's role as gateway to the region and the world into the skies. This would open up a wealth of economic opportunities decades later.

As economic activity, business services and infrastructural gateways converged, some groups came to dominate entire economic sectors and some spectacular fortunes were made. Colloquially referred to as *towkays*, men like Tan Kah Kee, Lim Nee Soon, Aw Boon Haw and Lee Kong Chian were the supremos of Singapore business in the inter-war years.

Of these four men, Tan Kah Kee alone attained the status of a legend in the Chinese community. Born in 1874, in Fujian Province in China, he emigrated to Singapore in 1890. In 1904, after the family business folded, Tan founded his own firm, Kheam Aik. In 1914, he made his first fortune from rubber and pineapple through some shrewd investments – he became a millionaire. In 1925, Tan was at the peak of his commercial success, making $8 million in that year alone. Tan Kah Kee & Co. was a conglomerate of its day. It owned rubber and pineapple plantations, rubber mills, pineapple canneries, factories that manufactured rubber products and other consumer goods – his canvas shoes with rubber soles were produced to the tune of seven million pairs a year and were sold all over Southeast Asia and China. His factories also assembled bicycles, concocted toothpaste and hair lotion, fired bricks and tiles and also produced chocolate, sweets and biscuits. And Tan sold all these through a chain of retail shops he owned and an extensive network of agents he worked with. He was an industrialist, a supply chain logistician and a consummate businessman all rolled into one.

His contemporary, Lim Nee Soon, a Teochew Straits Chinese was born in 1879 in Singapore. He too made his fortune from pineapple and rubber. Educated at Saint Joseph's Institution and Anglo-Chinese School, Lim was a pioneer in rubber and pineapple planting in Singapore, developing large plantations in rural areas in the north of Singapore. One of them, Nee Soon, bears his name which lives on today in the *pinyinsed* form 'Yishun' as the name of a large public housing estate built on his former plantations. He also ventured into banking and served as director of many companies.

The Politics Of Being Chinese In Singapore

Politically, the most powerful people in Singapore were the Governor, his retinue and the small number of British officials in the Malayan Civil Service. But economically, the most powerful people, were the Chinese *towkays*. The Chinese community respected the *towkays*. They had standing and influence. They looked up to them, listened to them and supported them. Therefore, to manage the Chinese community, the British needed the *towkays* on their side.

At the turn of the century, the Chinese in Singapore were generally an industrious and peaceful lot who kept to themselves, their businesses and their jobs. This changed in October 1911 as the Xinhai Revolution broke out in China. A sense of being 'Chinese', an identity that cut across dialect and clan lines emerged. With this came an identification with the idea of a Chinese nation and an affiliation or loyalty to the Republic of China. In 1919, the May Fourth Movement in China transformed this largely passive affiliation into an active identification with Chinese nationalism and open political activism.

On 4 May 1919, demonstrations and protests erupted in China at Tiananmen Square against a national humiliation that had taken place. At the Paris Peace Conference, the Allies rejected China's request to reclaim territories formerly held by Germany in Shandong, especially the port of Qingdao. Instead, they ceded the territories to Japan, adding to the list of humiliations that China had suffered at Japanese hands. The Chinese were outraged. In China, university students protested and demonstrated.

It did not take long for this sentiment to arrive in Singapore. Just days later, anti-Japanese pamphlets began circulating in Singapore. Influential voices in the Chinese community called for a broad boycott of Japanese products and businesses. Anonymous letters were circulated to the press to pressure and intimidate individuals into complying with the boycott. Things came to a head on 19 June 1919 when a full-scale riot broke out.

This outburst of political activism and the riot alarmed the colonial government. It responded with a series of repressive measures to limit Chinese political activity in Singapore. In 1920, the governor Lawrence Guillemard enacted the Education Ordinance to check political activism and subversion in Chinese schools. All schools, teachers and staff had to be registered. The government could inspect schools, their curricula and teaching materials. Any school could be declared illegal and closed if it could not explain why it was involved in political activities. Next, he introduced the Printing Press Ordinance to control publishers and those who ran the printing presses. Eventually, in July 1925, the Kuomintang (KMT) was banned.

In 1929, the Governor, Sir Cecil Clementi, extended these repressive measures. The KMT ban remained. Fund-raising for the

KMT in China was forbidden. Anti-colonial views in the Chinese press were censored. Immigration control was first used in 1930 to weed out political radicals. By 1933, the number of new immigrants was just one-tenth of that three years earlier. Next, an Aliens Ordinance was introduced to replace the Immigration Restriction Ordinance. An 'alien' was one who was not British or Indian. And the Malays, being the indigenous people of the land were not 'alien', so it became clear who the 'alien' was. This law gave the colonial government the power to register and control the 'aliens' who were resident in Singapore.

These crude and blunt measures were implemented when the Great Depression in 1929 brought about great economic hardship in Singapore. The Chinese Chamber of Commerce protested. The Straits Chinese did the same. The government, they charged, was anti-Chinese. The contributions of the Chinese to the development of Singapore and Malaya meant absolutely nothing at all. For the first time, the Chinese in Singapore, immigrant or Straits-born, were united against a government that obviously feared and distrusted them.

Still, the British were canny and sensible enough to know that, whether they liked it or not, they had at least to engage with the Chinese community leaders. The laws could only do so much. And they simply could not just ignore the people who controlled entire sectors of the economy and kept the colony running. They simply could not ignore someone like Tan Kah Kee.

But Tan was not just another successful Chinese *towkay* and multi-millionaire. There were many others like him in the Chinese community anyway. What made Tan stand out and what gave him a high level of regard and moral standing was his philanthropy. The Chinese expected that a man with wealth should give back to the community – having taken from society, one should give back to society. Tan did this to an extent that few were able to match.

Tan gave exceedingly generously to education, which was something the Chinese valued greatly. In Singapore, he co-founded three primary schools and two secondary schools, including the Chinese High School in 1919. In 1921, he founded the Amoy University in Fujian Province. Tan's name spread far and wide after this. It was estimated that by the mid-1920s, Tan had given some $8,000,000 to education. A further $200,000 went to other charitable causes such as hospitals and relief funds.

And since the British could not ignore Tan Kah Kee, they recognised him as a community leader. In 1918, they made him a Justice of the Peace, and in 1923, appointed him to the Chinese Advisory Board. More importantly, they endorsed Tan's political role in the Chinese community. In British eyes, Tan's non-partisan stance neutralised the political forces that were competing to lead the community. It was clear to them that Tan's energies were directed towards China-oriented causes and activities. He was a patriot and a moderate, not a subversive and certainly not one who endorsed violence for the cause. The British trusted him.

The British were tacitly supportive when Tan directed the community's response towards news of Japanese atrocities in Shandong in 1928. He directed a boycott of Japanese products as anti-Japanese activities gathered momentum. Pamphlets were distributed. Public speeches were made at gatherings. The Chinese press adopted an anti-Japanese stance and it comes as no surprise that Tan owned one of these newspapers, the *Nanyang Siang Pau*, that had a wide circulation.

Anti-Japanese feeling, never far from the hearts of the Singapore Chinese, erupted once again on 7 July 1937 when Japan invaded China. The KMT government appealed to overseas Chinese to raise funds and volunteer for the war effort. Similarly, the British initially supported Tan when he became the leader of fund-raising efforts in Singapore in 1937. By 1938, he was coordinating such efforts across Southeast Asia. With backing from Lee Kong Chian, the chairman of the Chinese Chamber of Commerce (a multimillionaire and philanthropist in his own right and also, incidentally, Tan's son-in-law), Tan set up a structure that raised funds in a methodical and organised manner. He organised fund-raising along dialect lines to ensure that all Chinese, including the Straits Chinese, participated in these efforts.

The Chinese showed their anti-Japanese emotions openly. They stopped buying from Japanese shops. The effect of this boycott was visible and palpable as trade with Japan shrank significantly in 1938. Japanese doctors, dentists and barbers lost customers in droves as the Chinese boycotted them. Some Japanese were even turfed out of their homes and business premises by their Chinese landlords.

All this unnerved the colonial government. They were particularly worried about how the communists would work their way into these relief efforts. These worries were not unfounded. After a setback in 1931 when the arrest of a French communist agent, Serge le Franc, broke the back of the newly formed Malayan Communist Party (MCP), it had recovered sufficiently by 1938 to infiltrate the relief movement. By 1939, the MCP rode on the rising tide of Chinese patriotism to transform itself into a patriotic, anti-Japanese movement that made inroads into schools and trade unions in the name of nationalism. The MCP was a political reality that the British could not wish away.

In late January 1942, as the fall of Singapore to the Japanese looked imminent, Tan was asked by the Governor Shenton Thomas to mobilise the Singapore Chinese. Under Tan's direction, a Singapore Chinese Mobilisation Committee was formed. A thousand volunteered to fight the Japanese. The British trusted Tan to the end.

Whilst the immigrant Chinese were engaged in overt political activism, their Straits Chinese counterparts generally stood above the political fray. They were the 'King's Chinese' and they were British subjects who exercised considerable influence through their appointments and the Straits Chinese Business Association (SCBA). The outbreak of the First World War in 1914 brought forth an overt and public show of loyalty to the British crown. Tan Jiak Kim, a prominent Straits Chinese community leader and public figure, donated $37,000 to the Prince of Wales Relief Fund that was used to fund the British war effort. In 1916, he presented a fighter aircraft christened (albeit rather unimaginatively) as 'Malaya No. 21' at a cost of £2,250 to the war effort. The Straits Chinese also participated in a Malaya-wide fund-raising campaign that furnished the Royal Air Force with a fleet of fifty-three aircraft. Straits Chinese youth were also encouraged to sign up for military service in the Singapore Volunteer Corps.

For the Straits Chinese, these public demonstrations of loyalty and recognition by the British hid a reality that excluded them from the higher rungs of government and the civil service. On the surface, they were the equals of any other British subject. After all, prominent Straits Chinese leaders held seats in the government – the Executive, Legislative and Municipal Councils. Of these leaders, Tan Cheng Lock, the scion of a wealthy Melaka family and a successful businessman, was active in public life. Tan first served on the Legislative Council from 1923 to 1934 before taking up appointment on the Executive Council from 1933 to 1935. He was a vocal and ardent advocate for more political representation and social reform. Many, like Song Ong Siang, were conferred honours by the British. But this seeming equality stopped there. The Malayan Civil Service was closed to them. They could only serve in the subordinate Straits Settlements Civil Service set up in 1934 to admit non-European British subjects into junior government positions.

The Beginnings of Malay Political Activism

The normally placid Malay community was astir as a contest was afoot over the leadership of the Malay community and over what it meant to be a 'Malay' in colonial Singapore. Together, these two contests set off the beginnings of Malay political activism in Singapore, an activism that eventually led to the emergence of a distinct style of Malay political leadership, community organisation and mobilisation.

The contest over who would lead the Malays arose because of simmering resentment towards the Arabs. The Arabs were spectacularly successful business-wise and they used their wealth to buy land, especially on the city fringes, where the Malays lived. Arab money had displaced the Malays from their kampungs and homes – this was something that no amount of Arab charity and philanthropy could assuage.

Who would lead the Malays? To lead a community is to advocate for its interests and to address or solve its problems. In Singapore during the inter-war years, this meant confronting, with honesty and candidness, the most pressing challenge facing the Malays – how should they respond to the displacement colonialism wrought? To a group of younger Malays, existing organisations such as the Persekutuan Islam Singapura (PIS) were incapable of rising to the challenge. The PIS, led by Arabs and Jawi Peranakans, was derisively painted as a 'rich man's association' that was entirely self-absorbed and incapable of even taking the least interest in the community's problems, much less deal with existential issues.

This group of younger Malays were, in many ways, the product of colonial modernity. They had a distinctly Singapore Malay outlook and were, in a way, the archetypes of the modern Singapore Malay. Mohamed Eunos Abdullah, educated at Raffles Institution, cut an active figure in public life. He was a Justice of the Peace, a member of the Muslim Advisory Board and the first Malay municipal commissioner.

Professionally, he was a journalist, first editing the *Utusan Melayu* and later, the progressive and urbane *Lembaga Melayu* which was also the sole Malay language daily from 1922 to 1931. Similarly, Dr. Abdul Samad, educated at King Edward VII College of Medicine, was Singapore's first Malay doctor. Tengku Kadir, a descendant of Malay royalty, was a known public figure. These men were urbane, professional, middle-class and also deeply religious. They were also politically astute – in 1921, as a riposte to the indolence of the PIS, they set up the Muslim Institute to advocate Malay issues.

In 1924, the colonial government decided to appoint an additional Asian representative to the Legislative Council. Naturally, the PIS insisted that a Muslim be appointed. The MI rejected this and stated, quite unequivocally, that the appointee must be a Malay. It was a bid to reclaim the leadership of the Singapore Malays. Ethnicity, and not faith, it insisted, should be the determining factor. In the end, the British went the way of the MI and appointed Mohamed Eunos as Singapore's first Malay Legislative Councillor.

Any person leading a community would need a base and an organisation that could mobilise manpower and resources to canvass support. For Mohamed Eunos to be effective in his work, he needed such a base. On 14 May 1926, the Kesatuan Melayu Singapura (KMS) or the Singapore Malay Union was founded. Eunos now had his base and the Malays had their first political organisation. The KMS held its first meeting at the Istana Kampong Glam – this was the highly symbolic Royal Palace of Sultan Hussein Shah. Only Malays, defined by ethnicity and culture, could be members. It was a Malay organisation for Malays. Non-Malay Muslims, including Arabs and Indian Muslims, were excluded. In the absence of a *raja*, the Singapore Malays would no longer let anyone else lead them. They would lead themselves.

Although political in its outlook, the KMS was not a political organisation. It had no interest in seeking power or in challenging the colonial government. It was conservative, openly loyalist and willing to work within existing political realities. The case of Kampung Melayu illustrates this well. In 1927, with the support of Tan Cheng Lock in the Legislative Council, Eunos proposed the establishment of a Malay Reservation known as Kampung Melayu. Modelled after Kampung Bahru in Kuala Lumpur, this provided Malays with a space to maintain their traditional lifestyles, away from the city. Much legwork went into the proposal before Eunos presented it. They got a sense of where the Singapore Malays stood on the issue before getting Eunos to propose it at the council. In this, the KMS was organised, thorough and professional as an advocate of the community's interests. In 1929, this vision became reality. Kampung Melayu was set up in eastern Singapore, just outside the city limits. It was a powerful moment for Singapore Malays. For the first time since the diminution of Sultan Hussein's bloodline from the political scene, the Singapore Malays were being led by one of their own once again.

Imperial Twilight – Overstretch

The end of the First World War signalled the beginning of a gradual decline of Imperial Britain. This might seem a little counterintuitive if we consider the following. The empire was at its greatest territorial extent ever, covering a quarter of the world's land area, and King George V reigned over 400 million people or a quarter of the world's population. However, size is not everything. The consequences of the First World War in the form of war weariness and a huge national debt that had ballooned some ten times to finance the war, all combined to weaken Britain's ability to maintain and meet its strategic commitments and liabilities globally. The Anglo-Japanese Alliance (1902) is a case in point. It was for a long time a fixture of British foreign policy in Asia, and it was allowed to lapse in 1923 as Britain sought closer ties with the emergent global power (and also its principal creditor), the United States of America. Britain's position as the leading power in Asia was dependent on a close partnership with the USA and the tacit recognition of this geopolitical reality. This partnership was necessary because Britain no longer had the resources to maintain both a Home Fleet and a Far Eastern Fleet that its strategic commitments demanded. At the same time, America's naval parity in the Far East was acknowledged in the Washington Naval Treaty (1923). British power in Asia therefore hinged on two elements. The first was the availability and willingness of the Americans to keep potential adversaries at bay in Asia. The second was Britain's ability to dispatch a fleet to the Far East in a period of tension. The first element would be in question if the Americans became isolationist in both foreign policy and outlook. The second element would be in question if Britain had to, at the same time when a fleet in the Far East was needed, fight a war in Europe on which its survival depended. Britain's

Far Eastern defence strategy thus rested on a hope and a prayer. And while Britain hoped and prayed that its strategic premises would hold, a naval base was needed.

In the 1920s, it was decided that Britain needed a naval base in Singapore to defend its imperial interests in the Far East. What use, however, was a naval base if there was no battle fleet assigned to the Far East? And what use was a naval base and a battle fleet if its approaches, air, land and sea, were undefended? As the 1930s approached, the international situation worsened with the rise of militarist Japan in Asia and Nazi Germany in Europe. Both powers were bent on challenging and upending the existing international order. Britain was, as it turned out, incapable of coping with these twin threats. It was strategically and militarily overstretched. Singapore's eventual capitulation to the Japanese on 15 February 1942 was sealed the moment the planning assumptions of Singapore's defence were laid.

The Singapore Strategy, as it came to be known, assumed the following. There would, first and foremost, be no permanent Royal Navy battle fleet stationed in the Far East. A fleet could be despatched and expected to reach Singapore within forty-two days. A small garrison, together with fortifications such as coastal gun batteries could defend and hold Singapore (because of the naval base) until the fleet arrived. The arrival of this fleet would deter any potential aggressor and engage it if necessary. These tenuous assumptions held for most of the 1920s in the absence of any significant threat in Europe and in the Far East. Based on these assumptions, Singapore was chosen as the site of the naval base in June 1921. In 1923, £11 million was allocated to build the naval base. The naval base was to be built in Sembawang and it was accessible via the Straits of Johor from the west. An airfield would be built at nearby Seletar.

Hyperbolically described as 'the Gibraltar of the East' and 'the bastion of British might', the naval base was finally completed in 1938. This hyperbole played up the obvious and neglected the subtle. The 'Gibraltar of the East' possessed impressive new dry docks, new airfields at Tengah and Sembawang, new barracks in Selarang for garrison troops and a network of coastal batteries that covered its seaward approaches. 'Fortress Singapore', another inflated moniker that was coined during this period, was assumed to be impregnable. The trappings of imperial power – the Command House, the Admiralty

House and the vast King George VI Dock opened in 1938 – merely papered over the paucity of British military resources in the Far East.

This impregnable fortress was however vulnerable to one thing – the shift in the international balance of power that was triggered in 1931 with the Japanese annexation of Manchuria and its exit from the League of Nations in 1932. Hitler's ascent to power in 1933 and his decision to withdraw Germany from the League of Nations shattered the inter-war international order. Soon after, Hitler moved to tear apart the strictures imposed on Germany by the Treaty of Versailles of 1919. In 1935, Germany began rearming. In 1936, it sent troops into the Rhineland, a demilitarised zone. In 1938, following a sham referendum in Austria, it effectively annexed Austria in what has become known as the *Anschluss*. And in October of the same year, it triggered a crisis over the Sudetenland in Czechoslovakia. The British government, led by Neville Chamberlain, bought time for itself by appeasing Hitler. By the autumn of 1939, Hitler was making similar provocative claims against Poland. War clouds loomed in Europe. Meanwhile, in the Far East, Japan launched a full-scale invasion of China in July 1937 following the Marco Polo Bridge incident. The assumptions of the Singapore Strategy were beginning to unravel.

The first sign of this unravelling surfaced when, in 1937, simulated war plans showed that any defence of Singapore had to take into account the defence of the entire Malay Peninsula. These simulations, drawn up by General Officer Commanding (GOC) Malaya, Major-General William Dobbie and his General Staff Officer 1, Colonel Arthur Ernest Percival, showed the Japanese landing in northeast Malaya. This was ironic given that it was Percival who ended up surrendering Singapore to the Japanese. His planning scenario, drawn up in 1937, would become his nightmare come 8 December 1941.

The second sign of this unravelling was in the gradual extension of the 'period before relief' from its initial 40 days to 70 days in June 1939. This was revised and extended to 180 days in September 1939, as war broke out in Europe. Singapore would have to defend itself for half a year before any naval reinforcements arrived. Prime Minister Winston Churchill would prioritise the defence of Britain over that of Singapore, Australia and New Zealand. And it would be his subsequent decisions and priorities over the allocation of military resources and assets that would doom Singapore.

The rapid collapse of France and the subsequent British retreat from Dunkirk in June 1940 marked the collapse of the Singapore Strategy. No naval fleet could be despatched to the Far East as Britain fought for its survival. British military planners decided that Singapore's defence would be helmed by the Royal Air Force (RAF) and with the army in support. Ironically, there were no aircraft to be spared for the RAF in Malaya. The army, in view of Britain's desperation, would be inadequately equipped and insufficiently trained for operations in Malaya.

Imperial Twilight – War

On 8 December 1941, when the first Japanese bombs were dropped on Singapore and Japanese troops landed in Kota Bahru, it became clear that Singapore's defences were but a fig leaf. The moment of reckoning had come.

Force Z, the much-vaunted naval fleet to the East, arrived earlier on 2 December 1941. Comprising a modern battleship, the HMS *Prince of Wales*, a battle cruiser, the HMS *Repulse*, and four small destroyers, the fleet looked impressive as it steamed into the Straits of Johor. Churchill thought that this would deter the Japanese, who by now had based bomber aircraft in French Indochina, well within range of Malaya and Singapore. In reality, a far larger fleet was needed to counter the might of the Imperial Japanese Navy. There was one other shortcoming in this naval fleet other than its size. Apart from anti-aircraft guns onboard the ships, Force Z had no air cover. On 10 December, having deployed with no land-based air cover, these proud ships became the first naval ships to be sunk by aircraft.

The Royal Air Force, on which the defence of Malaya and Singapore rested, was similarly anaemic. Only 336 aircraft were assigned to Malaya, out of the 582 aircraft recommended. Of these 336 aircraft, only 158 were in Malaya on 8 December 1941. Most of the aircraft were obsolete – the modern Spitfires and Hurricanes were not made available to Malaya. Similarly, the army was inadequately fitted out. Against a modern adversary such as the Japanese, the British army, which comprised Australian, British and Indian troops, had no tanks and few anti-tank and anti-aircraft elements. Churchill had, in the absence of any appreciation of the dire strategic situation in Malaya, decided to send spare tanks and Hurricane fighter planes to the Soviet Union instead. Ironically, the Russians had little need for these war materiel that would have made a huge difference in Malaya.

With the exception of a handful of units, the army was by and large unprepared for the fast-paced campaign the Japanese unleashed on them. GOC Malaya, Lieutenant-General Arthur E. Percival, who took command in May 1941, was dealt a bad hand. Though a brilliant staff officer and a humane person, Percival was no match for his adversary, Lieutenant-General Yamashita Tomoyuki. With ill-equipped forces at his disposal and a fractious command team, Percival could only do so much.

The Japanese advance down the Peninsula from 8 December 1941 was relentless. If British planning was characterised by complacency and dithering, the Japanese went about it in a systematic, focused and driven manner. Japanese planning for the Malayan campaign began in earnest in early 1941. The extent of Singapore's network of coastal defences, its guns and batteries, ruled out any frontal attack. The Japanese would instead attack Singapore from its north after they made their way down the peninsula.

Yamashita commanded three experienced and battle-hardened army divisions of 26,000 men. Though outnumbered by the British army, these crack troops would take Malaya in just a little over two months. Penang fell on 18 December 1941. Kuala Lumpur was next on 11 January 1942. By 31 Jan 1942, British forces had withdrawn to Singapore.

On 8 February 1942, the Japanese launched their invasion on Singapore. Dalforce, made up of poorly-armed Chinese volunteers, defended their posts in Jurong and Bukit Timah fiercely and doggedly but to little effect. On 13 February 1942, the day before Singapore surrendered, the outnumbered Malay Regiment fought bravely at the strategically important Bukit Chandu to frustrate the Japanese troops and give them a bloody nose.

Percival, encircled and embattled, decided to surrender on the morning of 15 February 1942, the first day of the Lunar New Year. Later that afternoon, a visibly worn-out Percival met with Yamashita at the Ford Motor Factory in Bukit Timah which served as Japanese headquarters. Insistent and aggressive, Yamashita was not open to negotiations – he wanted the British to surrender and for good reason. As brilliantly as his army had performed, it was running out of supplies. By 8:30 pm, the Malayan Campaign was over.

Percival would become the scapegoat for the fall of Singapore. Yamashita would be hailed as the 'Tiger of Malaya' and feted as a war hero in Tokyo. Churchill, the architect of military disaster, had wanted British troops to fight to the bitter end, down to the last man. To him, the honour of the British Empire was at stake. It is to Percival's credit that even though he was bound by his orders to resist to the end, he had sought permission to surrender. He had spared Singapore's defenceless civilian population from the orgy of rape and looting (as seen in Nanjing) that the Imperial Japanese Amy would surely have unleashed had the British chosen to fight to the last man.

CHAPTER FIVE

SYONAN

1942–1945

Why Was Singapore Important To The Japanese?

For the Japanese, as it was for the British and for the Malay rajas before them, Singapore's geographical location required it to be captured in any military invasion of Southeast Asia. For Yamashita, Singapore was nothing more than a forward base. Seemingly short-sighted, this view reflected the military aspects of Japanese war aims – to capture Singapore before invading the Dutch East Indies and eventually Australia. The Japanese government viewed things rather differently and more broadly. Other than Singapore's strategic location, they also considered Singapore's economic role. They wanted Singapore to be the capital of Japan's empire in Southeast Asia. Singapore, unlike other territories in Southeast Asia, was to be a permanent colony. Their primary aim was to get the place up and running after the ruin and destruction inflicted by the military campaign.

Governing Singapore

Two weeks after the surrender, it became clear how Singapore would be run. The Japanese set up the *tokubetsu-si*, the municipal government and the *gunseikan-bu*, the military administration. The *tokubetsu-si* was the apex of this administration and the *gunseikan-bu* sat below it, at least in theory. In practice, the *gunseikan-bu* rode roughshod over the understaffed *tokubetsu-si*. The first Japanese mayor of Singapore was Odate Shigeo and his deputy was Toyota Kaoru. Odate was subsequently replaced in 1943 by Naito Kanichi. The military administration was headed by Colonel Wataru Watanabe. A veteran of the Japanese campaign in China, Wataru maintained a hardline attitude towards the Singapore Chinese.

After the surrender and after the European civilians were interned and military personnel imprisoned as prisoners of war (POW), the Japanese went to work to make Singapore theirs. The Lion City was no more – it was renamed as *Syonan-to* or the Light of the South. Surely there was no small measure of irony to this name for the Japanese Occupation would be the darkest period in Singapore's history.

Littered with destruction and debris from the battle, Singapore had to be cleaned up and law and order restored. Those who worked at the electrical power plants, waterworks and other essential services were ordered to return to work. POWs were used to clear the streets of debris. The use of European POWs as white coolies was intended to humiliate them in front of the Singapore people. Looters were shot or executed on the spot. Their heads were displayed on spikes for all to see. Even in these early acts of brutality and summary justice, the Japanese provided the Singapore Chinese with a taster of what was in store for them. Chinese looters were beheaded on the spot whereas others were usually let off with a warning.

By early March 1942, most services were restored. A working but patchy water supply was restored. Radio broadcasts resumed. Newspapers were circulated again. A Malay newspaper *The Berita Malai* appeared with astonishing speed on 17 February 1942. The pre-war *Sin Chew Jit Poh* and *The Straits Times* were renamed *Syonan Jit Poh* and *Syonan Times* (eventually renamed again as the *Syonan Shimbun* in December 1942). Still, the radio programmes and the broadsheets carried mainly news and propaganda. Even so, the Japanese made sure that all radio sets could only receive certain frequencies. It was a crime to listen to foreign radio broadcasts.

On 20 February 1942, the Singapore people were introduced to the concept of the Nippon Spirit or *Nippon-Seishin*. The Japanese Emperor Hirohito was revered. His birthday was made a public holiday. Singapore's clocks were brought forward by an hour, putting them in line with Tokyo time.

Schools opened soon after. Singapore school children were mobilised to put up a mass display in April 1942. The occasion was to celebrate Emperor Hirohito's birthday. Yamashita himself reviewed this spectacle and he must have been beaming as thousands of school children marched past him carrying Japanese flags and singing *Kimigayo*, the Japanese national anthem. Beyond keeping the children occupied, the schools served a larger purpose – to inculcate a sense and consciousness of being Japanese in Singapore children. Unsurprisingly, Singapore parents were not fans of this sort of educational focus – at the peak, only some seven thousand children went to school. Preoccupied with survival, education, especially one that was designed to 'Nipponise' the population, tumbled down parents' priorities.

Managing The Singapore People

The Japanese adopted an obviously and openly racist and discriminatory position in managing the people of Singapore. Whilst they sought the cooperation of the Malays and Indians, they were anti-Chinese. The Japanese treated Singapore Chinese more harshly than Chinese in the rest of Southeast Asia. This was unsurprising given the concentration of anti-Japanese activities in Singapore in support of the Chinese war effort from 1937. The only other community to be treated with this degree of hostility and suspicion were the Eurasians. Even then, it paled in comparison to what was meted out to the Chinese. It must however be said that given the brutality and arbitrariness that underscored the Japanese regime, all racial groups suffered in the hands of the Japanese. Although there were some who collaborated with the Japanese for personal gain or in self-interest, the majority gritted their teeth and waited for their occupiers to be vanquished.

To say that the Japanese were inconsistent between their beliefs and their actions would be a gross understatement. In name, official Japanese policy was driven by their vision of a Greater East Asian Co-Prosperity Sphere. To them, all Asians were equal, and they wanted to cooperate with all Asians to build the new order in East Asia. The British policy of divide and rule was condemned as oppressive and restrictive. Universal brotherhood or *hakko-ichu* would bond all Asians together in an environment of mutual respect and tolerance. These lofty ideals were empty words. The Japanese pursued discriminatory policies that divided the people along ethnic lines more than ever. They were not the liberators they presented themselves to be. And the people could see that.

Coercion

What little good, if any, the Japanese ever achieved in their occupation of Singapore was forever eclipsed and overshadowed by their brutality towards the Singapore Chinese during Operation Sook Ching in the days following the surrender.

On 18 February 1942, Major General Kawamura Saburo, commander of the Singapore Garrison, was ordered to report to Army Headquarters. While he was there, Yamashita ordered him to begin mopping-up operations in Singapore. Together with the Kempeitai (Military Police) commander, Lieutenant Colonel Oishi Masayuki, they drew up the plans for screening and purging the Singapore Chinese. They were out to get members of the volunteer forces, communists, looters and those who had been identified as anti-Japanese elements. Operation Sook Ching (or purification through purge) was dubbed somewhat innocuously as *Dai Kensho* (or the great inspection) by the Japanese. Singapore Chinese men aged eighteen to fifty were ordered to report to one of the five major screening centres located around the island. At these centres, the men were screened in a haphazard and disorganised manner. There was no specific or defined criteria used to identify anti-Japanese elements. In some centres, those who wore spectacles or spoke English were taken away. In others, Hainanese were detained in large numbers – they were suspected of being communists. And at some, schoolteachers and journalists were seized. Collaborators, their faces hidden by hoods, pointed out supposedly anti-Japanese elements. We would never know if they actually knew these anti-Japanese elements or were driven by self-interest or a personal grudge. The lucky ones who passed through this screening were given 'examined' papers – when these papers ran out, they stamped the word 'examined' on clothing, or faces, or arms or shoulders. For those who were detained or taken away, death awaited. They were transported by lorry to massacre sites in Changi, Punggol, Tanah Merah, Katong and Sime Road to name a few. There, they were shot and bayoneted and buried in mass graves.

We will never know for sure how many perished in Operation Sook Ching – the Japanese claim that five thousand were killed whereas historians put the figure closer to twenty-five thousand. Regardless of the exact number, this deliberate and targeted policy aimed at the Singapore Chinese was crude and ineffective at best. Many important individuals, notably the leaders of the anti-Japanese activities before the war, had already fled Singapore. Tan Kah Kee hid out in Sumatra for the duration of the war. Lim Bo Seng made his way to India where he eventually assembled the nucleus of Force 136, a guerrilla force. Lee Kong Chian was in the United States. In early March 1942, the operation was called off. Its futility was obvious to the Japanese. Operation Sook Ching was in essence a gratuitous exercise that turned the Singapore Chinese against the Japanese. For the rest of the Occupation, they would have nothing but hatred for the Japanese.

Having ostensibly screened and purged the Singapore Chinese population of anti-Japanese elements, the Japanese now turned to extracting a levy from them. This move, the brainchild of Colonel Watanabe Wataru, was intended to raise funds to defray the costs of administering Singapore and also to make the Malayan Chinese atone for their past anti-Japanese beliefs and activities. This $50 million levy, dubbed a 'gift' by the Japanese, was a quarter of all currency in circulation in Malaya. The onerous and repugnant task of raising the money, of which $10 million was apportioned to Singapore, was foisted on the Oversea Chinese Association (OCA).

The founding of the OCA remains shrouded in controversy. To the Chinese leaders who served on the OCA, it was formed out of duress and torture in Japanese hands – its primary role was to ensure that $50 million was collected from the Chinese. However, Shinozaki Mamoru, a Japanese official who was the OCA adviser, has maintained that the OCA was formed to rescue prominent Singapore Chinese leaders during Operation *Sook Ching* and to protect the Singapore Chinese. He has also insisted that he was not involved in the fund raising itself.

Regardless, the sum still had to be raised. On a daily basis, Takase Toru, Watanabe's right-hand man, with the help of Wee Twee Kim, a notorious and vicious Taiwanese collaborator, used death threats to harangue and intimidate the Chinese community leaders. By June 1942, despite being supplied with tax and property records by the Japanese, only a third of the sum was raised via levies on individuals and properties. Eventually, the OCA had to borrow a sum of $22 million at a hefty 6% interest from the Yokohama Specie Bank – collateral had to be put up. Willy nilly, the Japanese would get their

$50 million, in cash or otherwise in kind. This act of extortion, accompanied by the use of torture and intimidation, only made the Singapore Chinese hate the occupiers even more.

Beyond these anti-Chinese measures, the Japanese resorted to coercion and fear in governing Singapore. Fear, cruelty and violence characterised the daily lives of the people. Collective responsibility was used to control the population from July 1942. Each family was required to have a 'peace living certificate' and the head of the household was responsible for the behaviour and actions of their households. A *jikeidan* (vigilance committee) was introduced to ensure that neighbours policed each other and, if necessary, rat on each other. Public beatings and random slappings by Japanese soldiers were part of everyday life. Brutality, a way of life in the Japanese army, became a way of life. Underscoring this brutality was the *Kempeitai* which enforced a reign of terror – people lived in fear of being reported by informers for crimes and misdemeanours, real and imagined. They used torture to break individuals. Beatings, electric shocks and water torture were but some of the more common methods used. Many died in their hands. The *Kempeitai* Headquarters at the old YMCA Building in Stamford Road became synonymous with torture, torment and death.

A World Turned Upside Down

Following the British surrender, Singapore's raison d'etre as a staple port and regional entrepot vanished overnight. Cut off from the international economy and its markets in the United States, the United Kingdom and Europe, Singapore's economic existence was imperilled. Singapore's entrepot trade with the region declined as well. Singapore could no longer count on imports, especially food, to meet its needs. It was thus unsurprising that official Japanese policy required Singapore to become a self-sufficient society.

Whatever the declared policy was, food shortages set in by April 1942. Rice imports fell from 370,670 tons in 1942 to just 94,102 in 1944. Prices started to go up and it was not just for rice. The prices of eggs and sugar went up as well. A *kati* (600 grams) of rice cost 50¢ in December 1942. By the end of the war in August 1945, it was going for $75 a *kati*. An egg went from costing 10¢ to $35. Sugar rose from 8¢ a *kati* to $120. Singapore's food security evaporated. The black market boomed as shortages worsened. This was exacerbated by a currency that got increasingly worthless as the Occupation wore on. The Japanese printed money liberally and money supply was uncontrolled. Poor-quality Japanese banana notes, named after the tropical fruit printed on them, bore no serial numbers and were thus susceptible to forgery. Inflation skyrocketed and the Japanese had no effective solutions. A fruitless 'Grow More Food' campaign was launched in 1942 but there was little enthusiasm for it. This irked the Japanese and by 1944, they had to coerce and intimidate the people into participating. Singapore never achieved anything close to self-sufficiency in its food supply. Malnutrition was common. As a result, diseases such as beri-beri, which resulted from Vitamin B deficiency, were prevalent.

Singapore society took on a certain manic and reckless character during the Japanese Occupation. The social order that defined colonial society in Singapore was gone. The British, who sat at the top of the social hierarchy, were held prisoner by the Japanese. Those who were privileged by the British by dint of social status or employment found themselves marginalised. Opportunities formerly denied to those in the lower classes were now available for picking, if one was willing to collaborate with the Japanese.

In this atmosphere where nothing seemed to be of any value, the black market thrived, and bribery and corruption were rampant. Some individuals profited and fortunes were made. Unsurprisingly, the Singapore Chinese continued to dominate the economy. However, as one observer put it, life coarsened during the Japanese Occupation. One's conscience could be had for a price – the deprivations and brutality of the Occupation triggered cynical self-interest. Betrayals were common. Profiteering on the black market was a way of making a living. Hoarding ensured that you possessed objects of value that could be traded for a high price when the time was right. It was certainly selfish and even unethical, but it was also about survival at all costs.

Collaboration And Resistance

It is in this context of survival, shortages and absence of values that the issue of collaboration has to be considered. Collaboration is often regarded as a moral failing. Collaborators in post-war Europe were humiliated publicly and often summarily executed. Making common cause with the enemy was traitorous behaviour. Such a line of reasoning, though common, is one-dimensional. Who these collaborators were and what they did for the Japanese remains a largely unexplored historical issue. However, sufficient historical evidence exists to show that the people, being a pragmatic lot, held their noses and did what they had to do to survive.

Collaboration was seen as necessary to provide a modicum of protection to the community, but it was at the same time, regarded as morally questionable. The OCA is a case in point. Coerced into leading the OCA, Dr. Lim Boon Keng reportedly pretended to be drunk throughout the Occupation to avoid cooperating with the Japanese in this role. Yet, the OCA also acquiesced to Japanese demands, for example, in helping set up a settlement in Endau, Johor for Singapore Chinese. Others trod a fine line between being a protector of the community and a Japanese collaborator. Lim Chong Pang of the OCA was tried and jailed by the British as a collaborator after the war. He was acquitted on the basis of 15,000 signatures on a petition saying he was not one. Dr. C. J. Paglar, of the Eurasian Welfare Association, suffered a similar fate but was acquitted on the account of a testimony by Shinozaki Mamoru. It was those who collaborated with the Kempeitai and the security services that drew the most disgust and became the target of reprisal killings after the Occupation.

For individuals, the Occupation was a morally ambiguous time. For the sake of survival, there was sometimes no choice but to work *for* the Japanese. But for some, working *with* the Japanese promised rich pickings and even power – enticements that they found difficult to resist. After the war, British investigators concluded that these were 'abnormal times'. They would therefore only prosecute a man if he 'had collaboratively wholeheartedly and beyond any extent'.

Just as there were collaborators, there were also those who found that resistance was the only way to live during the Occupation. Yet, Singapore was too small to harbour any resistance movement. The resistance movement operated mainly in the peninsula in the form of the Malayan Peoples' Anti-Japanese Army and, later, Force 136 led by Lim Bo Seng. Most members of the resistance were Chinese. Many were also survivors of Dalforce, the hastily assembled volunteer corps that fought the Japanese bitterly in Bukit Timah in the last days of the Malayan Campaign. Still, the resistance movement was limited in its scale and impact.

End of Occupation

In late 1944, the Singapore people could see that the tide of war had turned against the Japanese. American B-29 Superfortress bombers began daily air raids on the island in November 1944 and by July 1945, they were a daily sight in Singapore skies, flying at high altitude with light glinting off their silver skins. In July 1945, the Japanese put the people to work. Trenches were dug and air raid shelters rebuilt. Japanese civilians were also called up for military training, some of which took place in open view in front of City Hall. The signs were clear – the Japanese were on their last legs and they intended to fight to the last man in a last-ditch stand.

On 6 August 1945, the Enola Gay, an American B-29 bomber captained by Paul Tibbets appeared over the skies of Hiroshima and dropped 'Little Boy', an innocuously nicknamed explosive device. The atomic bomb devastated Hiroshima. On 9 August 1945, in the face of the Japanese refusal to surrender, a second bomb was dropped, this time on Nagasaki. Six days later, the Japanese Emperor Hirohito spoke to the Japanese people over the radio, announcing the Japanese surrender. It was the first time his subjects had heard his voice.

The last-ditch stand to defend Singapore never materialised, for all Allied plans to recapture the island were scuttled in view of the Japanese surrender on 15 August 1945. On 21 August 1945, the Japanese surrender was officially announced to the Singapore people. With this news, collaborators slipped away quietly. The OCA disbanded itself. The Japanese army retreated to an internment camp it had prepared for itself in Jurong. The island was gripped by a wave of reprisals against collaborators. Wee Twee Kim, the notorious Taiwanese collaborator, was eventually arrested by the British and died in Outram Jail.

On 5 September 1945, the British returned to an elated and jubilant Singapore people who lined a three-mile long route to welcome them with rousing cheers. But some were not so enthusiastic. Lee Kip Lin remembers that: 'it annoyed me to see the arrogant faces of some of the British officers. It was the same arrogance that you saw before the war.' Things had changed.

On 12 September 1945, a Japanese delegation led by General Itagaki, entered City Hall to sign a formal surrender to the British. A huge crowd was at the Padang to witness this. They cheered when Lord Louis Mountbatten appeared to accept the surrender. They jeered and cursed at the Japanese delegation. The Union Jack, the same one kept hidden during the Occupation, was raised over the city. A Royal Marines band played 'God Save the King' and Mountbatten led three cheers for the King. The Japanese were gone. The war was over.

The rapid collapse of the British defence in the Malayan Campaign and the Japanese surrender showed the people one thing – neither the British nor the Japanese were superior or invincible. There was nothing inherently superior to be gleaned from one's ethnicity. Even as they returned triumphantly, things would not be the same for the British. The people, having seen how even the mighty and haughty British had feet of clay, now sought to rule themselves.

CHAPTER SIX

THE CONTEST

1945–1959

Year Zero

As the atomic bombs detonated in Japan over Hiroshima and Nagasaki in Japan in early August 1945, the world changed profoundly. The old order built on colonialism was on its last legs. The Left was on the rise. All over the world, colonies began clamouring for independence. The powers that ruled the vast empires pondered their impending retreat and eventual demise, some more deliberately than others. 1945 was, as historians have so aptly put it, Year Zero. Beyond the revenge killings, reprisals, hunger, the physical reconstruction of bombed-out cities and destroyed infrastructure, 1945 represented an opportunity to rebuild the world sans colonialism. In September 1945, Singapore came under the British Military Administration (BMA). But whatever joy and happiness the people experienced in seeing the British as liberators quickly evaporated as the BMA was marred by corruption, maladministration and extensive black marketeering. Some even called the BMA the 'Black Market Administration.' Whatever goodwill the British enjoyed was gone in seven months. Life did not get any better for the ordinary people after liberation.

Giving It All Up? – British Decolonisation In Southeast Asia

The Second World War was undoubtedly the single event most responsible for triggering the process of decolonisation in empires worldwide. For the British Empire, one of the most consequential events arising from the war was the Atlantic Charter. This statement, which was issued jointly by American President Franklin Delano Roosevelt and British Prime Minister Winston Churchill on 14 August 1941 at the end of the Atlantic Conference, marked the point where the formal dissolution of the British Empire began. Included in the statement was an important clause on self-determination: 'the right of all peoples to choose the form of government under which they will live'. Decolonisation had begun, for the British at least. The French and the Dutch were not keen losing their empires and hung on until they were forcibly evicted by its subject peoples.

Decolonisation would define and drive politics in the colonial territories for the next two decades or so from 1945. What then is decolonisation? Was it a matter of simply giving it all up and walking away? The reality is rather more complex. Decolonisation is the process of giving up political control over a colony and handing over that control to its people. This process is subject to several assumptions. First, it would be a gradual process as the colonial power took the local people through a period of political tutelage. This meant a gradual shift to limited self-government, then full self-government and eventually, independence. Second, there was no fixed time frame to govern this process. Third, the colonial power would identify and cultivate a suitable local elite to hand political power over to. All these would be done in view of securing the strategic interests of the colonial power. Things, however, did not always go according to plan, as we shall see in Singapore's case.

Planning For Post-War Malaya

British planning for the post-war futures of Malaya and Singapore came under the auspices of the Malayan Planning Unit (MPU). What preoccupied the MPU was the issue of preparing Malaya for self-government. It eventually settled on its plan, dubbed the Malayan Union, in 1943. The Malayan Union comprised the Federated Malay States, the Unfederated Malay States, Penang and Melaka. Singapore was excluded from this plan and would remain a Crown Colony. This was principally because of its large Chinese population – it would be unpalatable to the Malay rulers who had to agree to this plan. Including Singapore would mean upsetting the racial balance in the peninsula in the long run.

However, the long-term vision was always to reunite Singapore with Malaya to form a bloc of British colonial territories as part of a 'Grand Design'. This bloc would be accomplished in two phases. Phase one would see the merger of Singapore with Malaya. Phase

Two would see the inclusion of Sarawak, North Borneo and Brunei. To the British planners, this was the best way to ensure regional stability and protect British interests. The 'Grand Design' was, for most part, a vision rather than a policy. There was no timetable for its implementation and certainly, no active planning for it.

As the war ended, the British planners swung into action to implement the Malayan Union. Sir Harold MacMichael was despatched to Malaya in October 1945 to arrange new treaty relationships with the Sultans. By 24 December 1945, he had secured the signatures of all the rulers – the outcome of nine weeks of secret discussions. However, the Sultans were unhappy with the browbeating and arm-twisting that the no-nonsense and mission-focused MacMichael subjected them to. The Malayan Union was already in trouble.

In January 1946, the Malayan Union was announced. This did not go down well with the peninsula Malays who opposed the equality it accorded to non-Malays in terms of citizenship and political representation. The Malays responded swiftly to this and formed the United Malay National Organisation (UMNO) to challenge it. Although the Malayan Union was inaugurated on 1 April 1946, it was eventually dissolved in 1948 and replaced by the Federation of Malaya.

In both iterations, the Malayan Union and the Federation of Malaya, there was one thing in common. Singapore was excluded. And although British planners nursed the hope of Singapore's eventual reunification with the peninsula, Singapore's political development diverged sharply from this point. It would develop a political style that was radically different from the Federation. Politics in Singapore would become ideologically driven, non-communal, non-communist, mass-based and characterised by open and robust debate. Getting Singapore and Malaya back together was going to be complex and difficult.

What Do We Do With Singapore?

Given Singapore's political, economic and military significance, the British were in no hurry to shepherd it towards independence and this remained so until the mid-1950s. In 1946, Singapore was granted a colonial constitution that retained the Governor's veto and reserve powers. The Executive and Legislative Councils were retained. Eventually, after much criticism for its lack of local representation, the makeup of the Legislative Council was reviewed. Most significantly, six members of the Legislative Council would be popularly elected by universal suffrage. On 1 March 1948, the new Constitution came into effect and shortly after, on 20 March 1948, Singapore held its first democratic elections. The first step towards political change, though small, had been taken.

The 1948 Constitution ensured that political change took place at an unhurried pace. Singapore's political development was led by the English-educated who believed that maintaining, if not actually prolonging, the political status quo was to its advantage. Nothing reflected this mindset better than the Singapore Progressive Party (SPP). Founded in 1947, the SPP was dominated by English-educated professionals, largely Straits Chinese, who were conservative about political change. They had no dreams or plans for independence. Their aim was to attain full self-government in 1963. Essentially, the SPP's programme was an extension of the glacial pace of political change under the pre-war colonial administration. This made the SPP the partner of choice for the British when it came to the business of handing over power in Singapore.

Unsurprisingly, the SPP did well in Singapore's first Legislative Council election in 1948 – it won three of the six seats up for grabs. In 1951, it reprised this performance when it took six of the nine seats available for elections. By 1954, it looked like Singapore was chugging along nicely in this scheme of gradual political change led by the SPP. But there was just one problem. The majority of Singapore Chinese were unrepresented in these democratic exercises – they were 'aliens' and not British subjects and not Singapore citizens because it did not exist then. They could not vote even if they wanted to.

But the people of Singapore were generally not interested in politics as the 1948 election showed. Few could vote – out of the population of 940,000, about 200,000 were eligible to vote. Of this group, only 22,443 bothered to register to vote. Though turnout was high at 63.2%, there were only 14,126 voters or 1.5% of the total population. The 1951 Election was a little better – 2.6% of the total population voted. Clearly, something had to be done to trigger more widespread voter participation.

Larger political forces soon emerged to disrupt the SPP's comfortable illusion of its dominant role in stewarding Singapore's political development. The British had concluded that political change was necessary in order to keep up with the aspirations of the people.

To them, when the time came to hand power over, the government-in-waiting had to demonstrate the ability to govern. It also had to represent *all* the people of Singapore and not just a select group of British subjects. This meant that it had to represent the under-represented Chinese. The SPP was ill-placed to do so.

To address this situation, Governor Sir John Fearnes Nicoll announced the formation of a commission in July 1953. Led by Sir George Rendel, it was tasked to review the limited and inadequate 1948 Constitution. The Rendel Commission, as it came to be known, met for the first time in November 1953. In early 1954, it submitted its recommendations. To encourage voter participation, voter registration was made automatic. To ensure that representation was broad-based, a thirty-two seat Legislative Assembly replaced the Legislative Council. Twenty-five seats were to be popularly elected. To provide experience in governance and administration, a nine-member Council of Ministers was created. The Governor would appoint three Ministers and the rest would be drawn from the majority party in the Assembly. The British also retained the portfolios of defence, finance and internal affairs. In essence, Singapore was given a form of limited self-government. Having accepted these recommendations, the Rendel Constitution was effected on 8 February 1955. On the same day, the colonial government announced that a General Election was to be held on 2 April 1955.

The other political force that the SPP was not ready for and not able to deal with was the rise of left-wing politics in Singapore, especially amongst the majority Singapore Chinese. The Singapore Chinese were not a happy lot. For one, many were poor and led lives of deprivation. They lived in overcrowded and unhygienic conditions. Families often lived in a cubicle or a room, in a dwelling crammed with other households. They had to share bathroom and kitchen facilities. Privacy did not exist. This was the reality uncovered in a study conducted by Barrington Kaye of the University of Malaya in 1955. These miserable conditions were aggravated by the feeling that the colonial government discriminated against them. Although Singapore was a prosperous British colony, unemployment was high, and wages were low. They had no opportunities for education beyond secondary school. They were shut out of civil service jobs. Those who were not born in Singapore were not citizens. And they certainly could not vote. Yet, at the same time, they were subject to the 1954 National

Service Ordinance, which compelled them to serve in the military for the colonial government. For them, to be anti-colonial, radical or not, was therefore a means to political change for a singular purpose – to address their socio-economic plight and redress their grievances. In this light, the Malayan Communist Party (MCP), proscribed since 1948, saw the Singapore Chinese as fertile ground. Its targets were the Chinese schools and Chinese-speaking trade unions. By 1954, it decided to infiltrate these bodies and transform them into front organisations that would achieve its political ends either by radical agitation or by winning elections.

So, when the Rendel Commission gave the Singapore Chinese a vote at the ballot box in the 1955 elections, they became a force that disrupted and transformed the nature of Singapore politics. The SPP and its ilk, the right-wing, conservative parties, were unable to connect with the Singapore Chinese voter. They could not detect, much less understand, the leftward shift in Singapore towards mass-based politics and the intensity of such a political environment. Their political assumptions would be entirely disrupted.

The Rise Of The Left – The 1955 Election

Two new parties on the political left dominated the elections – they were the Labour Front (LF) and the Peoples' Action Party (PAP). Both parties stoked the people's interest in politics and in Singapore's future. From 1955, both parties were engaged in a tussle for political dominance over Singapore's direction and pace towards self-government and eventual independence.

Formed in July 1954, the LF was led by David Saul Marshall, a Sephardic Jew from one of the smallest minority groups in Singapore. A lawyer trained at the University of London, Marshall had an active public life. He served on both the Executive and Legislative Councils, was a member of the SPP and was Chairman of the Jewish Welfare Board from 1949 to 1951. All these while he was a busy practising lawyer at Allen and Gledhill.

Together with Lim Yew Hock and Francis Thomas, Marshall founded the LF in 1954. Lim, a professional stenographer, had established the Singapore Trade Union Congress in 1954. Francis Thomas was a teacher. The LF presented a political platform that was anti-colonial and attuned to the needs of the political ground.

It campaigned for immediate self-government within the context of a merged Singapore and Malaya. It called for the Malayanisation of the civil service. The Legislative Assembly was to become multi-lingual. Some 220,000 Singapore Chinese would be granted citizenship. The Emergency Regulations that enabled the government to detain a person without trial were to be abolished. Even though it was openly anti-colonial and Malayan in its outlook, the LF suffered from one critical weakness – it did not become a mass party. Its sole attempt to do so, by making an overture to the newly formed PAP, was unsuccessful. It would struggle with this shortcoming for a long time.

On 21 November 1954, the PAP was inaugurated at the Victoria Memorial Hall. Its slate of convenors at this red-letter occasion was a remarkable concentration of talent, commitment and derring-do. Its leader, Lee Kuan Yew, a Cambridge-educated lawyer, was active in the Malayan Forum in London and was now a legal advisor to the unions. In the *Fajar* trial, Lee made his name by taking up the defence of the university students. Dr. Toh Chin Chye was a lecturer at the University of Malaya. Chan Chiaw Thor and Fong Swee Suan, both educated at the Chinese High School, were a schoolteacher and a union leader respectively. Fong was the general secretary of the Singapore Bus Workers' Union. Devan Nair was also a schoolteacher who became a union secretary in 1953. S. Rajaratnam was a journalist with *The Straits Times*. There were some names not on the slate of convenors. Goh Keng Swee and Kenny Byrne were both civil servants who had to stay above the political fray. And lastly, there was Lim Chin Siong. Charismatic, good looking and a powerful orator in the Chinese dialects, Lim was the secretary of the Singapore Factory and Shop Workers' Union. Lee had invited him to be a convenor, but he demurred and offered it to Fong instead.

Like the LF, the PAP was an anti-colonial and nationalist party. It opposed the Rendel Constitution. Pan-Malayan in its outlook, it believed in merger with the Federation and an independent and democratic Malaya. It opposed the Rendel Constitution because it was colonial. It called for industrialisation to replace the 'colonial economy' and the removal of the Emergency Regulations. True to its Malayan outlook, it advocated for Malay as the national language with Chinese and Tamil being recognised as official languages.

Crucially, the PAP's leadership knew that to succeed in Singapore politics, it had to capture the support of the Singapore Chinese. To do so, it did what the LF could not and did not do. It became a mass party by making common cause with militant, radical left-wing political elements affiliated with the Malayan Communist Party (MCP). Fong Swee Suan and Lim Chin Siong brought to the PAP the support of the Singapore Chinese – this enabled Lee to tap into the deep vein of political frustration and socio-economic grievances to generate support for the PAP.

Needless to say, neither of these parties with their anti-colonial, left-wing and strident nationalist credentials were at all kosher to the British. Their top choice in this contest was still the right-wing Singapore Progressive Party, the conservative epitome of the leisurely tea and scones type of politics. To say that the SPP took things for granted would be a gross understatement. Secure in the arms of their British backers, the SPP, acting like the favoured child of the establishment that it was, did not sense that the times were indeed, a-changin'.

As 2 April 1955 dawned, 300,000 people went to vote. Because of automatic registration, there were a lot more of them than the 79,000 in the 1951 election. Many of the new voters were the Chinese-educated. They were drawn to the left-wing parties by their staunch anti-colonial beliefs. To them, there was hope in the promises of change made by the LF and the PAP.

That night, as the election results came in, it became clear that the British had lost their grip on the direction and pace of political change in Singapore. Their favoured child, the SPP, had lost, and lost big. It won only four seats out of the eighteen it contested. Its leader, C.C. Tan, lost to David Marshall in Cairnhill constituency. Lim Yew Hock beat Chua Bock Kwee handily and took Havelock constituency with the biggest majority, 86%. No one, not the British and certainly not the SPP itself, expected it to be shunted into political oblivion in this election. The Singaporean people had rejected their conservative platform of maintaining the status quo. And they had shown that they were not just interested in participating in politics, they were able to create history.

If the SPP did not expect to lose, then the LF did not expect to win. It had won ten of the seventeen seats it contested, making it the biggest winner for the night but not big enough for it to be the majority party. David Marshall, as leader of the LF, would lead a minority government and would have to form a coalition with the UMNO-MCA Alliance, which won three seats, in order to govern. This, together with the limited and ill-defined nature of the Rendel Constitution, would give Marshall endless grief as he tried to govern Singapore.

The PAP came through that night as the clear winner, although it won only three seats; but it only contested four seats. Lee Kuan Yew won the Tanjong Pagar Constituency easily, taking 6029 votes or 78.3% of the popular vote, the highest number of votes won by any candidate that night. Lee would hold his Tanjong Pagar Constituency for the rest of his political career until his passing in 2015. Goh Chew Chua and Lim Chin Siong both won in Punggol-Tampines and Bukit Timah respectively. Although it contested only four seats, the PAP captured the imagination of the people. Its rallies drew crowds and it focused tightly on tearing down the SPP in its campaign. It demonstrated its political acumen by deliberately choosing to contest the election in a limited number of seats. This shielded them from the possibility of having to govern under the Rendel Constitution it opposed. Whatever the outcome, the PAP would be in opposition. Without the pressure of governing, the PAP would use the Legislative Assembly to make itself, its leaders and its beliefs known to the Singapore people.

With this unexpected election result, Singapore found itself in uncharted territory. The British lost their preferred partners, the SPP, whom they knew and understood. They could no longer control the pace or direction of political change in Singapore. Henceforth, the British found themselves in a rear-guard action of managing rather than driving political change in Singapore. The bottom-line was clear – British strategic interests, especially economic and defence interests, had to be protected.

Governing Singapore: David Marshall As Chief Minister

Charismatic, mercurial and strong-minded, David Marshall's appointment as Chief Minister on 6 April 1955 proved to be a challenge for the colonial administration. To begin with, Marshall neither expected nor wanted to become Chief Minister. However, having been given the job, Marshall from the onset refused to play the role of a deferential and subservient Chief Minister. He did whatever he could to confer dignity and respect on the office of the Chief Minister, which he likened to that of being Prime Minister. He was the elected representative of the Singapore people, a nationalist, not a hand-in-glove partner of the British. This immediately put him at odds with Sir John Nicoll, the Governor. To Nicoll, the Chief Minister was a title, an honorific, and not much else. Marshall's actions affronted him and the colonial government. He responded by treating Marshall with mildly disguised contempt and even derision.

Both Marshall's actions and Nicoll's responses are well documented in history. One of the most memorable clashes took place over the issue of the Chief Minister's physical office. The British assumed that Marshall did not need a separate physical office. His office at the Ministry of Commerce and Industry in Fullerton Building would also be the Chief Minister's physical office. Also, the British expected the Chief Secretary, and not Marshall, to continue to coordinate the ministries. Marshall chafed at these indignities. The Chief Secretary, William Goode, was the highest-ranking civil servant in Singapore, second only to the Governor.

Marshall's response was pointed. He told Nicoll that he would set up shop under the 'old apple tree' at Empress Place if he was not provided with an office. And if Nicoll declined to supply any furniture for that set up, he would supply them himself! All he asked for was a telephone line. Thankfully, Goode astutely stepped in and hastily arranged, over the weekend, for Marshall to have an office in the Legislative Assembly building – a small cubicle under the stairs. It was small and very modest, but huge in symbolism and set the tone of Marshall's administration.

Their mutual dislike aside, Marshall and Nicoll needed to get down to work in forming the government. This was another bone of contention. Marshall had to form a coalition government as the LF did not have a majority in the Legislative Assembly. Given that he did not want to work with the SPP and that the PAP were unlikely to partner him, Marshall tried to form a government by enlisting the UMNO-MCA Alliance. Despite his best efforts, he landed up four seats short of an overall majority.

The 1955 Constitution provided for four appointed unofficial members of the Legislative Assembly. This was Nicoll's prerogative. He alone could help Marshall secure an overall majority. Nicoll apparently relished in needling Marshall by reminding him of this reality. But this was patently ridiculous. If Nicoll had stalled on this issue and a government could not be formed, there would be a constitutional crisis and possibly even fresh elections. But, more importantly, Nicoll did not want to set a precedent for the future. He did not want minority rule to become a norm. In the end, Nicoll and Marshall compromised. Richard Chuan Hoe Lim and Francis Thomas, both key members in the LF, were appointed. Singapore's first elected cabinet of ministers was in business.

Besides dealing with Nicoll, Marshall had to contend with his own cabinet ministers and their political ambitions. As Chief Minister, Marshall was also Minister for Commerce and Industry. He appointed Lim Yew Hock as Minister for Labour and Welfare, Armand J. Braga as Minister for Health and Chew Swee Kee as Minister for Education. Chew was not enamoured with this post for he had to deal with a thorny problem – the political restlessness of the Chinese middle schools. Initially, Marshall appointed Francis Thomas, whom he trusted, as Minister for Local Government, Lands and Housing. He needed someone like Thomas because the ministry was allocated the largest budget and 'hence the most opportunities for corruption and kickbacks'. He appointed the UMNO-MCA leader, Abdul Hamid bin Haji Jumat as the Minister for Communications and Works. Marshall was eventually forced to switch Thomas and Abdul Hamid in their portfolios because his UMNO-MCA partners insisted on it.

Having now formed the government, Marshall wrestled with the vexatious problem that destroyed his government a little over a year later. This was the issue of internal security. To the British, a government that was able to maintain internal security and stability was one that could eventually protect their interests in the event of self-government and eventual independence. This was of paramount importance to the British now that the impetus for directing political change was no longer in their hands. The pace and form of Singapore's transition from colony to self-government and its eventual independence would hinge on this.

Singapore's internal security situation from the mid-1950s onwards was complex and volatile. Unlike the armed insurgency fought in the jungles of Malaya, Singapore's internal security threats came in the form of militant young people who were under the apparent direction of the Malayan Communist Party (MCP) and who were quite ready to organise and participate in strikes and riots if necessary. Trade unions, student unions and political parties alike were open to infiltration by these radical elements. Whoever governed Singapore must have the steel and appetite to deal with this lethal cocktail of socio-economic grievance, a deficit of social justice and the appeal of communism as a panacea to society's ills.

Shortly after Marshall's appointment as Chief Minister, he was put to the test. In May 1955, the Hock Lee Bus Riot broke out. More than any other event during his office, this riot challenged his personal and political beliefs. It also damaged his political standing with the British. The riots began over a dispute between the left-affiliated Singapore Bus Workers' Union (SBWU) and the Hock Lee Employees' Union (HLEU) over control of the latter. The police moved in on 12 May 1955 to disperse the crowd of striking students and workers – skirmishes took place and escalated into a riot shortly. In the face of this civil disturbance, Marshall appeared to be paralysed. On one side, he was pressured by the British to mobilise the security forces to quell the rioters. This he refused to do because, as he quite rightly pointed out, internal security was outside his purview as Chief Minister. And on the other, he was deeply and painfully aware that if he did so, he would lose all credibility in the eyes of the people. He would become a colonial stooge. Worsening this quandary was Marshall's deeply held belief that it was wrong to use force against the Singapore people. To him, the strike and the subsequent riot were symptoms of deep-seated grievances that had been hijacked by radical political forces for their political ends. The use of force would not address these grievances nor solve them. At best, the rioters would be quelled momentarily. But they would come back again, with more demands, more anger and in a more organised fashion.

Still, Marshall had little choice this time. Eventually, with escalating violence and the threat of disturbances spreading, he had to order in the police. Publicly, Marshall insisted that he had to use force because it was the government's duty to maintain law and order. At the same time, he cautioned the public about 'the dangers of being used for political ends by political opportunists' that were out to destroy the government. Although he had read the intentions of the radical left clearly, he could not grasp the cold ruthlessness and self-interest that drove their political calculations. Marshall was a political ingenue in this respect. He could not quite grasp how trenchant and uncompromising the radical left was. Their ideological beliefs and political dogma prevented them from settling for an outcome that served the greater good of society.

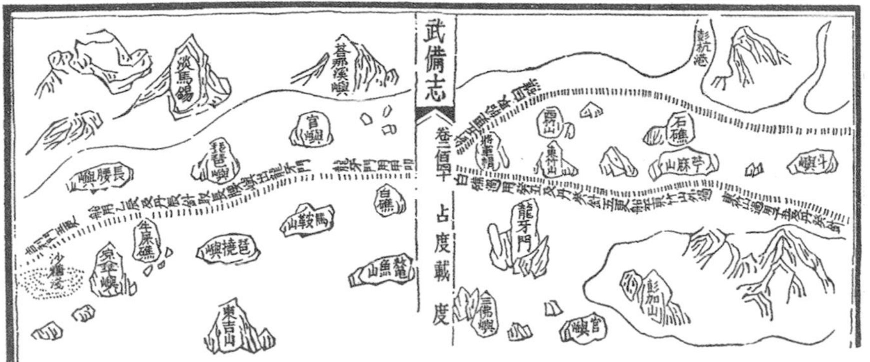

The *Mao Kun* map, or Zheng He's navigational map, was published in 1628. Singapore is marked on the map as *Danmaxi* (Temasek) on the top left hand corner. To the right of the centre of the map is *Lungyamen* (Dragon Teeth's Gate).

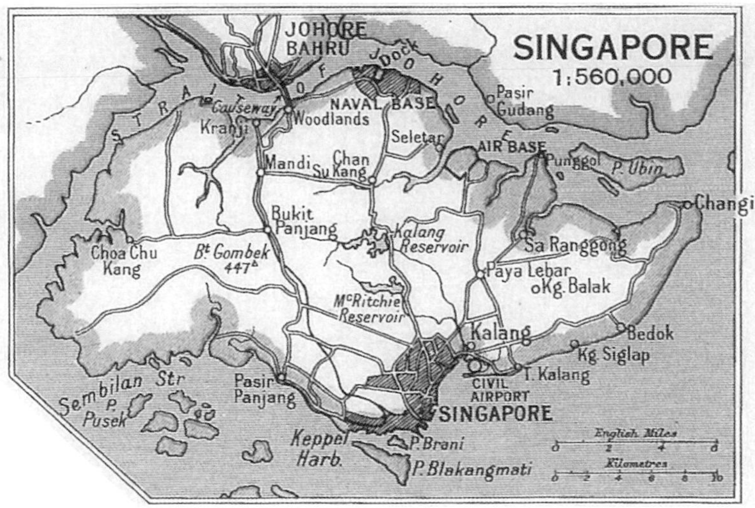

1930s map of Singapore. This map depicts the key gateways of Singapore such as the naval base in Sembawang, the Causeway, Kallang Airport and Keppel Harbour.

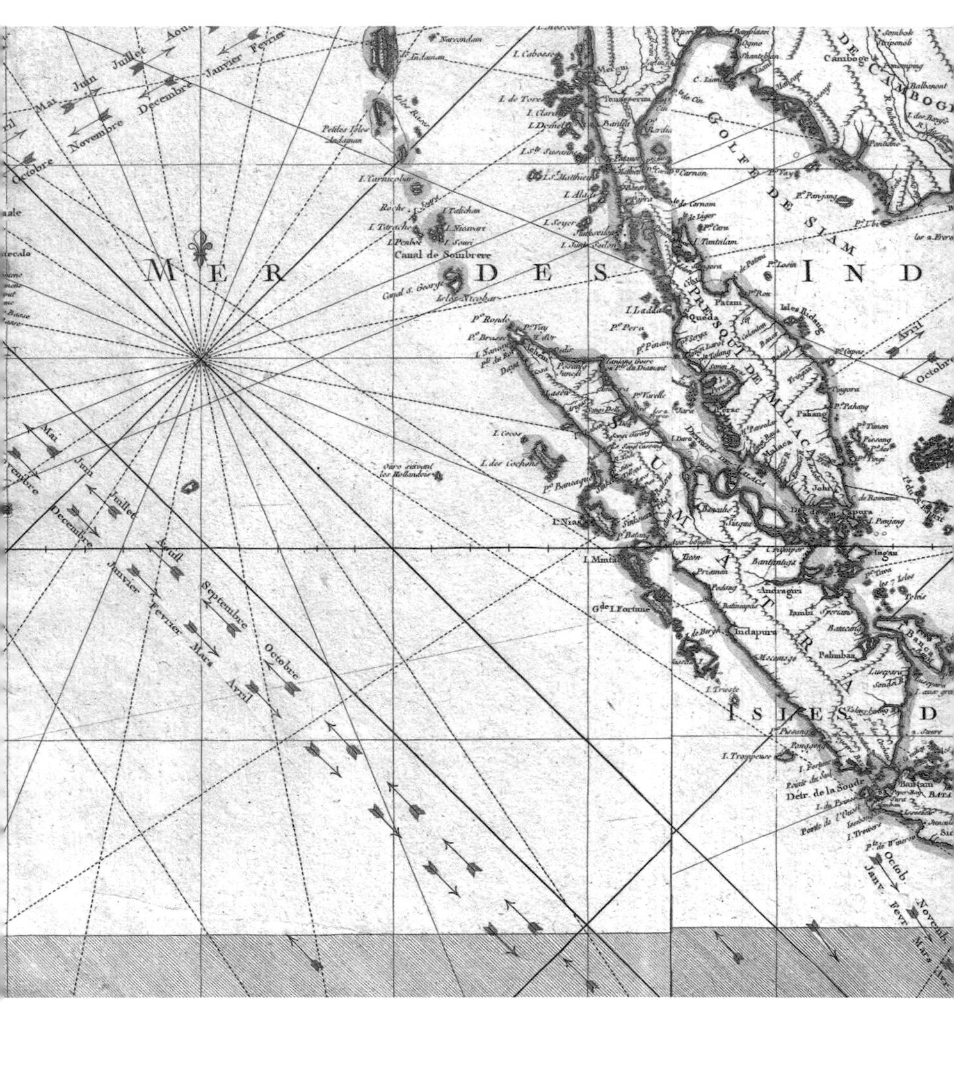
MER DES IND
GOLFE DE SIAM
PRESQU'ISLE DE MALACA
SUMATRA
ISLES D
Canal de Sombrere
Isles Nicobar
Petites Isles Andaman
I. Carnicobar
I. Nicavari
I. Souri
I. Tarache
I. Tilichan
Canal S. George
P.te Ronde
I. Cocos
I. des Cochons
I. Nias
I. Minta
Gde I. Fortune
I. Trieste
I. Trappeuse
Detr. de la Sonde
Bantam
Palimban
Indapura
Andragiri
Jambi
Malaca
Pahang
Queda
Patani
Tenasserim
Cambogé
I. Ladda
P.te Pera
I. Alab
I. Narcondam
I. Cabosse
I. de Tores
Janvier
Fevrier
Mars
Avril
Mai
Juin
Juillet
Aout
Septembre
Octobre
Novembre
Decembre

Rigobert Donne's (1727 – 1794) decorative maps of India, Ceylon and the East Indies from the late 18th century. The arrows depict the monsoon winds that changed direction every six months. The map shows the Strait of Singapore but the island itself is not labelled.

Francis Edward Rawdon-Hastings (1754 – 1826), 1st Marquess of Hastings. As the Governor-General of India, he authorised Raffles to search for a suitable location for a port south of the Straits of Melaka.

Sir Stamford Raffles (1781 – 1826). An official of the English East India Company, a naturalist and a scholar, he is best known for founding Singapore in 1819.

Major-General William Farquhar (1774 – 1839). He is regarded as a founder of Singapore and was also its first Resident (1819 – 1823). He saw the fledging colony through its precarious early days.

John Crawfurd (1783 – 1868). He was the second Resident of Singapore (1823 – 1926). A sensible and effective administrator, Crawfurd secured sovereign rights over Singapore for the British in 1824. He remained a lifelong advocate for the colony after his retirement.

Raffles Place in 1910. Previously known as Commercial Square until its renaming in 1858, Raffles Place was the commercial hub of colonial Singapore. This photo depicts (from left to right) the Shanghai Life Insurance & Co., Dr. S. I. Watsubo, G. Otomune & Co., Katzbrothers Ltd., and The Dispensary.

20th century street scene of South Bridge Road depicting trams, rickshaws and Chinese business advertisements.

20th century photo (circa. 1910) of the Singapore River, showing the iconic *tongkangs* and *twakows* (or bumboats) at Boat Quay. These wooden vessels played a vital role transporting goods from ships anchored off Singapore to warehouses along the Singapore River.

William Pickering (1840 – 1907). He was appointed head of the Chinese Protectorate and first Protector of the Chinese in 1877. Fluent in Chinese, Pickering also established the *Poh Leung Kok*, a refuge for women who had been forced into prostitution.

The Chinese Protectorate building in North Bridge Road. The Protectorate provided some recourse to official protection and justice for the Chinese, who were previously beholden to the secret societies.

A rubber tapper at work. Using the herringbone method invented by Henry Ridley, the tapper extracted raw latex from the rubber tree. The raw latex would be collected, processed and exported later through Singapore.

Postcard (c. 1900 – 1908) depicting a German mail steamer at Borneo Wharf, Keppel Harbour. This wharf was built by the Borneo Company, which was the first to build wharves at Keppel Harbour.

ALEXANDRA ROAD
HAVELOCK ROAD
OUTRAM ROAD
Criminal Prison
Lunatic Asylum
RAEBURN
KAMPONG BAHRU ROAD
Borneo Wharf Railway Station
PLANTATION
FLAGSTAFF
MOUNT FABER
Observatory
HOUSE
Railway
WHARVES & DOCKS
ST JAMES
BAY
DOCK
P & O WHARF
PULAU HANTU

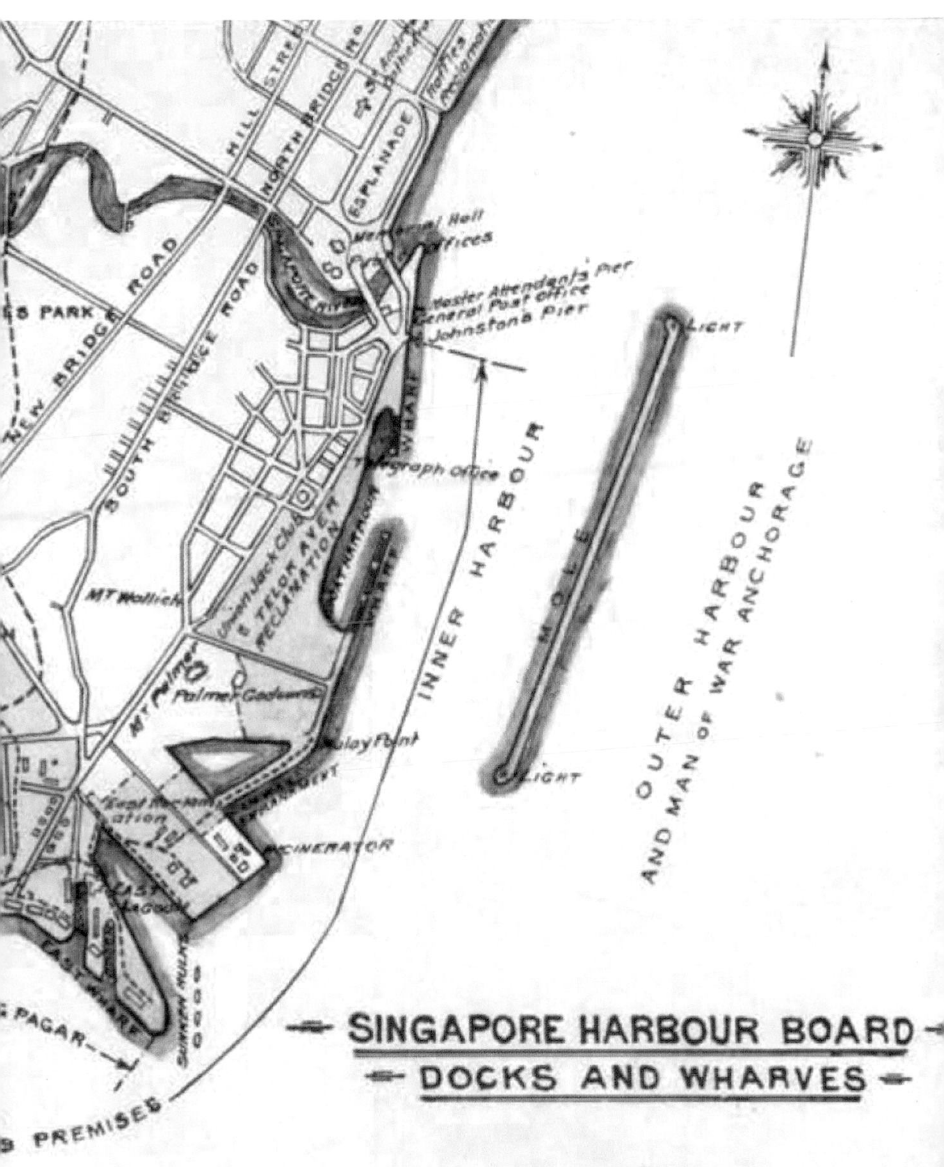

Map from the 1920s showing the extent of the Singapore Harbour Board's premises. The port of Singapore had more than three kilometres of wharves. There were also a range of docks such as the Empire Dock, which measured a kilometre in length and King's Dock, which measured almost 280 metres in length.

Lim Nee Soon (1879 – 1936) (centre) standing in front of a lorry that is laden with freshly harvested pineapples. The lorry bears the name 'Lim Nee Soon Rubber Factory'. Rubber and pineapples were the pillars of Lim Nee Soon's commercial empire.

A sailing ship and steamers in the Albert Dock in Keppel Harbour. The Albert Dock measured almost 150 metres in length.

Tan Kah Kee (1874 – 1961) owned one of the business conglomerates of the day. He was a noted philantrophist, educationist, political activist and community leader. He was a leading figure in the fund raising movement that mobilised the Singapore Chinese to give in support of the war in China.

The dignified and stately Supreme Court and Municipal Building fronting the Padang. These were visible and tangible symbols of British administration and power.

The Art Deco-style Kallang Airport Terminal Building designed by Frank Dorrington Ward. Hailed as the finest airport in the British Empire, it was the jewel of the Empire's aviation crown in the pre-war era.

1903 Straits Settlements Dollar with the bust of King Edward VII, King and Emperor, facing right. The denomination 'one dollar' is rendered in Chinese and in Jawi script on the reverse.

A Japanese 'banana note' worth ten dollars issued during the Japanese Occupation of Singapore (1942 - 1945). Formally known as the military yen, the currency was issued in large quantities, without security features and serial numbers.

General Yamashita Tomoyuki (1885 - 1946). Known as the Tiger of Malaya, Yamashita commanded the 25th Japanese Army that captured Singapore on 15 February 1942.

Lieutenant-General Arthur E. Percival (1887 - 1966), General Officer Commanding (GOC) Malaya. He commanded the Commonwealth forces defending Malaya and Singapore and surrendered to the Japanese on 15 February 1942.

Watched over by an Allied officer, Japanese General Itagaki signs the Instrument of Surrender at the Municipal Building in Singapore on 12 September 1945.

Chief Minister David Marshall tries out a Lee-Enfield rifle while visiting the Singapore Military Forces at Tanah Merah in July 1955.

Visit of the Secretary of State for the Colonies, Alan Lennox-Boyd in August 1955. In the photo are (from left to right), Alan Lennox-Boyd, Lady Anne Black, the Governor of Singapore Sir Robert Black, Lady Patricia Lennox-Boyd, Chief Minister David Marshall and Commissioner-General for Southeast Asia Malcolm MacDonald. This photo was taken at Kallang Airport.

National Day Parade 1969 at the Padang. President Yusof Ishak is inspecting a Guard-of-Honour mounted by the 3rd Battalion, Singapore Infantry Regiment. He is escorted by the Guard commander, Major Albert Tan.

Singapore's AMX-13 tanks make their debut at the 1969 National Day Parade at the Padang. Armed with a 75mm main gun, these tanks, bought second-hand from Israel, boosted Singapore's defence capabilities significantly.

Opposition Member of Parliament (MP) for Anson, Joshua Benjamin Jeyaratnam, arriving at the Istana to attend a National Day Reception hosted by President and Mrs. C.V. Devan Nair. Jeyaratnam was a member of the Worker's Party. He became the first Opposition MP to be elected since 1965, when he won the Anson constituency in a by-election in 1981. He was re-elected in 1984.

Rather naively, he thought that he could win the students and trade unions to his side through reason and negotiation – he was after all, an anti-colonial nationalist. He could not have been more wrong. The Hock Lee Bus Riot broke Marshall politically. He would never quite inspire confidence in the British in his views about internal security in Singapore. Internal security became the proverbial albatross around his neck. He remained in office but as Nicoll quite cynically observed, this was only because the political alternatives were unpalatable.

Marshall had long been wary of the Emergency Regulations Ordinance, first passed in 1948. This law provided the government with wide-ranging powers to deal with internal security threats. It could order and enforce a curfew, and preventively detain anyone without trial, in anticipation of a political or security threat. In August 1955, Marshall moved to repeal the Emergency Regulations Ordinance. This was good politics but bad policy. Marshall was once again caught between political reality and his personal beliefs. Marshall, the liberal, viewed such powers as an affront to his beliefs, especially the arbitrary manner in which they could be wielded and enforced. Marshall, the politician, however, had to ensure that he fulfilled his party's election pledges. And Marshall, the Chief Minister, knew that he needed these powers, which he disdained, to govern. Hemmed in on three sides, Marshall tabled the Preservation of Public Security Bill on 15 August 1955. He played this card well and it showed how agile and skilful Marshall could be as a politician. His aim, rather than a wholesale repeal, was to temper the excesses of the Emergency Regulations Ordinance. It placed limits on detention. It also placed the power of detention in the hands of a panel of three judges. The Bill passed in the Assembly by a vote of 19 to 4 on 12 October 1955 to become the Preservation of Public Security Ordinance (PPSO). The British would have none of this. They responded swiftly. In an extraordinary move which underscored that internal security was a non-negotiable bottom line, William Goode, the Chief Secretary, moved to pass the Criminal Law (Temporary Provisions) Bill in the Assembly. This restored many of the elements repealed under the PPSO and the colonial authorities were none the weaker when it came to powers to contain the radical left. The only difference was that the CL(TP) Ordinance was to be temporary in nature as it had to be reviewed every five years. It passed on the same day as the PPSO and remains in force, subject to regular review by the Singapore Parliament.

Marshall worked hard to close the distance between the government and the people. In June 1955, he began meeting with his constituents in the first Meet-the-People sessions ever. Very soon after, the other ministers followed suit. At these sessions, the constituents were treated as clients and once their problems or concerns were heard, then letters of reference to the relevant authorities or other necessary action was undertaken on the spot. No one left empty handed. The client would leave with his problem listened to and acted on, if not solved. Always one for the underdog, Marshall pushed for the establishment of the Legal Aid Bureau to provide the common man with legal assistance and counsel. On 6 June 1956, the Legal Aid and Advice Ordinance was passed – it was a landmark law that recognised that every person deserved the equal protection of the law. As a fervent nationalist, Marshall set up the Malayanisation Commission in August 1955 to systematically and more rapidly Malayanise the civil service, to replace British officials with local ones. This push bore fruit eventually in 1959, when almost all of the civil service was Malayanised. There was so much for David Marshall to do under such trying and difficult circumstances where every idea and proposal had to be fought for or finagled from allies and opponents alike. But Marshall, above all, inspired. His ideals, his belief in the common man, his love for Singapore – these are hallmarks of the Marshall government that history needs to remember.

The PAP In Opposition

Across the floor of the Assembly, the fledging PAP sat in opposition. Lee Kuan Yew, seated where the Leader of the Opposition would have been, now faced David Marshall, the Chief Minister, squarely. Both men were formidable debaters with sharp minds and equally acerbic tongues and their debates would make for robust and entertaining exchanges in the august chamber. Marshall, passionate and flamboyant, stood in sharp contrast to Lee, who was analytical and coldly rational. Lee and the PAP, having decided shrewdly to contest the elections in a limited fashion and having declined Marshall's entreaties to join the Labour Front in a governing coalition, now stood poised to reap a modest profit from these decisions.

Politically, Lee was as realistic as he was astute and shrewd. The political equations were clear to him. The Rendel Constitution was so limited as to make any sort of impactful governing a near impossibility. He avoided the risk of having to do so by contesting only a handful of seats. The Labour Front was to him a motley collection of political amateurs and adventurers who were cavalier and lacked any sort of substance. He avoided the risk of association by declining Marshall's entreaties. By the end of the 1955 Election, it was clear that no political party could alienate the Chinese in Singapore and hope for political success. To succeed politically, the PAP had taken the risk of allying with radical left-wing elements. And as with all risk-taking ventures, Lee would be preoccupied by it for most of 1955 and 1956.

Lee was a risk taker but a careful and deliberate one. His assessment of the political situation was cold, calculating and accurate. Mostly, he avoided the grand gestures that could have drawn him attention. Then again, was there a need for such political grandstanding? The PAP, its leaders and its branding, already stood out as a left-wing party that was markedly different from its peers. Its lightning symbol was an arresting sight. Its strategy of co-opting union activists and activism to build a mass party with the support of the Chinese-educated, was bold. All these also made it an easy target for its foes.

It was during the Hock Lee Bus Riot of April 1955, the same riot that destroyed David Marshall politically, that the nature of the political risk Lee had taken became apparent. Lee was taken aback by the mob violence. Lee had expected Lim Chin Siong and Fong Swee Suan to stir up the workers and students, but the orgy of gratuitous destruction was totally unexpected. In an emergency meeting called on 16 May 1955, Lee was cornered by both Marshall and Goode. Lee found that whatever accusations were being hurled at him, he could not condemn Lim Chin Siong and Fong Swee Suan. They were the instigators of the riot but also the nucleus of the PAP's powerful radical left faction. They carried with them the Chinese supporters of the PAP; the very reason Lee took the gamble in the first place. But Lee could not defend them either. To do so would be to commit political suicide for he would have been pilloried as a communist sympathiser and the PAP cast as a communist front organisation.

Goode attacked and castigated Lee and the PAP for fomenting and instigating the riot that wrecked the city. As far as he was concerned, Lee lost control of the PAP to the radical left. Lee was clearly under pressure now – he needed the radical left's support for the PAP's survival, yet he was now under pressure to purge them from the PAP.

If Lee had caved in, then the PAP would split and that would have put paid to its political ambitions. Caught in a corner, Lee responded nimbly, and narrowly saved the day for the PAP, for at least that moment. Lee began by restating the PAP's stand – to use non-violent methods to take down the colonial system. The PAP, he insisted, would fight the communists or anyone who threatened the existence of an independent, democratic and non-communist Malaya.

Marshall would have none of this from Lee. In Marshall's words, Lee was a cat's paw for Lim. For Lee, this was a perilous moment. The Emergency Regulations hung over him and the PAP like the Sword of Damocles. Detention and proscription were both distinct possibilities. Regardless, Lee had no choice but to continue to walk the political tightrope and balance, no matter how precariously, his moderate faction and the radical left in the PAP. There was no other option. But Lee took away an important lesson from the Hock Lee Riots. He learnt that when the PAP came to power, it could not govern like Marshall – it had to prescribe political solutions to what was essentially a political problem: a radical left that wanted to realise, at all costs and by any means, its vision of a communist Malaya.

Marshall's Constitutional Crisis

Marshall cannot be faulted for being complacent in forcing the British to rethink their attitudes toward Singapore's political future. He acted assiduously to force the British to adjust the timetable for Singapore's political development. As the visit by the Secretary of State for the Colonies, Alan Lennox-Boyd, drew near, Marshall made his move. He asked the new Governor Sir Robert Black, who took office in June 1955, to appoint four assistant ministers. Black responded by offering to appoint two assistant ministers instead. Marshall shrewdly used this as an opportunity to precipitate a constitutional crisis. To do so, he argued that behind this issue was the more fundamental question – was it the Governor or the ministers who ran the country? Marshall disagreed with the view that the Governor was not bound to accept the Chief Minister's advice. He threatened to resign.

Black responded sensibly and calmly, and he must be given credit for not dismissing Marshall's threat as an outburst of petulance. Black recognised that Marshall's *fait accompli* would have blown the constitutional crisis into calamitous proportions. If Marshall actually resigned, there would have to be a fresh election. Given the radical left's show of strength in the interminable strikes and recent Hock Lee Bus Riot, it was entirely possible that a pro-communist political party, as the PAP was then perceived to be, would be returned to power. This would be a disaster for the British and far worse than having to deal with a government led by Marshall. After all, the bottom-line was always to safeguard British political and economic interests. Marshall crossed this tripwire with his threat.

On 22 July 1955, Marshall tabled a motion for immediate self-government in the Assembly that passed without difficulty. In a press interview that followed, Marshall wielded the threat of resignation as a political sledgehammer. He would have done so, however, if the British adopted an open attitude towards Singapore's political evolution and were prepared to contemplate speeding up the pace of this evolution. Faced with these threats, the British were confronted with the possibilities of having to hold a fresh election if they did not agree.

Marshall had therefore cleverly framed the agenda before Lennox-Boyd arrived in Singapore on 31 July 1955. On 18 August, the British responded. Though they did not agree with Marshall's interpretation of the 1955 Constitution, they were willing to go along with it. They accepted that the Chief Minister's advice to the Governor was binding – Marshall had his four assistant ministers. More significantly, Marshall gained control over the pace, direction and timetable of Singapore's path to self-government and independence. The constitutional talks would be held much earlier. He was ebullient.

Towards Self-Government – The First Steps (1955 – 1956)

In April 1956, as the All-Party Merdeka Mission headed to London for talks on self-government for Singapore, internal security would make or break these talks. As a staunch nationalist with an anti-colonial outlook, Marshall was expected to adopt a strident and uncompromising stand when it came to Singapore's political future. After all, he had campaigned on a platform that promised to husband Singapore towards self-government and eventual independence. Indeed, as events have shown, no political party that showed a lack of urgency in this respect would have any traction with an electorate that was impatient for political change. Marshall's single failing in this matter was not being sufficiently astute and nuanced in his reading of both the British government and the members of his own mission. He was once again stymied and hobbled, caught between his beliefs and dreams for Singapore and a hard political reality. And it was not just this seeming lack of political acumen that failed him. Behind Marshall was a fractious and splintered group of political parties that did not rally behind him. His own party deserted him at the closing stages of the fraught negotiations. Certainly, his political skills fell short. There was no common line as they sat at the negotiating tables and this was something that the British government was well placed to exploit.

Soon after arriving in London, the thirteen-man all-party delegation realised that it was not an opportune time for talks on Singapore's constitutional future. The stakes were high. Before flying off, Marshall stated that he would resign if he failed in his mission to get self-government for Singapore. He believed that if he did so, his entire government would follow suit, thus precipitating a fresh election. He was certain that the British wanted to avoid this at all costs. Marshall, as it would turn out, had assumed wrongly.

If Marshall went to the talks with a set of wrong assumptions, then Lee went with his eyes wide open. Lee's assumptions were built on a realistic read of the political situation in Singapore and, perhaps more crucially, in Britain. He was under no illusions about the British, whom he knew were in no mood to make any significant concessions to the Singapore delegation. The PAP's aims were therefore more limited than those proposed by Marshall. For one, they accepted the reality that the British had every right to revoke or suspend the constitution if they had to. This was a fact. Asking for and chasing after an elusive independence was, to Lee and the PAP, akin to tilting at windmills. This was the line that Lee held at the conference.

On 23 April 1956, the talks opened at Carlton House in London. Alan Lennox-Boyd, the Secretary of State for the Colonies, led a twenty-two strong delegation and he made the British position quite clear. He set the negotiating boundaries quite clearly. He was firm but not unwilling to compromise. Lennox-Boyd asserted the joint control over internal security and external defence was non-negotiable. They would not risk Singapore falling into communist hands and being, as Lennox-Boyd would put it, 'a colony of Peking'. They would hold on tightly to the power and step in should the need arise. The Singapore delegation had very little wriggle room.

Marshall responded rather blisteringly. Clearly in a fighting mood, he presented his position to Lennox-Boyd in a similarly trenchant manner. Just as internal security and defence were non-negotiables for the British, it was the same for Marshall when it came to self-government and independence. Marshall proposed that internal security be separated from external defence. The Singapore government would be responsible for the former while a proposed Defence Council would be responsible for the latter. To address and allay British fears, he put in a mechanism that enabled the government to call on the Defence Council and draw on its military resources should such a need arise. Marshall's proposals were rejected. They were unwilling to budge. There was no surrendering their final say over internal security in Singapore.

Marshall tried ways and means to get around this vexatious problem by tweaking the composition and form of the proposed Defence and Security Council (DSC). The DSC proposed by the British consisted of the UK High Commissioner, the Council of Ministers and the Commissioner of Police. Most significantly, the UK High Commissioner would chair the DSC and also held the casting vote in the event of a tie. Marshall counter-proposed. He wanted a six-year term limit on the DSC and the removal of the UK High Commissioner's casting vote. He reasoned that in a worst-case scenario, the Constitution could be suspended. This was unhelpful and unrealistic since the suspension of the Constitution was not something to be taken lightly. Once again, Marshall's fixes were turned down. The British simply could not trust nor bring themselves to trust Marshall with responsibility over Singapore's internal security, stability, law and order. The spectre of the Hock Lee Bus Riot haunted Marshall even in London. Marshall's final proposal for the Chairman of the DSC to be a nominee from the Federation of Malaya was similarly shot down.

For all their stubbornness and intransigence over internal security, the British were generous and open to all other proposals put up by the delegation. They were willing to abolish the ex-officio and nominated members in the Assembly. They were willing to open up all seats in an expanded Assembly of fifty to the popular vote. They agreed to a Singapore citizenship, the Malayanisation of the Civil Service and the replacement of the Governor with a High Commissioner, who would act on the advice of the Council of Ministers. The Singapore delegation was willing to accept this offer. But Marshall and Lim Chin Siong refused.

To Marshall, all these were sweeteners. Real power, in terms of the ability to deal with subversion, disorder and internal security, remained firmly in the hands of the British. This was not what he came to London for. It was an affront to what he sought for the people of Singapore, which was nothing less than full sovereignty. Soon after, on 15 May 1956, the delegation put out a communique announcing the breakdown of talks. Marshall's time as Chief Minister was up.

Just as Marshall's political star was rapidly fading away, Lee's began rising. He had made a good impression on the British – his intelligence, his reputation as a firebrand and his ability, were evident to the British. He was, in many of their eyes, the coming man in Singapore politics. For Marshall's successor, Lim Yew Hock, and for Singapore, the British assessment of Lee would have profound consequences.

A Man Cannot Serve Two Masters: The Lim Yew Hock Government (1956 – 1957)

Marshall's resignation after the Constitutional Conference cast a pall of sobriety over Singapore politics. Marshall's hankering after a sensation of independence had left Singapore without a crumb of self-government. Shorn of his exuberance and passion, whom some derided as erratic, Singapore politics entered a new phase. There was no alternative. After all, David Marshall was one of a kind – there was no one quite like him.

On 8 June 1956, his successor, Lim Yew Hock, was sworn in as Chief Minister. He was seen, at that point, as a sober and sensible leader. While Lim was not Marshall, he faced the same challenges. How was he to deal with Singapore's internal security situation without becoming unpopular with the people, especially the Chinese community, which had by now became the bastion of the radical left? The schools, the trade unions and the rural areas were the sources of its support, and also its power bases. To strike at any of these would be politically dangerous. To strike at any of these and then take responsibility for it would be political suicide. Lim would end up doing both. He needed to have his political cake and eat it. The British, he reasoned, would need to be convinced that unlike Marshall, he was able to make the hard decisions to straighten Singapore out. He would learn that it was impossible for a man to serve and please two masters, the British and the Singapore people. Cutting through this Gordian

Knot was to prove beyond the LF. In the wings stood the PAP, waiting for its breakout moment.

In September 1956, Lim moved against the radical left, striking at the heart of its power. He dissolved the Singapore Chinese Middle Schools Students' Union (SCMSSU). He wanted to send the signal to everyone that he was a tough man who was unafraid to act against the radical left. Lim knew he had the power to deploy a range of security forces and legal instruments to curb the radical left. And he relished using it.

Lim's strike against the radical left was a calculated move that he hoped would secure his political ambitions. Unsurprisingly, the PAP now found itself squarely in Lim's crosshairs. Its leaders were incensed. Lee accused Lim of trying to destroy the PAP's credibility and appeal by painting it as a communist open-front organisation. Lim denied this. But he was shrewd. He knew that he could not ban the PAP outright as that would have ended his political career. The PAP's leadership, its organisation and its supporters were, however, fair game. Lim could not kill the PAP off completely, but he could slowly chip away at its machinery and cripple it as a political force.

In October 1956, Lim launched Operation Liberation against striking Chinese Middle School students. He issued an ultimatum to them – either disperse from their schools which they had occupied for two weeks or the government would disperse them, by force. The students were unmoved. They had union support, they expected this confrontation and they had steeled themselves for this. While the students held their posts, a PAP rally was taking place at Beauty World Park in Upper Bukit Timah on the evening of 25 October 1956. Lee Kuan Yew, Lim Chin Siong and Devan Nair were all there. On stage, Lim Chin Siong worked the crowd. Tensions escalated and riots soon broke out at the Chinese High School and Chung Cheng High School, spreading to Geylang, Rochor and other parts of the city. Busmen and factory workers went on a sympathy strike.

But unlike Marshall, Lim Yew Hock was ready. The riot police moved in with batons, tear gas and dye grenades. The army was on standby, ready to man roadblocks and enforce a curfew. Police cars were deployed en masse. And Lim used all these to great effect. There was no chance that things would spiral out of control. Detentions under the PPSO followed – the pretext was clear. Lim, Fong, Devan, Woodhull and Chan, the nucleus of the PAP's radical left leadership, were taken in. Lim was proud of what he had done. He had stared down the radical left and taken them on. He was tough. He could govern. He was not Marshall.

With the PAP's leadership hollowed out by the detention, Lim must have thought that he had dealt them a crippling blow. He was, by his own estimates at least, in a strong political position. Having assured the British of his internal security credentials, he was almost unassailable. But Lim had miscalculated. He had weakened the PAP but not broken it. He underestimated the resilience and will of the PAP moderates led by Lee.

In many ways, his miscalculations were, on the surface at least, valid. In the aftermath of the SCMSSU riots, the PAP was cast and painted as a subversive force and a political front for the communists. Public opinion was hostile to the PAP, and at the same time, public opinion approved of Lim's handling of the riots and his strong stance on law and order. The Chinese, however, saw Lim in a dark light. Lim had struck at the cherished symbols of Chinese identity and culture in Singapore, the two top Middle Schools, Chung Cheng High School and the Chinese High School. He was no leader but a mere colonial stooge and the puppet of colonial oppression.

Lim, however, felt that the odds were in his favour. After all, he had decapitated the PAP. He believed that he could convince the people that he had acted rightly and responsibly, especially since he had all the media tools, especially broadcast radio, at his disposal. Lim believed that he held the upper hand. After all, some 260,000 Chinese, those who would likely support the PAP's radical left, still did not have the right to vote, since they were not British subjects. If fresh elections were held there and then, Lim and his Labour Front would win, perhaps even handsomely.

Not for the first time since the PAP's founding, and certainly not for the last, Lee found himself on the defensive. He knew that the PAP had been weakened and its public image had taken a hammering. The government had detained the very people he depended on to mobilise the support of the Chinese masses. This posed a mortal threat to the PAP – why should the Chinese voters continue to support them? To retain the backing of the radical left, Lee had to show that the PAP was still a viable political partner, one that could win elections.

On 5 November 1956, Lee moved in the Assembly to condemn and deplore the arrest and detention of the radical left leadership of the PAP. Lee made it very clear that he was a nationalist. He then delivered a clear-eyed and no-holds-barred analysis of the Singapore political situation. Singapore's political future was driven, he reasoned, not by leadership but by whoever was willing and able to advance a cause. Whoever could do so would be able to mobilise the leaders in a revolutionary situation – a people mired in socio-economic grievances drawn by an ideology that promised the answers. The communists, Lee declared, would make common cause with anybody, 'whether he is Communist, non-Communist or anti-Communist, who helps to advance their cause is used'. This was the political reality that all parties had to realise they were contending with.

But even before this, Lee argued, it was necessary to wrest from the British the control and responsibility over internal security in Singapore. Not to do so would render any party or government politically vulnerable. This was a salvo aimed in the direction of Lim Yew Hock, whose Labour Front government had no control over internal security and yet willingly took responsibility for putting down the riots. To this, Lim insisted that he had no regrets. Time, he insisted, would show that he acted correctly. Lee was under no such illusions for himself or the PAP. Unlike Lim, he did not believe that any government that used internal security forces it had no constitutional mandate over could continue to hold the people's trust and support.

Towards Self-Government: The Next Steps (1957 – 1958)

Beneath this gloomy political cloud, the parties readied themselves for the 2nd Constitutional Conference scheduled for March 1957. Just eleven months had lapsed since the abortive round of talks in May 1956. No one was keen to see a rerun of that fiasco. This time, the delegation adopted a low-key, cool and realistic approach. They focused on the do-able, the possible and the attainable, with no drama and histrionics. The bottom line, once again, was internal security.

In the run-up to the talks, Lim Yew Hock called for an All-Party Meeting on 7 Feb 1957, the first of eight such meetings. As late as December 1956, Lim remained ambiguous and non-committal about this All-Party approach, but this changed only because Lennox-Boyd and the Colonial Office had ostensibly intimated that they would not have it any other way. Having no choice, Lim demurred. In these eight meetings, the differences between the parties were thrashed out and solutions devised.

Two important and consequential proposals were put forth. The first, which Lee insisted on, was a new citizenship law that would give the vote to the 260,000 'alien' Chinese, who were not British subjects. This also meant that the earliest elections could only take place in May 1958 – this took the heat off the PAP (and everyone else). Second, the proposed Internal Security Council (ISC) was to share responsibility jointly between three UK members, three Singapore members and one member from the Federation of Malaya who would also hold the casting vote in the event of a tie. The Federation Prime Minister, Tunku Abdul Rahman, had agreed to this arrangement earlier on 18 December 1956.

When the delegation flew for London, their mission was quite clear – 'to secure from Her Majesty's Government the status of a self-governing state with all the rights, powers and privileges pertaining to internal affairs, and the control of trade, commerce and cultural relations in external affairs'. There would be no more talk of independence. This was a modest proposal for full self-government. It was well within the realm of the probable rather than the mere possible. And this modesty extended to the size of the delegation as well. Previously, it comprised thirteen members; it was now down to five, with two from the Labour Front, one from UMNO, one from the Liberal Socialists and one from the PAP. A modest delegation, with modest goals, negotiating in a modest, moderate fashion. This set the tone for the talks.

Unsurprisingly, the talks, held from 11 March to 11 April 1957, concluded predictably and amicably. The British acceded to the proposals marshalled by the delegation. There would be a Legislative Assembly of fifty-one elected members from which the Prime Minister and Cabinet would be chosen. The head of state would be a Malayan-born *Yang di-Pertuan Negara*, who would be the Queen's representative in Singapore. The British retained responsibility for defence and foreign affairs. The proposed ISC would jointly manage internal security matters. The sober, reasonable atmosphere of the talks must have helped for the British were willing to acquiesce to the ISC proposal – it was novel and almost a gamble – but given the political circumstances, the best possible compromise.

Still, if there was any inkling that the British had niggling doubts about the internal security arrangements, it did not show until

Lennox-Boyd introduced a non-negotiable provision, Clause 30, on 10 April 1957. This Clause barred anyone who had engaged in or been detained because of subversive activities from running in the forthcoming elections. Both Lim and Lee openly expressed reservations about this provision, but they decided to put it before the Legislative Assembly for debate rather than let it derail the talks. Both men were briefed prior to this announcement and had expressed their views to Lennox-Boyd – they would not accept the clause, but neither would they demur nor object if the British insisted on it and took responsibility for it.

Predictably, back in Singapore, Marshall came out with his guns blazing against the outcome of the talks. He described it colourfully and disparagingly as a *tiga suku busok merdeka* (three-quarters rotten independence) on 26 April 1957 in an Assembly debate. Paradoxically, although Marshall rejected the terms of the constitution, he openly declared that he was in favour of Clause 30. Now, whether this was an honest mistake or not, the point is moot. Marshall's stand and his subsequent aborted move to challenge Lee to a by-election (which took place anyway) further discredited him politically. Marshall resigned his seat in the Legislative Assembly three days later on 29 April 1957. He also announced that he was withdrawing from the by-election. But this was not his final farewell from politics – he still had some fight left in him, as we shall see.

At these talks, Lim Yew Hock had, to his credit, showed that Singapore politics under his Chief Ministership was indeed the art of the possible. Unlike Marshall, Lim did not chase after the impossible. Yet, Lim was overshadowed by the eloquent and incisive Lee, who cut an impressive intellectual and sartorial figure at the talks. But for Lee, regardless of what the British thought of him, the fight for the PAP had just begun.

Regrouping And Rebuilding: The PAP (1957 – 1958)

As the dust from Marshall's unexpected by-election challenge settled, Lee and his lieutenants in the PAP leadership prepared to contest it. The question on their minds was predictable –could the PAP survive politically without support from the radical left?

Even though Marshall had withdrawn from it, the by-election still had to be held. The by-election would be a useful barometer of where the PAP's political fortune stood. Things were tense within the PAP. The moderates were trying to re-establish their political footing. The radical leftists were restive, itching to influence the by-election in Tanjong Pagar. In a display of solidarity and resolve, Toh Chin Chye and Ong Pang Boon showed that they would have none of that. Offers to canvass votes were rebuffed and rejected. They had to determine that they could win on their own.

The by-election results were heartening – Lee had polled, not unexpectedly, 67.5% of the votes cast. As Lee observed the rush of the voters in the evening, he had remarked 'the people are behind us'. The PAP proved that it could survive without the electoral boost from the radical leftists. The people knew the PAP, knew what it stood for and where it stood and rallied decisively behind it. It did not look so good for Lim Yew Hock's Labour Front though. His candidate in Cairnhill was defeated by the widely derided Liberal Socialists and came in third, behind an independent candidate backed by David Marshall. This defeat did not go unnoticed. Lim and his government were fatally wounded.

Lee's next move was to secure the moderates' hold over the PAP itself. In Lee's words, the moment had come to flush out the communists. The radical left moved first. In a show of what Lee termed 'adventurism', they threw down the gauntlet. The intention was to capture the PAP's Central Executive Committee (CEC), its highest decision-making body. This move, bold as it was, required some delicacy and finesse in execution.

Lim Chin Joo (Lim Chin Siong's younger brother) was in charge, as the first-line leaders were all under political detention. Party members packed the Annual General Meeting (AGM) on 4 August 1957 at the Singapore Badminton Hall with their supporters. The PAP's laxity in managing its membership cards and admission cards played to their advantage. The hall was packed with people who had been instructed to vote 'the right way': to capture a majority in the CEC and keep the moderates in key positions. This would maintain the illusion that the moderates remained in control. The PAP would thus be transformed into a true political front for the radical left which would be able to carry every motion and resolution in the CEC, exerting a grip over party organisation, policy and direction.

But Lee, Ong, Byrne and Toh had not been idle. Before the AGM, they engineered a leak to the press that exposed the radical left's plans.

The headline 'Stage is Set for the Big PAP Showdown' was splashed across the papers on 1 August 1957. Lee and his team, with their vision of 'an independent, democratic, non-communist, socialist Malaya', had put themselves on the ballot. They would force the radical left into the open and face them in a fight. The battle lines were drawn. On 4 August 1957, they fought to a draw. Lee and the moderates took six seats and the radical left six seats on the CEC. The CEC was split down the middle.

Not all was lost for the moderates. The biggest advantage Lee and his moderates offered the radical left was political cover, which was critical. As long Lee and his team remained in the CEC and held key positions, Lim Yew Hock could not proscribe the PAP as a security threat. Lee's final card was obvious – if he and his team refused to take up key positions in the CEC but instead remained within it as ordinary members, then the radical left would lose its political cover. They would be exposed and vulnerable. This was exactly what Lee and his team did. On 6 August 1957, they issued a statement that they would not take office in the CEC. They had shown their hand.

The political adventurers suddenly found themselves outflanked and naked. They needed Lee to compromise. To do so, they offered Lee and his team a majority of one via the process of co-option. This offer, made on 9 August 1957, was rejected. A working majority in the CEC, Lee reasoned, was not an overall majority. He would not have control over the party's policy and direction. On 13 August 1957, with no solution in sight, Tan Chong Kim and T. T. Rajah had no choice but to take up the posts of Chairman and General Secretary respectively. The radical left had overplayed their hand.

On the night of 22 August 1957, Lim Yew Hock acted. Mass arrests were launched at Middle Road, home of the trade unions. Eighteen PAP members, including five of the newly elected CEC (except for T. T. Rajah), and thirteen trade unionists, were detained under the PPSO. They were, in Lim's eyes, not just a security threat but also a political threat. The radical left under Lim Chin Joo was, at this point, simultaneously working to absorb the Trades Union Congress (TUC) into the leftist Singapore General Employees' Union (SGEU). For Lim, this was personal. The TUC was, after all, his political base in the labour movement.

Lim must have felt encouraged by what he had achieved with this round of detentions. Once again, he had acted decisively. He made it look like Lee had deliberately abandoned the radical left. This would surely shatter any support that Lee and the PAP enjoyed. He had also secured his mass base in the labour movement – the radical left's attempts to subvert the TUC were halted.

But once again, Lim had miscalculated. He inadvertently did Lee and his moderates a huge political favour by arresting the radical left and not proscribing the PAP. The PAP did not break. Lee and his team did not lose control of the PAP to the radical left. For now, they had a moment of respite, of reprieve, to regroup and reorganise. And Lee would make it count.

On 8 May 1958, the PAP re-registered all its members. There would be two classes of membership – cadres and ordinary members. Cadre members could attend and vote at party conferences. For an ordinary member to be promoted to the rank of a cadre member, approval from the CEC was required. And the cadre members were the ones who elected the CEC. This reform, inspired by the Papacy, ringfenced the CEC against any infiltration and subversion by the radical left through its membership base. Its purge was finished and done.

Lim Yew Hock: Out Of Time & Out Of Ideas

As 1957 wore on, Lim Yew Hock's political fortunes took a beating. On 10 October 1957, any electoral advantage he enjoyed vanished overnight. The 260,000 'alien' Chinese who up till then had no right to vote, could now do so as the Singapore Citizenship Ordinance was passed. Under this law, all who were born in Singapore or the Federation of Malaya were eligible to become Singapore citizens. For those who had resided in Singapore for ten years or more, citizenship by naturalisation was offered. These were the voters whom Lim had alienated and marginalised with his politically flat-footed crackdown on the radical left, the trade unions and the Chinese Middle Schools. They finally had a chance to make themselves heard in the next general election. The doomsday clock had begun counting down for Lim Yew Hock and his Labour Front.

Even without taking this bloc of voters into consideration, it was clear that Lim Yew Hock was on decidedly shaky ground by the end of 1957. If Lim needed any convincing that the PAP was still politically alive, enervated perhaps but still alive, he had only to look at the outcome of the City Council election on 21 December 1957. For the political parties concerned, this was a critical election, even though it was for local government. Whichever party won the election would have a platform from which to convince the people that they could deliver a better quality of life, be it in terms of housing, standpipes or electricity supply. For the PAP, this was the moment to show Lim Yew Hock, the radical left and the Singapore people that the party was alive. It still had its political groove and it was in fighting form. For Lim Yew Hock, it was a litmus test – how much political damage had he inflicted on the Labour Front in the last eighteen months? Had all his calculations and machinations come to nought?

The results for the thirty-two wards were telling for Lim Yew Hock. The Labour Front was decimated. It took only four of the sixteen seats it contested. The PAP won handsomely, taking thirteen of the fourteen seats it contested. With the support of two seats from UMNO, the PAP now had a simple, working majority. And with this, Ong Eng Guan took office as the first elected Mayor of the City of Singapore.

The people had spoken, but Lim remained truculent, at least publicly. In January 1958, when reporters asked him about the City Council results, he remarked rather testily, 'the Council was elected by 30% of the people, the 70% are still uncommitted'. To him, low voter turnout skewed the election results in favour of the victors. His silent majority did not speak up in that election. Regardless of what he said publicly and regardless of how defiant he sounded, the political reality was clear. Lim Yew Hock was out of time and out of ideas.

But Lim was not about to give up his political ambitions without a fight just yet. For a man who was almost out of time, Lim used the power of incumbency to his advantage. Citing vague justifications, the general elections would not be held until 2 April 1959, at the latest. He used Sir William Goode's last Governor's Address in April 1958 to make this known.

Still, whatever Lim's hopes, dreams and expectations were, it was clear to the British, by May 1958, that Lim was out of political capital and was a spent force in Singapore politics. At the 3rd Constitutional Conference held in London from 13 to 28 May 1958, it was clear that the British saw Lee not just as the leader of the PAP but also the leader of a government-in-waiting. They were convinced that the PAP would win the next election and that Lee was the man who was leading the team that had the resolve and ability to carry out the tasks ahead.

The talks, the final step in the road to full self-government, were in some ways, a formality, the inking of an agreement that had been sorted out beforehand. Singapore was set to become a full self-governing state with total control over domestic affairs under this new constitution.

The controversial Clause 30, non-negotiable at the previous talks, had been removed. On 1 August 1958, the State of Singapore Act was passed with royal assent. Whoever won the next election in Singapore would become the first elected government of the State of Singapore. This was a big political prize. And compared to 1955, the stakes were much higher.

Deprived of the political endorsement of the British, Lim attempted to reboot and strengthen his political base by forming a coalition, the Singapore Peoples' Alliance (SPA), on 10 November 1958. By 2 December 1958, the SPA had morphed into the SPA/UMNO-MCA Alliance coalition, undoubtedly an attempt to inject new political capital by showcasing Lim's close ties with politicians from the Federation of Malaya, especially its Prime Minister, Tunku Abdul Rahman. In mid-1958, the Liberal Socialists made a series of public statements once again questioning the PAP's anti-communist credentials. A line in the sand had been drawn. To vote for the PAP, Lim and his allies insinuated was to vote for communism.

1959 – 'The People's Verdict Is Clear And Decisive.'

As 1959 began, the lines of battle were being drawn and the political parties began staking their positions. Lim Yew Hock and Lee Kuan Yew crossed swords heatedly in the Assembly on 11 February 1959 over the Legislative Assembly Elections (Amendment) Bill. This opening exchange, coming just four days before the PAP's inaugural pre-election rally, saw both men claiming that victory in the upcoming election was theirs. Lee declared, brimming with confidence, that victory was 'a foregone conclusion'. Obviously, Lim could not be seen conceding so early in this contest. Lim reciprocated with his own chest beating – he too claimed that he was bound to win.

Four days later, on 15 February 1959, the PAP's takedown of Lim Yew Hock and the SPA began. Speaking to a crowd of five thousand at Hong Lim Green from a platform formed by two lorries, Dr. Toh Chin Chye, the PAP Chairman, delivered the first of what would be the fatal blow for the SPA. This was the beginning of the Chew Swee Kee scandal – Chew Swee Kee was the Minister for Education who was a key player in the LF and the SPA. The PAP's relentless messaging focused on one thing – the SPA was corrupt, incompetent and utterly untrustworthy. Thereafter, whatever the SPA said, or rather, regardless of what it said or did, the Singapore people would view it through the lens of this scandal. The PAP had decisively and ruthlessly seized the opportunity to frame the political discourse for this election. In Lee's words, they were 'playing to win'.

The PAP's attacks on the SPA and Chew Swee Kee finally paid off when he resigned on 4 March 1959 before debates over the allegations began in the Legislative Assembly. This was as good as an admission of guilt by the erstwhile Minister for Education. On 2 April 1959, the Governor appointed Justice M. Buttrose to chair a Commission of Inquiry (COI) into the matter. On 26 May 1959, just four days before the election, the Commission reported on its findings. The facts were stark. Chew had apparently received political gifts totalling $701,593.47 from a foreign source in 1957 and 1958, when he was with the LF. The PAP's relentless charges that the SPA and its ilk were a corrupt lot of carpet baggers, hangers-on and political opportunists had stuck. It mattered not one bit that technically, a political gift did not constitute a bribe. Corruption or not, the implication was clear: Chew had colluded with foreigners and sold Singapore down the river. This slur stuck. And the SPA never recovered from this.

Amidst this hubbub, the electoral machinery ground on. Earlier, on 31 March 1959, the Governor dissolved the Legislative Assembly that had run its full four-year term. Nomination Day was on 25 April 1959 and the General Election was scheduled for 30 May 1959. Lim Yew Hock was finally out of time. On 6 April 1959, the Liberal Socialists (Lib-Socs) finally agreed to enter into a coalition with the SPA/UMNO-MCA Alliance. The Lib-Socs came onto the political scene in 1956 when the SPP merged with the Democratic Party. There was little in common between the coalition partners beyond being an anti-PAP front. It was a classic case of too little, too late and it became something of a joke. Even though they were anticipating political oblivion, they could not agree on the most basic tactical rule of political contests – how to avoid splitting the vote. On 28 May 1959, two days before the elections, the coalition held urgent talks to discuss this. These fell apart and a blame game began. It became farce rapidly. As they bickered, the PAP ridiculed them. Toh Chin Chye, the PAP Chairman, put it quite rightly when he described it as 'a motor car with many drivers.' And this car was going nowhere because the drivers could not agree on who was driving and where they were going.

With its opponents in disarray, the PAP ran a tight and disciplined campaign that targeted them and captured the attention, if not the imagination, of the people. The joys and sorrows of the people were its joys and sorrows. And the PAP was obviously well prepared. On 25 April 1959, it unveiled its five-year plan for Singapore. In its campaign manifesto, aptly and soberly titled 'The Tasks Ahead', the party outlined its plans for the economy, its labour policy, housing, rural development and even women's rights. No other political party had such an extensive, coherent and practical programme for Singapore.

And the PAP was everywhere, day and night. PAP candidates shook hands with voters, listened to them and made themselves heard at mass rallies and street meetings all over Singapore, including its 'odd corners', as Lee put it. The PAP put on an impressive display of how it could mobilise its supporters, energise its volunteers and draw the crowds. And their supporters came with flower garlands, offers of lorries to be used as rally platforms, offers of electricity and a technician or two to rig it all up, at no charge at all. The working class and the Chinese-educated, often enthusiastic, came in large numbers to these rallies, which were noisy, entertaining and almost festive affairs. Having eschewed mass rallies altogether, the SPA and Lib-Socs must have found these rallies to be quite an intimidating sight that might well have broken their spirits and demoralised them.

In the end, late in the night on 30 May 1959, the PAP was swept into power with a landslide victory. It won 43 of the 51 seats it contested, securing 53.4% of the votes, and 84.3% of seats in the Assembly. The SPA and its allies, the Lib-Socs, were wiped out politically. The SPA won four seats. The Lib-Socs won none. It was a crushing defeat for the governing party and its allies. That night, Lee declared to the people of Singapore: 'We have no personal future apart from your future. Your joys and sorrows are ours. We share the same future, be it good, indifferent or bad. It is our duty to see that it is a bright and cheerful future'. Optimistic words but sober ones and for the right reasons. The next six years would be the PAP's toughest yet.

CHAPTER SEVEN

Becoming Singapore

1959–1965

'Let's Get Together, Sing A Happy Song, Malaysia Forever, Ten Million Strong' – Towards Merger

'Merger' – a word that evokes strong, almost visceral reactions in Singapore and Malaysia even today. Once seen as a solution to the political and economic problems that confronted Singapore, the eventual separation of Singapore from Malaysia on 9 August 1965 signalled the dissolution of a grand vision and the cutting of kinship and cultural ties that spanned the Federation. The people of Singapore and its leaders were now faced with the unimaginable – Singapore had to go it alone. And they had to do this whilst the nation was confronted by trauma and anguish, emotions that have defined independent Singapore's psyche and ethos ever since.

On 3 December 1959, Yusof bin Ishak was sworn in as the first Malayan-born *Yang di-Pertuan Negara*. Yusof's inauguration was the first act of National Loyalty Week that took place from 3 to 10 December 1959. Singapore's state flag, crimson and white with five stars and a crescent moon, was unveiled, together with the national anthem, *Majulah Singapura*, (Onward Singapore). The state crest was also introduced to the people. Consisting of a shield adorned with five stars and a white crescent moon and a banner emblazoned with the words '*Majulah Singapura*' below it, the shield was supported by a lion on the left and a tiger on the right. This was symbolic and significant. The lion of course represents Singapore. The tiger symbolised the historically close ties between Singapore and the Federation of Malaya. This symbolism also represented the hope of a closer association or union in the future.

This hope took a little longer to come to fruition. Then came 27 May 1961. While speaking to a roomful of correspondents at a luncheon of the Foreign Correspondents Association of Southeast Asia, the Tunku made some remarks that stunned everyone in attendance. He had chosen the time, place and audience well – after all, what better way to get news out than release it to a roomful of newshounds? In an almost offhand manner, he announced that a closer association between Malaya, Singapore and the Borneo territories was a distinct possibility. Although short on the details, the Tunku's very public announcement upended the calculations of Singapore politicians and British officials and sent everyone scrambling. The seemingly impossible was now possible.

Singapore politicians, beginning with Marshall in 1955 and then Lim Yew Hock, had courted the Tunku assiduously about Singapore's merger with the Federation. Time and again, The Tunku had demurred and rebuffed them. As late as April 1961, no one expected any movement in this particular political direction. And the Tunku was not just calling for a customs union or a common market or a loose association of states but a political union, the integration of disparate states, political systems, ethos and their peoples, into a single political entity, the Federation of Malaysia. The Tunku, it appeared, had decided to consider the impossible. Why?

To those correspondents in the room, and to anyone hearing the news then, it was a bombshell. The Tunku was long known to be lukewarm towards any form of association with Singapore. The issue of the Chinese and the racial balance in the Federation was never far from his mind. The Tunku was known to be cautious and deliberative, not known for sudden moves. After all, Federation politics was defined and driven by race and the dictum of Malay political domination. The Tunku had no choice but to play the politics of compromise, cajolery and patience.

To insiders, this was not an inexplicable about turn on the Tunku's part. Consider this: in June 1960, a full year before the announcement, at a meeting of Commonwealth Prime Ministers, he had remarked to Lord Perth of the Colonial Office that he was open to a merger if some sort of package deal could be offered. This 'package deal' was the 'Grand Design' that lay as a paper exercise in the filing cabinets of the Colonial Office. One does not need to be a terribly astute politician to see what this deal would bring. It would expand the Federation of Malaya considerably in terms of territory, resources and population. And it was the issue of population – the inclusion of Ibans, Dayaks and the other indigenous Bornean peoples – that made the issue of the number of Chinese in Singapore more palatable. In short, Borneo was the spoonful of sugar that made the bitter pill of Singapore somewhat easier to swallow for both the Tunku and his colleagues. Strategically, 'Mighty Malaysia', ten million strong, would serve as a counter-weight to the other regional Malay behemoth, Indonesia.

Putting aside the package deal and sweetener, it was developments in Singapore that prompted the Tunku to think differently. What the Tunku saw in Singapore in early 1961 must have worried him greatly. The PAP's political ground, so firm in mid-1959, was slipping from underneath it. When the PAP candidate Jek Yeun Thong got trounced by Ong Eng Guan of the United Peoples' Party in the Hong Lim by-election on 29 April 1961, despite intense campaigning by cabinet members, alarm bells went off in the Tunku's head. The pro-communists, it appeared, were gaining the upper hand. If the PAP government collapsed and the pro-communists took power, whether openly or via a proxy, the Federation would risk having a communist Cuba at its doorstep. As British officials put it, a 'batik curtain' would descend across the Straits of Johor and behind it, in Singapore, lay political elements and forces beyond the Tunku's reach. The Tunku also knew that by 1963, like it or not, Singapore was likely to gain independence in the next round of constitutional talks. This would put the island beyond his or Britain's reach. The moment of decision had come, for the Tunku, Lee Kuan Yew and the British. Ultimately, having made the first move, the Tunku held all the cards. The pace, direction and nature of the entire merger enterprise was controlled by him. The Tunku would make this work in his favour.

For Lee Kuan Yew and the PAP government, this announcement, could not have come at a better time. It was as if the Tunku had just thrown them a life-line. But merger was not a quick fix, nor a matter of political expedience for the PAP to save itself. Lee and the PAP had always been keen and ardent advocates of merger. Lee himself felt that an independent Singapore was a 'dangerous illusion' – a resource-scarce Singapore without a hinterland was an impossibility, economically or otherwise. Merger was more than reconnecting with the Federation because of shared history, geography, culture and kinship. It was also about survival, in this case, economic survival. Singapore needed jobs, many jobs, for its fast-growing population.

Dr. Goh Keng Swee, the Finance Minister, was keenly aware of this reality. It was a sight he took in each time he drove past a school and saw it teeming with students who would eventually graduate and need employment. Singapore's economic lifeline since its founding, entrepot trade, was on the decline. It could not provide the mass employment that Singapore needed. In his mind, industrialisation would solve this problem. Therein, however, lay another problem. An industrialised Singapore would need markets. Since Singapore's domestic market ranged from small to non-existent, the island needed to look outwards. The solution, it seemed, was across the Causeway, in the form of a common market. This would come about as part of merger. Economics aside, politics mattered. Independence, *through* merger, not just independence, was a key plank in the PAP's 1959 general election campaign. Promises made would have to be kept. Whether it was delivering jobs or independence through merger, the PAP would have to make good its pledge to the people.

Twelve Radio Broadcasts: The Battle For Merger

On 13 September 1961, Lee took to the airwaves to speak to the Singapore people directly in the first of a series of twelve radio talks dubbed 'The Battle for Merger'. From the time of the Tunku's announcement in May 1961, the PAP's grip on power had becoming increasingly tenuous. The grim prospect of Singapore being ruled by the staunchly anti-communist Federation government in Kuala Lumpur had spooked the anti-merger forces in the PAP and forced them come out of the woodwork. A battle loomed. Within the PAP, battle lines soon emerged as pro and anti-merger positions hardened. By this point, Lim Chin Siong had worked himself back into the political mainstream after his release from detention on 4 June 1959. Lee had appointed him as Political Secretary to the Ministry of Finance but this did not contain him nor his political intentions. He became one of the 'Big Six' group of trade union leaders that made their demands known on 2 June 1961, firing the opening barrage in the battle for merger. Unsurprisingly, they called for the abolition of the Internal Security Council and for control over Singapore's internal security. Five days later, forty-two trade unions issued a statement echoing these demands. All these sent a clear resounding message: the radical left was anti-merger. They knew that upon merger, the

Federation government would lock them up and snuff them out of their political existence.

For Lee, the moment of destiny had come, for him and for the PAP. He chose to break with the radical left faction decisively, openly and publicly at a rally held on 14 June 1961, the eve of the Anson by-election. For the first time, speaking to a crowd, Lee charged that the radical left would 'go to any lengths – even to destroying the party with which they are ostensibly associated' to derail merger and make sure it never happened. The PAP would have to split. Not since 1957 had Lee and the PAP faced a political crisis of this magnitude. The Anson by-election came and went. David Marshall of the Workers' Party won thanks to the covert support of the radical left. Things were not looking good for the PAP. It was the second by election it had lost in less than two months.

Lee had to act. He knew that this moment would come sooner or later, and he was ready. And in a way perhaps, he would rather it came sooner, before Lim Chin Siong had more time to sway wavering elements in the PAP to his side. On 21 July 1961, Lee took a gamble to clean house once again. At 3 a.m., in the Assembly, he moved a motion of confidence so that 'the PAP Assemblymen can publicly declare where they stood'. Lee was forcing an open confrontation. Stand up and be counted. Were you with Lee or otherwise? This was a huge gamble. If the government failed to carry the motion and lost the vote, it was game over. The consequences would have been dire. Lee and his colleagues knew what was in store for them if they were defeated. In the end, the government prevailed. But there were sixteen abstentions, thirteen from the PAP. They chose not to take a stand by abstaining, but this spoke volumes. They were unwilling to stand with Lee, with the existing PAP leadership, with merger. The thirteen Assemblymen from the PAP were expelled. The uneasy and risky association with the radical left was over. The PAP had split.

On 13 August 1961, the thirteen defectors, led by Dr. Lee Siew Choh and Lim Chin Siong, formed the Barisan Sosialis (Socialist Front). Earlier, on 18 July 1963, they met with Lord Selkirk, the British High Commissioner, at his official residence, Eden Hall. At what has become known as the Eden Hall Tea Party, Lim Chin Siong secured reassurances from Selkirk that the British would not intervene so long he played by the rules of the Constitution. This must have emboldened him to split with the PAP to form the Barisan.

Although the PAP was now rid of the radical left, Lee was not entirely out of the woods yet. The PAP now had a majority of just *one* seat in the Assembly. It was in a position more precarious than ever. In the absence of anti-hopping laws, Assemblymen who resigned retained their seats and could either cross the floor to join another political party or form a new political party without triggering a by-election. This was how the PAP's parliamentary majority was whittled away.

So, when Lee took to the airwaves in the evening of 13 September 1961, he was ready to counter the anti-merger forces. Lee was not out to threaten, to frighten or to warn. Rather, speaking in what has been described as homely tones, Lee sought to persuade, to convince, win hearts, minds and loyalties on the merger issue. Between 13 September and 9 October 1961, Lee spoke to the people of Singapore over Radio Singapura on Monday, Wednesday and Friday in Mandarin at 6:30 p.m., in English at 7:30 p.m., and in Malay at 9 p.m.

Lee spoke to the people in calm and reasoned tones. He outlined the benefits of merger, but he also explained the internal security threat. To make this more compelling, he named names.

Each broadcast ended with the listener wanting more. Translated also into Hokkien, Cantonese and Tamil and transcribed for print in the local newspapers, the entire exercise was a political masterstroke that tapped into the imagination of the people, reassured them and whetted their appetites for more. With these broadcasts, Lee recaptured the political initiative for merger in Singapore.

'Full Merger': The Barisan Boxed In

The Barisan, inaugurated on 17 September 1961 with Lim Chin Siong as Secretary-General and Dr. Lee Siew Choh as Chairman, soon found itself boxed in. Lee had made an open case for merger. The people had been told that they were being misled into making a wrong decision. He had made it clear that the Barisan were proxies of the communists who were trying to influence their views. Whatever way the Barisan chose to respond, they would find themselves fenced in and caught on the wrong foot. For an anti-merger party, its position would be, as it turned out, remarkably inconsistent.

The Barisan position was built on two pillars. The first was its bid for 'full merger' with the Federation. The second was to show that the

PAP had committed to less than a 'full merger', thus shortchanging the people of Singapore. The Barisan knew very well that the Tunku would never agree to 'full merger' because of what it entailed. 'Full merger' meant that Singapore citizens would *automatically* become Federal citizens and enjoy the same rights, including voting rights, as everyone else in the Federation.

Dr. Lee Siew Choh, Chairman of the Barisan, speaking at a radio forum on merger on 21 September 1961, made clear his party's stand on 'full merger' readily. Dr. Goh Keng Swee, having already sparred with Dr. Lee over the issue of a referendum, pounced on his opponent's position and ripped it apart. Dismissing the Barisan's position as 'absolute nonsense', Dr. Goh rather cunningly asked Dr. Lee whether 'he and his friends had made a study of this subject'? Walking right into this trap, Dr. Lee responded by saying: 'I think Dr. Goh, in fairness, you being such a specialist on this subject like that, I think we all would be enlightened and glad to hear from you'. Dr Goh then sprung the trap. Describing Dr. Lee's response as a 'confession of ignorance', he revealed that 'full merger' would cause some 300,000 Singaporeans, around half of the population, to become disenfranchised. This was Dr. Goh's own bombshell. Coming right after the radio broadcasts, Dr. Goh had exposed the Barisan's position as ill-considered, and it was obviously ill-prepared as well. Dr. Lee, it seemed, had no clue about the implication of this legal reality. He was completely blind-sided. On 23 September 1961, Lee acknowledged that this citizenship issue would have to be addressed and sorted out. This would eventually be one of the PAP's greatest trump cards.

The White Paper Debate: One Step Closer

On 11 November 1961, Command Paper 33 of 1961, the White Paper on merger, lay on the Table, ready to be debated by the Assembly. The White Paper, a development from the in-principle agreement of August 1961, stated the terms on which Singapore would merge with the Federation. Singapore would enjoy autonomy in education and labour but it would relinquish control over internal security, defence and external affairs. It would have 15 seats in the *Dewan Rakyat* and not 25 seats, as it was due in proportion to its population size. This was in return for increased autonomy.

Singapore citizens could only vote in Singapore and would only be Malaysian nationals, not citizens. The White Paper did not address the financial and economic issues.

With this, Singapore inched one step closer to merger. The debate ran from 17 November to 3 December 1961, dragged out by the Barisan' filibustering. Marathon speeches were made, all in the hope of stymying the vote. Dr. Lee, undeterred by Dr. Goh's very public demolition at the Radio Forum, predictably took up the citizenship issue once again. This time round, Lee took it upon himself to tear the Barisan position apart in a scathing and no holds barred speech in the Assembly on 24 November 1961. The Barisan, Lee declared, would never be satisfied, no matter what terms and conditions were agreed upon and no matter how generous these were. Its intention, Lee further charged, was to frustrate merger, not because merger was bad for the people but because there was no way the Barisan could come out and say that 'merger is no good for the communists'. This political tour de force carried the day for the PAP. The White Paper was eventually passed thirty-three to zero, with eighteen opposition members, including the Barisan, absent. But aspersions had been cast. Dr. Lee put it somewhat luridly by alleging that 'the Federation (was) taking on three wives in Borneo, while Singapore was not to be a fourth wife, only a mistress'. Singapore citizens, being 'the children of the mistress', were 'illegitimate with no right to federal citizenship'. The PAP would have to, somehow, fix this issue over citizenship that was causing great unease and put it to rest.

The Singapore National Referendum: Second Class No More

If the radio talks and the debate over the White Paper, both of which took place in the last quarter of 1961, were setbacks for the Barisan, then the debate over the Referendum Bill took the wind completely out of its sails. Referenda, superficially, look like an easy way to reach out to the people and get a sense of what they thought about issues and where they stood in relation to these issues. However, a referendum can go very wrong if voters are given simplistic, dichotomous choices as to where they stood on complex, layered issues. Lee and the PAP took no chances and planned meticulously for it. Willard A. Hanna, in a report for the American Universities Field Staff, described the PAP strategy as 'Machiavellian brilliance'. Machiavellian or not, the entire referendum exercise was, from start to end, a thoroughly clever and wily PAP plan.

During the debates over the Singapore National Referendum Bill, which began on 27 June 1962, Dr. Lee Siew Choh proposed that the merger be held on a basis of a straight 'yes' or 'no' vote. The Assembly rejected this proposal with 30 'noes'. Tun Lim Yew Hock of the SPA then proposed that the merger be structured around three questions. The Tun had once again done the PAP an inadvertent favour. Lee Kuan Yew was delighted. This was exactly what he had devised, a referendum on the forms of merger, not whether there should be merger or not. The Barisan now found itself trapped.

Not all was smooth sailing for the PAP though. During the debate, it was a minority government. Hoe Puay Choo, on 3 July 1962, apparently 'lost her nerve' and resigned from the PAP. The PAP now held only twenty-five votes in a house of fifty-one. It was close. Over the next eight days, positions were stated and restated, just to make a point. Some sessions were drawn out, lasting till past midnight. In the end, the Bill passed but only with the support of the SPA and UMNO. Clearly, they wanted to see this exercise through and keep things on track – political self-interest was at work here.

Dr. Lee remained dogged and defiant. On 13 July 1962, he tabled a motion of no-confidence in the government. Describing the government as 'discredited', he accused it of selling out the interests of the people of Singapore and blasted it for 'unreasonably and desperately wanting to railroad the so-called merger arrangements'. The motion was defeated. The Barisan had lost two critical votes, while the PAP had crossed two hurdles; Singapore inched another step towards merger. The Barisan was running out of time.

On 1 September 1962, at 8 a.m., the people of Singapore went to vote at one of the 345 polling stations. Two weeks of heated campaigning had come to an end. It felt almost like a general election. For the PAP, it was the climax of a campaign that began a year ago in September 1961. This was not just a merger referendum but an opportunity for them to find out, by proxy of the merger alternatives, where they stood in the hearts of the people. For the Barisan, it was a moment of reckoning; did they have the masses with them or not?

In the voting booth, the voter, held in his hands a ballot paper that offered three alternatives. He knew what Alternative A meant;

there was the Singapore state flag next to it. He had been told that Alternative B meant that he ran the risk of losing his citizenship. As for Alternative C, he could neither recognise the flag of the Borneo territories or nor figure out what it even meant.

Just two weeks earlier on 14 August 1962, Lee gave a critical boost to Alternative A. As he announced the referendum date, he dropped his own bombshell. At *his* request, the Tunku agreed on 30 July 1962, that 'all citizens of Singapore will become citizens of Malaysia'. This agreement would be followed through *only* if Alternative A came through as the majority choice. Therein lay the political genius behind the entire referendum exercise.

With this, the Barisan position, built around 'full merger', collapsed completely. It was an utter shambles; whatever doubt it had cast in the hearts of the Singapore people about becoming second-class citizens were vanquished. Lee had, in one stroke, rendered Alternative B a sham. Desperate now, Lim Chin Siong called on voters to cast blank votes in protest. But this had all been anticipated. The Referendum Act provided that all 'unmarked or uncertain' ballot papers, that is, blank or spoilt votes, would count as a vote *for* merger, the majority option. In the end, 71% of Singapore voters decided in favour of Alternative A. The blank votes were not needed after all.

Towards Coldstore

With the referendum in the bag and Singapore's political position stabilised for now, both Lee and the Tunku began to ponder the long-term prospects of having Singapore in Malaysia. Henceforth, the two men and the British would find themselves at odds with each other over the most vexatious and immediate issue: what to with the radical left in Singapore? Matters had certainly become more complex since the Barisan came into the picture in July 1961. Any security operation in Singapore against a registered, legal political party with sitting Assemblymen would immediately draw allegations and accusations that it was politically motivated, even if sanctioned by the Internal Security Council. The word most commonly bandied around in relation to this matter was 'odium'. The Tunku did not want to incur any odium from his own people by going ahead with merger while Singapore's radical left remained at large. Lee certainly wanted to avoid any odium arising from locking up his political opponents; he most certainly did not want to become another Lim Yew Hock. The British, serving as honest brokers, did not want to incur odium by sanctioning any security operation that smacked of even a hint of self-interest. A clear and present *security* threat was needed before the British would agree to anything. The political reality was, however, very clear. Both the British and Lee wanted and needed merger to happen. The Tunku knew this. He would use this as leverage and press it home to his advantage.

Odium aside, self-interest in terms of long-term political prospects and survival also came into play. The calculus was, in a way, simple, if a little circuitous. If Lee discredited himself by locking up his opponents before merger, then the political parties that the Tunku favoured, namely the SPA and UMNO, stood to benefit. They would supplant the PAP. Lim Yew Hock could even become Prime Minister, as Lee himself surmised. For Lee, this political threat outweighed the desire for any quick and easy solution to deal with the radical left. It was in his interest to ringfence the PAP and either defer any such operation until after merger or refuse to act unless it was a joint operation under the auspices of the ISC. Lee had not shepherded the PAP and the Singapore people through the entire merger battle only to be politically cast aside.

On 8 December 1962, the Brunei Revolt broke out. This turned out to be perfect political cover for a security operation. Perhaps it was bad timing or perhaps it was sheer coincidence, but Lim Chin Siong was seen with the Brunei's Partai Rakyat leader, A.M. Azahari, in Singapore just days before the revolt. The optics were not good for Lim. As if this was not bad enough, the Barisan issued a statement in support of the revolt. So did the CPM. These expressions of solidarity and sympathy gave sufficient cause for concern. The British, weighing the events and the choices in front of them, shed their reluctance to support any security operation in Singapore. Edwin Duncan-Sandys, the Secretary of State for the Colonies, informed Lord Selkirk, the High Commissioner, on 12 December 1962, that the British Prime Minister Harold Macmillan had given his personal approval for such an operation. The deck was cleared and the ISC began to move. The next day, the three governments met to 'consider the immediate arrest of Barisan leaders' in Singapore. Operation Coldstore was set for 16 December 1962, a Sunday. It never happened.

The Tunku was furious. Overnight, the latent suspicions and unspoken mistrust between the Tunku and Lee surfaced. Lee was worried that if he moved ahead with Operation Coldstore, he would have played his last card. With the radical left put away, he felt that the Tunku no longer had any incentive for Singapore to merge with Malaya. The Tunku, on the other hand, had deep reservations about arresting sitting members of his parliament. Both men refused to act despite British pressure to go ahead with the operation.

The damage was grievous. The Tunku was 'almost persuaded that Malaya's interest would be best served by taking North Borneo and Sarawak... into the new Federation and leaving Singapore out'. Lee was coldly resigned to this – unless the Federation took the initiative, the Singapore government would not bear joint responsibility for any arrests. On 17 December 1962, the Federation withdrew its representative from the Internal Security Council, leaving it in limbo. The British were aghast. To them, dealing with the odium of such an operation was preferable to the Tunku scuttling the merger plan altogether. On 28 December 1962, Lord Selkirk cabled Duncan-Sandys, warning him that 'there must be a real danger that the Tunku [would] not be prepared to include Singapore in Malaysia.' A compromise would have to be reached.

In the early hours of 2 February 1963, Special Branch officers fanned out across Singapore and detained more than one hundred people, including the leading lights of the radical left, Lim Chin Siong and Fong Swee Suan. This decision was taken only the day before, and only after much negotiation and persuasion on the part of the British. They had to persuade and convince Lee to mount the operation. At the same time, on 30 January 1963, the Tunku had told Geoffroy Tory, the British High Commissioner in Kuala Lumpur, in no uncertain terms that 'if this operation failed, merger with Singapore was off'. Tory underscored the Tunku's adamant stand – he warned everyone that 'this was positively the last time'. Everyone had to put their reservations aside. The British, especially Lord Selkirk, had to cast aside their objections. The Tunku had to give Lee another chance. And Lee would have to remount the arrest programme since the others were willing to compromise on this matter. Just before the operation was approved, Lee asked for Lim Chin Siong to be given the choice to leave Singapore. Lee's request was granted. But Lim chose to stay. Operation Coldstore broke the radical left, broke the Barisan and in essence broke the PAP's political opposition in order to fulfil the Tunku's precondition for merger. It was a high price to pay.

Becoming Part of Malaysia, Finally

The execution and conclusion of Operation Coldstore did not, however, make the road to merger any smoother and neither did it make merger any more inevitable. If anything, with the radical left in detention, the Tunku felt that he had the upper hand in negotiations. After all, Singapore needed Malaysia more than Malaysia wanted Singapore. For the Tunku, there was no longer a threat of a radical left government taking power in Singapore. But for Lee, merger was something he and the PAP had fought so hard for that they *had* to deliver it. The PAP's political future was over otherwise.

Even though the final Malaysia Agreement was concluded in London on 9 July 1963, after two weeks of negotiations, the months preceding it were marked by wrangling and manoeuvring on issues that would inevitably have political repercussions. For example, who should control Singapore's revenue collection and disbursement? How much should Singapore contribute to the Federal budget? More ominously, the Tunku had sent two of his senators from the Malayan Chinese Association (MCA) to Singapore to meet with invited Singapore businessmen to participate in the rejuvenation of its branch in Singapore.

The relationship between the two men was cool, often prickly. Lee's open style of negotiation, which entailed stating his positions to the press and in public, did not endear him to the Tunku. But Lee had to show the Singapore people he was fighting to secure the best terms for Singapore. More critically, in making his positions known to all and sundry, he was committing the Tunku to what had been decided.

In this political climate, it was unsurprising that by 5 July 1963, just days before the signing, the talks were on the brink of collapse. It was clear that merger was not a done deal. Lee was in a tricky and delicate position at the talks. He had to keep merger on track and, at the same time, show the people of Singapore that their faith in him and in the Alternative A they voted for was not misplaced. Lee recalls in his memoirs that Dr. Goh and he were 'prepared with supplies of sandwiches and beer' – he believes that 'the supply of food kept (their) stamina up throughout the gruelling night'.

A compromise was reached in the end, the British having been stretched to their limits as the 'honest brokers' in this act of political midwifery that had dragged on for close to twenty six months. Singapore agreed to pay 40% of its total revenue to the federal government. It would disburse a $150 million loan to the Borneo territories; $100 million would be interest-free for five years. The common market would be implemented over twelve years. Singapore citizens would retain their Singapore citizenship, become Malaysian citizens but they could only vote in Singapore. Malaysia Day was set for 31 August 1963. The agreement was finally inked on 9 July 1963.

But Malaysia Day did not take place as planned. In view of Indonesian opposition, it was postponed to 16 September 1963 in order for a United Nations mission to ensure that the people of North Borneo and Sarawak really wanted merger. Regardless, Lee went ahead. On 31 August 1963, the original Malaysia Day, Lee stood in front of a crowd at the Padang in Singapore and unilaterally declared Singapore's independence. This was not just an act of political showmanship; it was an adroit and calculated move intended to ensure that merger actually came about. After all, Lee had not consented to the postponement of Malaysia Day. On 16 September 1963, coincidentally Lee's fortieth birthday, he once again stood in front of a crowd at the Padang and this time proclaimed Singapore as part of Malaysia. Pledging his loyalty to the Central Government, the Tunku and his colleagues, Lee asked for 'an honourable relationship between the states and the Central Government, a relationship between brothers, not a relationship between masters and servants'. It was a political statement laced with a fervent, perhaps misplaced, hope.

The Snap Election – September 1963

Even before Malaysia Day, fateful decisions were made that shaped and defined Singapore's relationship with the central government in Kuala Lumpur in the worst way possible. On 3 September 1963, Lee prorogued the Legislative Assembly and called for a snap election in Singapore. The political parties had nine days, the minimum allowed under the law, to find, cajole and persuade candidates in time for Nomination Day on 12 September 1963. Then, on that day, he announced that Polling Day was set for 21 September 1963. Once again, the political parties had nine days, the minimum allowed under the law, to campaign, to persuade and convince the people to vote for them. The election would be a hotly contested and fast-paced affair. The political air in Singapore was electric and thick with political anticipation.

For Lee and the PAP, this was not really a snap election. The push for merger since mid-1961 and the merger referendum in September 1962 were, in effect, rehearsals for the general election campaign. They had gained for the PAP maximum exposure as the defender of Singapore's rights. But what mattered, and perhaps unsettled Lee, was the 25% of voters who cast blank votes in the merger referendum. These were the hard-core Barisan supporters who lived in the rural constituencies of Singapore. So, in November 1962, Lee took it upon himself to visit each and every one of Singapore's fifty-one constituencies, beginning with these rural districts in places such as Lim Chu Kang and Jalan Kayu. Lee was greeted, garlanded then feted during these visits. With him were government officers who were there to listen to and record views, take note of requests and accept petitions. With each visit, Lee and the PAP became a more real and more tangible presence in the lives of the people. And they were not just a presence. They attended to these requests and petitions promptly and visibly; roads were surfaced, streetlamps put up and standpipes installed. Community centres were opened, complete with *di rigeur* television set and ping pong table. Sometimes, Lee was roughed up, but he pressed on in his Land Rover, speaking to the people through a loudspeaker. For ten whole months, he was a one-man election campaign, bringing the PAP brand of being a can-do, responsive and responsible government to the people. By the time he called the snap election, Lee had visited every one of the fifty-one constituencies.

Predictably, every political party in Singapore cried foul at how Lee exploited the power of incumbency by calling a snap election. In truth, they were quite ready for it. The Barisan in particular was ready for the fight. Operation Coldstore had dealt it a heavy blow but the Barisan was not entirely crippled. The same could not be said for the Singapore Peoples' Alliance which was in disarray as was its Malay partner – Singapore UMNO. As it turned out, the PAP was, amongst all the parties, the readiest and most prepared for the elections.

The hustings began on 13 September 1963. Without skipping a beat, Lee drew the battle lines vividly and starkly. The choices were obvious. 'Vote for corruption, vote for decadent government – vote for the Alliance. Vote for chaos and anarchy – vote for the Barisan', he declared as he exhorted the Singapore voter to reject both parties. Still, no one was quite sure how things would turn out for the PAP. This election would be close.

The Barisan, being the PAP's rival and also the underdog, fought an organised and well-resourced campaign. It claimed to have drawn a crowd of 50,000 at its first rally in Shenton Way on 13 September 1963, although official figures put it at closer to 8,000. The Barisan was sharp and canny in its strategy. It exploited the absence of its detained leaders to its advantage. The faces of Lim Chin Siong, Fong Swee Suan and others on campaign posters reminded the voter that the Barisan was the underdog. It was fighting back even though it had been hit hard and unfairly by Operation Coldstore. It chose to focus on knocking out the PAP ministers in their constituencies and to do so, it deployed its resources most heavily in the urban areas, canvassing for every single vote. And it could do so because of the substantial and safe vote bank it held in the rural districts.

Its manifesto was uncomplicated. It was an anti-PAP platform aimed squarely at shredding the PAP's appeal and credibility by taking on issues that resonated with the people. It condemned the locking up of its leaders which it characterised as the arbitrary detention of anti-colonial politicians, patriots and nationalists. Unsurprisingly, it painted Lee Kuan Yew as an unprincipled politician who sold Singapore out first to the British, then to the central government in Kuala Lumpur. Finally, the four years of PAP government were labelled as a 'misrule'. The promises the PAP made in 'The Tasks Ahead' in 1959 had not been kept.

The PAP pulled out all the stops in its campaign. For a political party that had everything going for it, it was fighting to win every single vote. It trotted out a string of achievements and numbers to impress the voter: 24,000 housing units, a budgetary surplus of over $400 million in only four years, Jurong, the list went on. Surely, these were the sort of achievements that would deliver the votes. Its record was further enhanced by its success as the architect of Singapore's merger with Malaysia. And it had not sold Singapore out, but it had, as its record showed, negotiated and fought for the best possible agreement for Singapore. And in case anyone forgot, the Malaysia Day festivities, smack in the middle of the hustings, were a powerful reminder. Surely, having delivered on this, the PAP reasoned to the voter, it was the only political party that could and would fight to defend and protect Singapore's interests. No other political party could do this. And Lee warned that if the Barisan or the Singapore Alliance should win, then all bets were off.

Still, it was going to be close. Contemporary observers were not positive in their outlook about the PAP's prospects. By 20 September 1963, the eve of polling day, the British High Commission reported that a Barisan win was 'a distinct possibility'. The Australian High Commission shared these sentiments. The Barisan was positive that it would win perhaps 35 seats. Lee, however, remained confident and upbeat. He was right to be so.

Decision 1 – The Tunku Intervenes

As the results trickled in on the night of 21 September 1963, a pattern soon emerged. The PAP was on track for 'a sweeping victory'. It secured thirty-seven out of the fifty-one seats it contested; it had retained its majority by a comfortable margin, never mind that its vote share of 47% was down from 1959. Its strongest rival, the Barisan, picked up thirteen seats and with 32.9% of the popular vote, could claim to be the PAP's strongest opponent and also the master of the Chinese-speaking ground. Two cabinet ministers on the PAP ticket, K.M. Byrne and Tan Kia Gan, lost their seats. Ong Pang Boon, Yong Nyuk Lin, S. Rajaratnam, all cabinet ministers and PAP leaders, and the Deputy Prime Minister Toh Chin Chye himself, won only with slender majorities. Only eighty-nine votes saved Toh Chin Chye from defeat. It was *that* close. The Barisan' strategy was shrewd, but it did not translate into quite enough votes at the ballot box.

If the Singapore voters' rejection of the Singapore Alliance alarmed the Tunku, then the votes of the Singapore Malays in the three Malay-dominated constituencies shocked him utterly. In Geylang Serai, Kampung Kembangan and the Southern Islands constituencies,

Singapore UMNO candidates were completely routed. Singapore Malays had decided to vote in a non-communal manner for the non-communal PAP. Shaken to his core, and terribly angry with the outcome, the Tunku felt betrayed. He had assumed that with merger, Singapore Malays, the minority in Singapore, would switch their political allegiance en masse to UMNO. Instead, they had thrown in their lot with the PAP.

On 24 September 1963, an UMNO leader, Syed Ja'afar bin Albar, speaking in Johore Bahru, singled Lee Kuan Yew out as UMNO's political nemesis. A week after the polls, on 27 September 1963, the Tunku spoke at a protest rally at Singapore UMNO's Kampung Ubi branch. 'In future, I will play an important part in the elections', the Tunku announced after berating those who had betrayed UMNO. The fateful decision was made; the Tunku would henceforth personally oversee Singapore UMNO. He made sure, quite deliberately, that race would be a factor in Singapore-Malaysia relations. It was an open challenge to the PAP; UMNO would be a force to be reckoned with in Singapore politics.

Decision 2 – The PAP Crosses the Causeway

After the September 1963 election, UMNO could not be placated, no matter how conciliatory Lee appeared to be or how restrained and reassuring he was in his manner and pronouncements. All along, the Tunku had intended to contain Singapore politics and its intensities to Singapore. He gave Singapore a large measure of autonomy and recognised this by accepting that Lee would remain Prime Minister and not become *Menteri Besar* (Chief Minister) of a state. In return, the PAP would have to live with a shrunken political footprint in the *Dewan Rakyat* (Peoples' Assembly; the lower house of the Malaysian Parliament) and the peninsula. It had to be contented with its fifteen seats and not seek more by participating in the Federal elections. This quid pro quo, or a gentlemen's agreement between the Tunku and Lee, eventually became a bone of contention.

On 1 March 1964, DPM Toh Chin Chye announced that the PAP would participate in the April 1964 Federal elections after all. This decision, made by the PAP's CEC, shocked and surprised many, especially UMNO. UMNO accused the PAP of breaking the tacit understanding that had existed about the PAP's participation in the

Federal elections. The PAP was equally trenchant in its response: had not the Tunku personally intervened in the September 1963 election in Singapore by speaking at a rally? Whatever the case, UMNO was nervous and anxious about the PAP's intentions and Lee's ambitions. It would be a bruising campaign for the PAP as it kicked off its foray into peninsular politics on 22 March 1964. It would soon learn that Queensbury rules did not matter as much as race and personal animosities in this campaign and that these toxic political forces would force its hand as its campaign unfolded.

However, no one should have been totally surprised by the PAP's decision. For one, the PAP had adopted a pan-Malayan outlook since its founding in 1954. Its founding outlook aside, the PAP's political reality after Malaysia Day had shifted significantly. The nexus of power was the Central Government in Kuala Lumpur, not the Legislative Assembly in Singapore. Even though the PAP enjoyed considerable autonomy in governing Singapore, it would have been politically naïve to assume that this state of affairs would last forever. Slowly but surely, the Central Government would further contain the PAP politically and impose its conservative and communal-based model on Singapore. For the PAP to restrain itself and focus on being the best 'town council' in Malaysia was to choose death via slow strangulation. It had no choice. It had to break out of the arena of Singapore politics and make its democratic socialist, non-communal brand of politics known to Malaysia. It was a case of when rather than if.

From late 1963 onwards, the PAP leaders considered their options. They could choose to sit out the 1964 Federal elections, and in doing so, honour its end of the 'agreement' with the Tunku. Its next window of opportunity would be the Federal elections in 1969, five years later. If a day is a long time in politics, as it is often said, then waiting five years is an eternity. In five years, the PAP would have withered into political nothingness. This was the frame that guided the PAP leaders in their decision making. By late February 1964, while Lee was away on a goodwill mission to Africa to sell Malaysia, the CEC decided. Now, 1964, would be the best time. There was no better time. There was no other time.

Toh made the PAP's intentions very clear from the outset. The PAP did not want to challenge or dislodge UMNO from power. It recognised UMNO's leadership as indispensable in Malaysia. Its intention was to 'fight the pro-Indonesia, pro-communist and anti-Malaysia parties'. Also, the PAP had to become a *national* party in order to build Malaysia. Lastly, its strategic considerations were obvious. It chose to field a small slate of candidates to establish a toehold in Federation politics, just like it did in 1955 General Elections in Singapore. This was an exercise in positioning and building the PAP to become a serious political force in the Federation. It would show UMNO that the PAP could capture the vote in the cities and towns in Malaysia, where the Malaysian Chinese were concentrated. By 1969, the PAP would become either UMNO's partner or UMNO's opponent. The PAP was certainly not out to challenge or dislodge UMNO. Its sights were instead trained on the MCA.

No matter how he had chosen to couch it, Toh's position was received badly by Alliance leaders. Sure, they reasoned, the PAP was not out to challenge UMNO *directly*, but by challenging its partner, the MCA, it was doing so *indirectly*. The subtle political distinctions that the PAP made were entirely lost on them. Tan Siew Sin, on 2 March 1963, was clearly miffed when he responded to the PAP's ostensible challenge. 'The PAP claims it wants to fight not the Alliance, not the Central Government, not UMNO. By a process of elimination, it leaves only the MCA and MIC and your guess is as good as mine', Tan said publicly, with a touch of peevishness. This was telling, as Toh did not once refer to the MCA by name. However, the Tunku was with Tan on this. In their minds, once the PAP was done with the MCA, it would destroy UMNO. UMNO's destruction would signal the end for the entire political enterprise founded on Malay rights and supremacy. The Tunku did not want or need a new political vision for the Federation. He needed someone like Tan who knew his place in the Alliance and the place of the Chinese in the Federation. The PAP looked like it had declared war on the Alliance. In this war, race was an issue that was politicised and weaponised. And in the end, race broke Malaysia.

The PAP was routed in the end. Only one of its candidates, Devan Nair, won a seat in the *Dewan Rakyat* by a majority of 808 votes. The Federation voters chose to stick with the familiar Alliance. *Konfrontasi*, the anti-Malaysia insurgency launched by Sukarno in 1963, turned out to be the trump card that swung the vote massively in its favour. The PAP and the novel political vision it espoused at crowded mass rallies failed to gain traction. The PAP had ventured much, gambled big but gained little when the chips were cashed in. The Alliance now dominated the *Dewan Rakyat* and enjoyed a two-thirds supermajority; it could pass laws and amend the Constitution at will. The political environment looked more perilous than ever for the PAP and it would only get worse.

Decision 3 – UMNO Crosses the Causeway

During the hustings for the Federal election, UMNO leaders did not hesitate to paint the PAP as an anti-Malay party. It did not hesitate in using race as a weapon to turn Singapore Malays against the PAP. For extremists such as Albar, who was also UMNO Secretary-General, their moment to take on the PAP and smash it to smithereens had come. The election might have ended but the racial issues brought into the open and stoked enthusiastically by UMNO extremists led by Albar did not abate. There was to be no let up. Just three days after the election, UMNO launched an anti-PAP campaign designed to destroy it politically in Singapore.

On 28 April 1964, in the cool air of Fraser's Hill, a mountain station favoured by the British, the Tunku met Lee for a post-election meeting. The Tunku told Lee that he wanted Singapore to become 'the New York of Southeast Asia'. This was shorthand for Lee and the PAP to keep out of Federal politics and focus on transforming Singapore into an economic and financial powerhouse. Kuala Lumpur, in the meantime, would be Washington D.C., where power was exercised by the central government. In exchange, the Tunku would keep the MCA out of Singapore politics. Tan Siew Sin was there too at this meeting – this must have been music to his ears. The Tunku's strategy of containing the PAP in Singapore and insulating Malaysia from the PAP was but one part of the story. The other more sinister and more dangerous part was just unfolding. UMNO would, through Singapore UMNO (SUMNO), poison the well in Singapore by showing Singapore Malays that the PAP was keeping them down. It would turn them against the PAP. And it would present itself as the defender of the Singapore Malays. What UMNO wanted was to inflame and rouse racial tensions for political gain. Perhaps they knew how ugly it could get but they appeared quite ready for the worst to happen.

From May to July 1964, the *Utusan Melayu*, an UMNO-owned Jawi newspaper became UMNO's mouthpiece of choice. Using a tried and tested playbook, it launched a relentless barrage of scurrilous and poisonous accusations and allegations. It picked on issues that exploited the minority status of the Singapore Malays – for example, resettlement or Malay education. It then attacked the PAP government by blowing the issue out of proportion or by exaggerating and inflating the facts to portray Singapore Malays as victims. It then showed that SUMNO was there for them. Fear not, SUMNO would take up the issue for you with the Tunku, with Albar. Fear not, if SUMNO was not enough, UMNO would step up for you. Rally behind UMNO, the *Utusan Melayu* urged, and the PAP would not be able to ride roughshod over you.

Using this script, the *Utusan Melayu* blew the Kallang River Basin resettlement plan out of proportion under the headline '3,000 Malay Residents Threatened'. The reality was that out of the 2,500 families affected, only 200 were Malays and not 3,000 as reported. The *Utusan Melayu* used the refrain, 'oh well, when one has a stepfather...' constantly and to good effect. The insinuation was clear. Only SUMNO, with *Bapak Malaysia* at its helm, would treat you like his own children.

Against this backdrop of endless allegations, emotionally charged asides and politically driven action, Lee had to try to contain things. Privately, he was worried. This sort of communal politics did not bode well for the future of Malaysia and its survival as a united political unit. On 31 May 1964, he visited the constituencies most affected by resettlement to explain to them the reasons behind slum clearance. Yet, when rebutted with fact and reason, the *Utusan Melayu* would neither issue a correction nor retract its reports. Since it was running a campaign based on deliberate disinformation, one would suppose that accuracy and truth were only of second rank importance. It kept at it. *The Utusan Melayu* painted Lee's responses as deception and intimidation and as an attempt to split the Singapore Malays. It kept reporting, accusing, alleging and sensationalising. And why should it stop? After all, when Lee pleaded with the Tunku to rein in this inflammatory agitation, didn't he laugh it off and say that Lee 'was imagining things, there was really nothing to worry about'?

Collision – The Singapore Riots

At 9:30 am on 12 July 1964, at the New Star Cinema in Pasir Panjang, Syed Ja'afar Albar got ready to speak. Once on stage, he launched into a diatribe accusing Lee of being an oppressor and alleging that 'the fate of the Malays is even worse than it was during the Japanese occupation'. Praising Singapore Malays for their unity, he worked the crowd up into a frenzy and declared to an increasingly excited audience of several thousand that 'if there is unity, no force in this world can trample us down… Not one Lee Kuan Yew, a thousand Lee Kuan Yew… we finish them off…' The crowd responded enthusiastically with cries to arrest Lee, to arrest Othman Wok, to crush them and kill them. They were baying for blood. Albar's intention was clear. He was not here to give a speech at a convention. He was here to incite, to agitate, to stir things up and to cause Lee to be removed from office. Also, he was not acting on his own. He had Federation Deputy Prime Minister Razak backing him.

Albar did not let up even after this rabble-rousing speech. On 18 July 1964, just before Lee met with representatives of Singapore Malays, Albar remarked that 'if some undesirable incidents should happen… Lee Kuan Yew should not blame the *Utusan Melayu* or the Malays but he himself should take full responsibility'. Clearly, Albar *expected* something to happen. And he *expected* Lee to be destroyed by whatever happened. On 19 July 1964, Lee went ahead with the meeting. He took in their views in an even-handed and understanding manner. Expectedly, SUMNO boycotted this meeting. But Lee was clear about one thing; he would listen, he would seek to understand but he would not cave in to public pressure over special rights for the Singapore Malays. On 20 July 1964, the *Utusan Melayu* ran a provocative and nasty headline 'Challenge to all Malays – UMNO Youths; Lee Kuan Yew Condemned; Teacher forced student to smell pork – Protest'. This was no coincidence. For the next day, 21 July 1964, was the Prophet Mohamed's birthday, a red-letter day for the Singapore Malays. The fuse was lit. It would blow soon enough.

Racial riots broke out in Singapore on 21 July 1964 during a procession to mark the Prophet Mohamed's birthday. After an altercation between Malays in the procession and Chinese bystanders, communal violence spread. Four people were killed and 178 injured at the end of the first day. The government declared an islandwide dusk-to-dawn curfew. But it was not enough. Clashes resumed when curfew was lifted. The PAP government, with internal security out of its hands, could only look on helplessly as it waited for the Tunku and his deputy, Razak, to deploy the police and the army to restore order in Singapore. This was a lesson it never forgot.

Pushback – And Then Things Fall Apart

In the aftermath of the Singapore riots, a two-year political truce was declared. On 25 October 1964, Khir Johari, who oversaw the Singapore Alliance, ordered a reorganisation of the political grouping. The reorganisation meant only one thing: UMNO leaders had not given up on their campaign to destroy the PAP. They were preparing the Singapore Alliance to take on the PAP and win the Singapore state election due in 1967, a mere three years away. The Tunku endorsed his excuse: the truce only covered communal issues in politics, it did not extend to such activities. In this case, since UMNO could reorganize, then the PAP could do so too. The truce, if there was ever one in spirit, was over.

Now that there was no truce and it was clear that UMNO was still bent on destroying the PAP, the niceties of trying to accommodate and compromise on the part of the PAP leaders were no longer needed. The Alliance's political model, in which the Malaysian nation was defined by different races co-existing under Malay political dominance and leadership, would be openly and formally challenged. The PAP did not simply restructure itself to do so. It built an entire new coalition of like-minded partners. This coalition rejected Malaysia as an extension of old Malaya and its belief was captured in the term 'Malaysian Malaysia'. It was used for the first time, on 27 April 1965, when Toh announced that a group of political parties had convened in Singapore as a 'Malaysian Malaysia' body. UMNO now faced not only a political threat but one with existential consequences.

The Malaysian Solidarity Convention (MSC) met in Singapore on 9 May 1965. It was the PAP's pushback and counterpunch and the Alliance's nightmare. Tellingly, on 15 May 1965, at its 18th General Assembly, UMNO delegates were out baying for blood. To a man, they passed a resolution demanding that Lee be arrested and detained. A line was crossed that day. The Tunku balked at this. Arresting Lee would only martyr him and do no one, least of all the Alliance or Malaysia, any good at all.

On 31 May 1965, in the Dewan Rakyat, Lee hit back at UMNO extremists and repaid Albar in full for the provocative and incendiary speech on 12 July 1964 at Pasir Panjang. At the end of the debate on the King's Speech, Lee moved a motion of regret, the first ever since Malaya's independence in 1957. Prior to doing this, Lee delivered a cogent and coherent case for a Malaysian Malaysia. Taking UMNO extremists to task by reading excerpts from the *Utusan Melayu*, Lee called on the central government to 'disown Syed Ja'afar Albar' and state openly and unequivocally that it was in favour of a Malaysian Malaysia. Throughout his entire riposte on this matter, Lee had switched to speaking in Malay. Lee, Prime Minister of Singapore, a Chinese, was speaking eloquently in Malay, about Malay issues, about Malaysia's dichotomous ideological choices, in the heart of Malay power, to a Malay elite audience. The Tunku was aghast. This was the point of no return. Singapore was on the way out.

'Singapore is Out'

The Tunku, while being treated for shingles in a London clinic, pondered the situation in Malaysia. On 29 June 1965, after a lengthy cost-benefit analysis running into several sheets of paper, he decided that breaking up with Singapore was the only viable way forward. On the same day, Razak and Ismail, his number two and number three in government respectively, apparently arrived at the same conclusion. On 13 July 1965, Goh met with Razak and eventually came around to agreeing that 'disengagement could only be based on complete separation'. A week later, on 20 July 1965, Goh met Razak again, this time to hammer out the details on how to effect separation. 'The only way out was for Singapore to secede, *completely*', Goh made it clear to Razak. Five days later, the Tunku cabled and gave the go-ahead for the separation agreement to be drawn up. Having been greeted by a sea of 'Crush Lee' placards at the airport a day earlier, the Tunku met with his colleagues on 6 August 1965. They concurred that separation was *inevitable*. Lee gathered his team, Othman Wok, Toh, Ong and Raja, in Kuala Lumpur. Toh, Ong and Raja, all Malaysian-born and with deep kinship ties, needed some persuading and convincing. At Lee's request, the Tunku wrote a note to Toh, asking him to accept that separation was the only way out. The alternative was bloodshed. On 7 August 1965, the Singapore government signed the Separation

Agreement. And even in their moments of anguish, they did not forget about the Water Agreements. Lee had ensured they were worked into the Separation Agreement, just to be safe. On the morning of 9 August 1965, as the bill made its way through the Dewan Rakyat on a certificate of urgency, Lee got ready to make the announcement to the people of Singapore. At 10 a.m., he met with the British, Australian, New Zealand and Indian High Commissioners. At noon, in a television studio on Caldecott Hill, Lee spoke to the Singapore people, soon to be Singaporeans in a moment. Visibly emotional in front of television cameras, a roomful of reporters and an unsettled nation, Lee announced that Singapore was out. Overcome by a torrent of emotions, Lee choked up and wept.

CHAPTER EIGHT

'We, the Citizens of Singapore' 1965–2015

Starting Over

At the end of it all, after the radio announcements proclaiming Singapore's independence, after meeting the representatives from Singapore's diplomatic partners and after that emotion-laden press conference, Lee had one last person to meet: the UK High Commissioner. Lord Anthony Head, whom Lee regarded highly, flew in from Kuala Lumpur to meet with him at Sri Temasek, Lee's official residence in the Istana. Head, however, brought neither information nor instructions from London for him. The UK would only recognise the newly independent country on the next day, 10 August 1965. There was one other loose end to tie up. Meeting with Toh, Ong and Raja, who were the convenors and leaders of the Malaysian Solidarity Convention (MSC), Lee informed them that with Singapore out of Malaysia, its membership in the MSC must end. To continue participating in the MSC would be to interfere in the domestic affairs of Malaysia, which was now a foreign nation. The grand and idealistic Pan-Malayan vision of a radically different political future was no more.

Across the Causeway, the Tunku and Razak appeared non-plussed about things. In the Tunku's mind, if Singapore misbehaved, they could just threaten to cut off the water supply from Johore and bring Singapore to heel. The Tunku and Razak thought that the new nation would beg for reunification soon enough. This was a threat Lee and his successors would never forget.

Also, Malaysian troops were still stationed in Singapore at Camp Temasek. Lee feared that extremist elements in UMNO would instigate a coup using these troops to reverse Singapore's independence – to them, 'Singapore should never have been allowed to leave Malaysia, but should have been clobbered into submission.' It was a delicate, if not dangerous, moment for the new nation.

As a first-line defence against attempts at 'reunification', forcible or otherwise, Singapore needed the international community to recognise its independence and sovereignty. On 9 August 1965, the Ministry of Foreign Affairs (MFA) was set up and this was its first and most pressing task. Recognition soon came in, first from Malaysia. On 6 September 1965, Singapore established its first diplomatic mission, in Kuala Lumpur. Ko Teck Kin, who had served in the Federal Senate, was named Singapore's High Commissioner to Malaysia. Next, Singapore formally took up its seat at the United Nations on 21 September 1965, becoming its 117th member state. As the Singapore flag was raised outside the UN building in New York, it became part of the international community as an independent and sovereign nation. Then, on 15 October 1965, Singapore joined the Commonwealth as its 22nd member. Finally, Singapore was an independent country, well and truly separated from Malaysia.

Beyond diplomacy, the new nation needed some form of military defence, if not the ability to exercise some form of military deterrence. On 9 August 1965, the order of the battle of the Singapore Army comprised two infantry battalions, some signal and artillery elements, two small naval vessels – the RSS *Panglima* and the RSS *Singapura* – and no air force at all to speak of. Dr. Goh Keng Swee took charge of the Ministry of Interior and Defence (MINDEF) and began to build up an army from scratch. On 30 December 1965, the People's Defence Force (PDF) Act was passed in Parliament. Essentially a volunteer part-time militia, the PDF was an important stopgap defence unit till Singapore could muster the means and resources to build up its defence forces.

What about jobs for the people? The choices were few and not promising. Entrepot trade was declining, and it declined further as Malaysia and Indonesia stopped sending their goods to Singapore for processing. The colonial economic model which had been in play since 1819 was now defunct. Jobs had to be created in large numbers. Singaporeans had to pull together. They needed to be more disciplined, more cohesive, rugged. They needed to look beyond the tried and tested. There were no easy or instant solutions. Singaporeans would have to invent or acquire new means, new capabilities and set new standards. As Lee put it in his memoirs, 'we had to be different'. There was no choice to be otherwise.

On 24 August 1966, one year on from separation, Singapore students recited for the first time, the National Pledge: 'We, the citizens of Singapore, pledge ourselves as one united people, regardless of race, language and religion, to build a democratic society, based on justice and equality, so as to achieve happiness, prosperity and progress for our nation.' Drafted in English and translated into Chinese, Malay and Tamil, the National Pledge captured in thirty-eight words the beliefs, values and aspirations of Singapore as a multiracial, multicultural nation. These were what made Singapore fundamentally different from Malaysia then. And this still holds today.

Building a Democracy, Singapore Style

Suddenly, things went quiet. As thirty-six PAP Members of Parliament (MP) took their seats in the Parliament chamber on 8 December 1965, they were greeted by rows of empty red seats opposite them. The Barisan had derided Singapore's 'phoncy independence' and decided to boycott the opening of independent Singapore's first Parliament. Dr. Lee Siew Choh, who gave the orders, intended to take the struggle to the streets. With this, the implosion of the Barisan and of opposition politics in Singapore began. In October 1966, Barisan MPs resigned their seats. The opposition benches were now mostly empty. And things certainly became quieter after.

Never one to let a good crisis go to waste, this time round triggered by the British withdrawal announcement in January, Lee called for snap general elections to be held on 13 April 1968. Politically, the timing was impeccable. Dr. Lee Siew Choh, clinging obstinately to his Maoist-inspired beliefs, decided that the Barisan would boycott the elections. On Nomination Day, only seven of fifty-eight seats were contested – these were Tanjong Pagar, Jalan Kayu, Nee Soon, Farrer Park, Moulmein, Geylang Serai and Kampong Ubi. The PAP returned to power easily. In those seven contests, the people rallied behind the PAP in a show of support and confidence. It secured 84.4% of the popular vote and won all seven seats. Dr. Lee's obdurate stand did not just doom the Barisan, it also spelt the end of political opposition in Singapore. One-party rule had begun. General elections were held again in 1972, 1976 and 1980. And the PAP repeated this performance every time, making a clean sweep of all seats. Each election was won by a landslide. The Barisan tried to make a comeback in 1972 but failed miserably. It marked the end of a once proud and confident political party. With the main opposition party having elected to put itself out of the running, Singapore in the 1970s became an administrative state, as a contemporary observer put it. Singaporeans gradually become depoliticised. Politics, the man in the street felt, was best left to the politicians. After all, the PAP could be trusted to deliver the goods.

However, for a small handful, the concern was not whether the PAP could be trusted to deliver the goods – it was evident that they could – but the form, function and quality of the goods and the availability of serious alternatives. They formed the nuclei of a small but vocal group – Singapore Planning and Urban Research (SPUR) – formed on 13 October 1966. It looked like a study group but in function, it was an independent advocacy group that contested and challenged official wisdom about urban planning and development in Singapore. Although non-political and non-partisan, SPUR's position – that urban planning projects and decisions should be subject to public consultation *before* decisions were made – was irksome to the government.

On 15 August 1967, the government took issue with SPUR over this. In a letter to the press, it stated in no uncertain terms that 'an elective representative Government given the mandate to carry out policies does not need to go back to the people every time it adopts a proposal for implementation.' SPUR's call was derided as 'naïve' and they were labelled as 'armchair critics' unworthy of being 'taken seriously' given that 'planning for urban renewal (was) a full-time, exacting in its demands and deserving of the efforts and talents of highly-trained professional officials in many disciplines.' In other words – the technocrats knew better. But SPUR did have some serious ideas that ranged from the theoretical to the concrete. The most memorable and perhaps consequential was its very public call in February 1971 to relocate Singapore's international airport from Paya Lebar to Changi. This would free up valuable land beneath the flight corridors and enhance the safety of people living beneath them.

Politically unfettered by an opposition, the PAP government effected an agenda built around and driven by the politics of survival. The trade unions were curbed, pro-business labour laws were passed and the issues of wages, benefits and working conditions de-politicised. The role of the press was restricted – it would be a partner in nation-building, not an institution to keep the government in check. For Lee, 'the freedom of the press, the freedom of the mass media, must be subordinated to the overriding needs of the integrity of Singapore and to the purpose of an elected government'. In September 1974, the government passed a comprehensive law in the form of the Newspaper and Printing Presses Act. This law regulated the funding sources, shareholding and licensing of all publications in Singapore. In 1984, the broadsheets were all consolidated under the Singapore Press Holdings. There was now literally a single source of truth in Singapore.

Ideologically, the PAP moved steadily away from the radical socialism of its early days as it become more pragmatic, driven more by tangible economic outcomes than the ideological rhetoric and dogma. In May 1976, the PAP left the Socialist International. In a statement delivered by C.V. Devan Nair, it caustically rebuked 'the lunatic liberal fringes of West European social democratic parties to make common cause with our communists and fellow-travellers, and tell us how we ought to run affairs.' The PAP was confident of its model of socialism, which was premised on anti-communism, economic growth, and development. Socialism – as defined by the PAP – was what worked for Singapore and for Singaporeans.

On 31 October 1981, a by-election was held in Anson constituency, hitherto a secure PAP stronghold. Going by its track record, this should have been a shoo-in for the PAP. But the unexpected happened. At 10:53 pm, at the packed counting centre at Gan Eng Seng School, Returning Officer Richard Lau announced the results. Pang Kim Hin, the PAP candidate, had lost to Joshua Benjamin Jeyaratnam, the Workers' Party candidate, in a three-cornered fight. JBJ, as he was popularly known, took 51.93% of the vote, a majority of 7012 votes. The PAP was stunned. Just a year earlier, C.V. Devan Nair had romped home with 84.1% of the vote. With this loss, Pang made history by becoming the first PAP candidate to lose an electoral contest since 1965. The PAP's perfect track record was no more. It had lost just one seat, but it felt like a political earthquake. Was this a fluke or was it a sign that the political ground was beginning to shift?

In hindsight, Anson was the year the PAP's electoral invincibility began to crack. And it was the harbinger of things to come at the 1984 General Elections. The General Elections aside, 1984 was a landmark year for other reasons. It was a year Singaporeans celebrated 25 years of self-government and the PAP celebrated 25 years of being in power. It had been an impressive twenty-five years. But in 1983, several policy missteps were made, especially with the Graduate Mothers' Scheme. It led to charges of governmental arrogance and elitism. The people would not forget how these stung.

The central plank of the PAP's campaign as Singaporeans went to the ballot box on 22 December 1984 was, of course, its twenty-five years of sterling achievements. That day, the PAP lost two seats, in Anson to Jeyaratnam and in Potong Pasir, to Chiam See Tong of the Singapore Democratic Party (SDP). Chiam's victory deserves some telling. During the hustings, Lee sold Chiam's opponent hard by comparing the two men's academic results. He said: 'Mah Bow Tan, age 16, took his 'O' Levels – six distinctions, two credits. Mr Chiam, age 18 – six credits (*sic*), one pass'. The people of Potong Pasir went for Mr. Chiam, who took 60.28% of the votes. He would hold onto Potong Pasir for the rest of his parliamentary career until 2011. With the loss of two seats came a nationwide swing of 12.9% of the popular vote against the PAP. For the first time since 1965, the PAP lost seats in a General Election. The political ground had clearly shifted. The politics of survival was losing traction with a younger, more demanding electorate that was unwilling to take the PAP's policy prescriptions unquestioningly.

Important as these events were, what was more consequential was how the PAP responded to them. The PAP assumed that Singaporeans did not really want to turf them out but wanted more representation in Parliament; more voices and more space for more views to be heard. It also assumed that a 'freak' election result, one in which the PAP was accidentally turfed out of power, was a distinct possibility. To address this, a series of political innovations were introduced from July 1984. The first – the Non-Constituency Member of Parliament (NCMP) scheme – ensured an opposition presence in Parliament. In 1988, to guard against the 'freak' election result that diluted or reduced minority representation in Parliament, the Group Representation Constituency (GRC) was introduced. It gave the incumbent PAP government many advantages that made them seem electorally unassailable until 2011. In 1990, it introduced the Nominated Member of Parliament (NMP) to bring in non-partisan views, expert knowledge, and over time, the views of special interest groups. Finally, the Elected Presidency was introduced in 1991 to protect the reserves from a rogue government (elected as a result of a 'freak election') bent on raiding the reserves to finance populist policies.

The General Election aside, 1984 was also the year that the PAP's political renewal moved towards completion. The New Guard, as it was then known, the second generation PAP leadership team was in place. On 30 December 1984, they met for a night-time gathering in Tony Tan's home. Tan entered politics in 1978 via a by-election in Sembawang constituency, and had served as Minister for Education and Minister for Trade and Industry. Over light refreshments of coffee, juice and chocolate cake, the second-generation leaders chose Goh Chok Tong, then first Deputy Prime Minister, as the next Prime Minister. Before entering politics, Goh, an economist, was General Manager of Neptune Orient Lines, the national shipping line. In 1976, he contested and won Marine Parade Constituency, which he has held since. Also present at this meeting was thirty-two year old Brigadier-General (Reservist) Lee Hsien Loong, fresh from his maiden electoral contest in Teck Ghee constituency. He was now a Cabinet appointee designate. Prior to this, Lee had a successful career in the Singapore Armed Forces, serving tours of duty as an artillery battalion commander and eventually as Chief of Staff (General Staff).

Kinder and Gentler?
The Goh Chok Tong Administration (1990 – 2004)

On 28 November 1990, the founding Prime Minister, Lee, stepped aside and handed power over to Goh Chok Tong. The final act in the PAP's political renewal had taken place. Goh was determined to be his own man. In his first National Day Rally speech, in a specific reference to Lee, Goh said that 'I am not going to follow his act. I am going to walk my own way'. Avuncular, genial, and soft-spoken, Goh carried on his towering frame a toughness that belied his public image. It was on his watch that Operation Spectrum, an internal security operation designed to round up members of a 'Marxist Conspiracy' was executed, in May 1987

Nevertheless, Goh's stated desire was for a kinder, gentler Singapore led by a more consultative form of government. The first year of Goh's administration reflected such a belief and desire. In January 1991, the White Paper on Shared Values was released. In essence, this was an attempt to identify and agree on a framework of ethical and moral values that cut across racial and religious lines, for Singaporeans. Next, the government went public with its long-term vision for the country – 'Singapore: The Next Lap' – in February 1991. After this, on 20 June 1991, in a landmark speech at the inaugural National University of Singapore Society (NUSS) lecture, Brigadier-General (Reservist) George Yeo, the Acting Minister for Information and the Arts, described the state as an overarching banyan tree. Continuing with this metaphor, he noted that 'we have to prune the banyan tree, but we cannot do without the banyan tree', concluding with the caveat that 'we need some pluralism but not too much because too much will destroy us. In other words, we prune judiciously'. 'Prun(ing) judiciously' became an apt metaphor for the government's attitude towards alternative or opposing views in the 1990s. While it was more open and more consultative, it was not about to surrender its firm grip on politics and power just yet. The banyan tree was staying put.

In August 1991, Goh called for a snap general election. He wanted Singaporeans to endorse his style of government, to give him a mandate to govern more consultatively. But Chiam See Tong, the leader of the SDP and MP for Potong Pasir, with his seven examination credits, offered Singaporeans a beguiling proposition. They could continue to enjoy the fruits of a PAP government, with its promised openness, and at the same time, have more voices to represent them in Parliament. This was the genius and logic behind the by-election strategy – the PAP was returned to power on Nomination Day in every General Election until 2006, when the opposition changed tack. While it did little for the opposition in the long-run, it delivered for them in 1991. The PAP lost two more seats to the opposition – this made for an opposition bench of four, the largest since 1965. Its vote share slid to 61% which was then its lowest ever. Personally, 1991 was a let-down for Goh. He decided that the move towards a more open political system would adopt a slower pace. In other words, pruning would not only be more judicious, it would be slower and more managed.

And it showed. Sound alternative views within official structures were encouraged and recognised. In 1994, Nominated MP Walter Woon became the first private member to move a Bill in Parliament – the Maintenance of Parents Bill became law. Other views, expressed by critics outside such structures, drew robust responses from the government. Such a critic came in the form of local writer Catherine Lim, who was deemed to have violated the 'out of bounds' (OB) markers in her piece 'The PAP and the People: The Great Affective Divide'. Goh was making it clear that there were limits to political criticism in Singapore. A new term – the 'OB' marker – thus entered the national political lexicon. Critics should either express their political opinions or dissent through channels such as the Feedback Unit or join a political party. Sniping irresponsibly or cavalierly from the sidelines was frowned upon.

Electorally, Goh had a wily and ultimately effective counter to Chiam See Tong's beguiling strategy. In the January 1997 General Elections, Singaporeans were reminded that their votes had real consequences. This election, fought by the PAP under the banner 'Singapore 21: Make It Our Best Home', was an election about HDB estate upgrading. A national election was fought almost solely and purely on local issues. The voter had two choices. Vote for the PAP and your housing estate would be prioritised in the upgrading programme – your HDB flat, your most valuable asset, would become even more valuable. Vote for the opposition and you will get nothing in return – your un-upgraded HDB flat would become relatively less valuable in relation to upgraded ones. Between their most valuable asset and their political ideals, Singaporeans, being a pragmatic lot, went for the PAP, which achieved its best results since 1984. The PAP also took back two of the seats it lost in 1991. In the face of the PAP's strategy, the opposition more or less imploded.

This implosion was a severe setback. After all, the opposition's star was fairly bright after the 1991 General Election. Chiam was seen as the unofficial Leader of the Opposition and the SDP had the air of a respectable, credible political party. But two of its MPs, Cheo Chai Chen and Ling How Doong, were lacklustre and disappointing. Momentarily, when a certain Dr. Chee Soon Juan joined the SDP, its political potential and future looked much brighter but this optimism was short-lived. Chee eventually ousted Chiam as Secretary-General of the SDP. But Singaporeans did not take to his confrontational and adversarial form of politics. Though Chiam continued to hold his seat in Potong Pasir, he was politically weakened by this episode. To date, the SDP led by Chee remains in political wilderness.

The Lee Hsien Loong Administration (2004 – 2015)

On 11 August 2004, Lee Hsien Loong took over from Goh Chok Tong as Prime Minister after fourteen years as his deputy. Soon after, on 6 May 2006, he took the PAP on his first General Election outing, with a manifesto reminding Singaporeans of the importance of 'Staying Together, Moving Ahead', with the PAP. This time, the opposition abandoned the by-election strategy that it devised in 1991 and contested forty-seven out of eighty-four seats in straight fights – they had coordinated amongst themselves to avoid three-cornered contests. For the first time since 1988, the PAP did not form the government on Nomination Day. Still, this did not matter – thirty-seven seats remained uncontested in any case. In the end, the PAP, given the first past-the-post electoral system, won 82 out of 84 seats with a respectable 66.6% of the popular vote. For the opposition Worker's Party the years spent working the ground were beginning to show results. It secured 38.4% of the popular vote and expanded its winning margin in its Hougang stronghold. In Aljunied GRC, its team ran against, George Yeo, the Foreign Affairs minister, and secured a credible 43.9% of the vote. It even fielded a team of six political novices in the PM's own constituency. Its political gumption, campaign strategy and a thoughtful, well-prepared 52-page manifesto – 'You Have A Choice' – distinguished the WP from the other opposition parties and signalled its political coming of age.

The General Elections also had its lighter moments. Responding to government regulations over political broadcasts on the Internet, the 'blogfather' of Singapore, 'mr brown' began a series of eleven 'Persistently Non-Political' podcasts on 25 April. He insisted, tongue in cheek, that they did not contain 'persistent political content.' Episode 6 – the Bak Chor Mee Man – which riffed off a popular local noodle dish to obliquely comment on the PAP's response to an opposition party candidate's insistence over the validity of his candidacy papers, became hugely popular. Blogs played a major role as alternative news sources. They posted photographs of the huge crowds at WP's rallies, taken from vantage points at HDB flats near the rally grounds, which were a stark contrast against those published in the newspapers. Together, these were historic developments pushed the political boundaries and marked the entrance of the Internet into political campaigning and politics in Singapore.

And 2011 was a disaster for the PAP. It was not a good time for an election. The ground was decidedly sour, given the socio-economic impact of six years of liberal immigration policies. There were also several decided mis-steps in its campaign which called for 'Securing Our Future Together.' PAP candidate Tin Pei Ling became the target of an online smear campaign by netizens who criticised and mocked a video of her posing with a branded handbag – she quickly became the poster girl of a PAP that was out-of-step with national sentiments. Days before Polling Day, when speaking to reporters on a constituency visit on 30 April 2011, Minister Mentor Lee Kuan Yew warned Aljunied voters that they would have 'five years to live and repent.' This went down very badly with Singaporeans who were put off by the religious overtones of Lee's finger wagging warning.

The opposition went for broke in this election, contesting all but one seat. They also fielded a highly credible slate of well-credentialed candidates of whom Chen Show Mao and Nicole Seah became the most talked about. Strategically, Low Thia Khiang, the WP's leader, left his safe seat in Hougang to contest in Aljunied GRC, where it had made inroads in the previous election. It paid off. On 7 May 2011, the WP made history – it became the first opposition party to defeat the PAP in a GRC. It took down a heavyweight PAP team, comprising the Foreign Minister, the Second Minister for Finance and Transport, a Senior Minister of State, a member of Parliament and a new candidate touted as being of ministerial calibre.

On 3 May 2011, with days left to Polling Day, Lee Hsien Loong apologised to Singaporeans, twice, during the PAP's lunchtime rally at Raffles Place. 'If we didn't get it right, I'm sorry. But we will try better the next time'. As a senior political journalist observed, 'Mr Lee's speech was remarkable for its public mea culpa. And it was remarkable for its -- there is no other word for it – humility.' Nevertheless, the PAP saw its vote share slide to 60.5%. It was its worst electoral performance ever. The aftermath was sobering and unprecedented. Less than a week later, Lee Kuan Yew and Goh Chok Tong resigned from cabinet. Three unpopular ministers – Mah Bow Tan, Raymond Lim and Wong Kan Seng – were retired. At a press conference, Lee Hsien Loong explained to Singaporeans that he 'wanted a fresh start and that's why (he) called for radical change.'

The PAP swung into problem solving mode soon after the election. In 2011, Minister for National Development Khaw Boon Wan announced a ramped up building programme for the HDB – it intended to build 26,000 flats a year for the next two years. This far outstripped the total of 30,000 new units built from 2006 to 2010. Property 'cooling measures' such as stamp duties, additional stamp duties on second or third properties and tweaks to debt servicing ratio were introduced to rein in rising property prices. More importantly, new HDB flat prices were in 2011 de-linked from the resale market and priced separately. Through a slew of subsidies and grants, they were kept affordable. New MRT lines were announced. New MRT lines were opened. A fleet of 800 new buses, out of which the government provided funding for 550, was procured and rolled out over five years. Eight new bus routes running parallel to MRT lines were introduced – this reversed earlier policy. The intention was clear – public transport in Singapore was run for the benefit of Singaporeans, not public transport operators with an eye on their share prices and market valuations.

Months later, in August 2012, the government launched the 'Our Singapore Conversation' (OSC) to put its finger on the pulse of the nation, through a series of dialogues with a cross-section of Singaporeans. Around April 2013, the hugely popular Deputy Prime Minister Tharman Shanmugaratnam commented that the ideological nexus of the PAP had shifted left-of-centre. Singapore's social welfare measures were being scrutinised, examined and recalibrated. For a party as pragmatic as the PAP, the shift arose not because of any deep ideological realignment. Rather, as a local academic put it quite bluntly, the PAP realised that 'the party that continues to harp on individual responsibility and self-reliance may run the risk of defeat.' Whilst it retained its fundamental beliefs in a neoliberal economic model, it knew that the political and social consequences – inequality, decreasing social mobility and increasing social structural stratification – must be addressed. It knew that ignoring them would be politically perilous.

The Passing of An Era

On 21 February 2015, the Prime Minister's Office released a brief statement – Singapore's founding father, aged 91, had been in intensive care at the Singapore General Hospital (SGH) for about a fortnight. Soon after, Singaporeans started leaving cards, flowers and their good wishes at SGH's premises in Outram Road. The nation, it appeared, was saying its long goodbye to the man synonymous with Singapore's survival, growth and prosperity. Early in the morning on 23 March, PM Lee, visibly tearing, grieving and emotional, announced that Lee Kuan Yew – Singapore's founding father and his father – had passed on.

There was a week of national mourning and a lying-in-state at Parliament House. But there was something that the organizers, which met regularly to plan for such an inevitability, did not expect – the number of Singaporeans that would show up to pay their respects. The national atmosphere was sombre. And there was something awe-inspiring in the entirely unscripted manner which Singaporeans decided to show up, queue for hours just to file past, bow, salute or even kneel momentarily at the foot of Lee's casket to pay their last respects. Singapore had never seen anything like it. The line wound around the Civic District for several kilometres. MRT trains ran for twenty-four hours. The Padang was turned into a public queuing area. Soldiers handed out bottles of water and army medics tended to the unwell. In total, 454,687 people turned up for the lying-in-state. As one MINDEF executive put it quite candidly, 'we didn't expect so much emotion.'

This wave of national grief and emotion turned into national pride when Singapore hosted the Southeast Asian Games in June. On 9 August 2015, Singapore celebrated its Golden Jubilee in grand style. A month later on 11 September at the General Elections, the feel-good factor from this trifecta of events led to a landslide victory for the PAP. Its vote share increased to 69.6% and it even recaptured Punggol East from the opposition. It was at once an expression of gratitude to Lee Kuan Yew and also an endorsement of PM Lee's policies on housing, transport and immigration, which were seen to have heard and addressed voter concerns. A Pioneer Generation Package comprising healthcare and other benefits for elders born before 1949 was greatly popular.

The PAP fought this campaign in 'presidential' style – PM Lee's portrait was displayed alongside all PAP posters across the island. The anger and discontent that was so palpable at the rallies in the previous election was palpably gone. For the opposition, this was a difficult election to fight. The WP maintained its edge as the leading opposition party in terms of campaign organisation, its candidates and its messaging – even then, it was dogged by difficulties. Was this an anomalous election result, boosted by once-in-a-generation events or was Singapore still headed for a 'new normal' in its political development? Or was it, as an observer put it, an act of 'democratic backsliding?'

CHAPTER NINE

'To Achieve Happiness, Prosperity & Progress'

1965—2015

Happiness, Prosperity & Progress

Jobs, Jobs, Jobs – Singapore's Economic Story

Singapore's post-independence economic story rightly begins not in 1965 but in 1959 when it attained full internal self-government. Lee's team ran the country like the government of an independent nation-state, not as the political tutees in a colony awaiting independence. Even at this stage, they thought differently. Its lens was trained not on the short-term, winning of votes or pandering to populist voices, but on the medium to long-term, and its policies reflected this. True, many of these policies hinged on one tenuous assumption – a common market with the Federation. But at the same time, they were realists. And even as the PAP awaited this anxiously, it was not prepared to hold up Singapore's economic development for the Tunku to change his mind.

Upon taking over, Dr. Goh Keng Swee, one half of the economic brains trust behind Singapore's economic development, found out that the Lim Yew Hock government was not only running a budget deficit, but it had practically maintained no reserves. Consternated by this, Goh cut the salaries of member of cabinet and civil servants. This drastic move became the first tenet of Singapore's financial philosophy: You should maintain a balanced budget. Better yet, run a surplus. To raise capital to fund infrastructure development, Goh opted to borrow from the people of Singapore through the Central Provident Fund (CPF) – Singapore's compulsory national savings plan. The CPF was instructed to buy long-term government bonds. This reduced the need to rely on foreign development aid (which often came with its own conditions) or on borrowing from the financial markets. This was the second tenet: You should borrow judiciously and spend wisely.

The other half of the economic brains trust was Dr. Albert Winsemius, a Dutch economist who arrived in Singapore on 5 October 1960 as part of a United Nations Development Programme mission. He ended up being Singapore's chief economic advisor, without pay, until 1984. In June 1961, Winsemius submitted his report. He made two recommendations. First, the communist threat had to be eliminated (he figured that the 'how' was not his job). Second, 'let Raffles stand where he stands', at the Singapore River. Together, these actions would signal to the world that Singapore was politically stable and was not governed by rabid, anti-colonial nationalists. Investors could be sure that their money was safe here. These aside, the report advised the government to set up a body to coordinate and implement Singapore's industrialisation programme, which should focus on manufacturing and specific industries such as engineering and ship building. This was the basis for the First Development Plan (1961 – 1964).

The Goh-Winsemius partnership represented a meeting of technocratic minds. Both believed that economics should never be dictated by ideology. In May 1961, the Economic Development Board was set up with an initial funding of $100 million, to coordinate, direct and develop Singapore's industrialisation plans. On 1 September 1962, the foundation stone for the National Iron and Steel Mills (Natsteel) was laid in the estate set aside for Singapore's industrialisation – Jurong. Mocked by detractors as 'Goh's Folly', Jurong in time became of Singapore's industrial hub. Decades later, upon Winsemius' passing in 1996, Lee Kuan Yew paid tribute to his role and contributions, saying that 'Singapore is indebted to Winsemius', which was no small accolade.

Singapore's two years in Malaysia brought very little by way of economic development. The entire economic agenda came to a standstill. Each time Goh tried to push the central government towards establishing the common market, he was rebuffed or given conditions that were near impossible for the Singapore government to meet. The Federal Finance Minister, Tan Siew Sin, was not about to do Singapore any political favours and he was certainly not about to do Goh, who was his cousin, any personal ones either. When Singapore separated from Malaysia in 1965, it was very much where it was economically in 1963.

On 9 August 1965, the reality of independence made economic priorities crystal clear for Lee and his team. The most important goal was to provide jobs for Singaporeans and improve their lives. To do so, Singapore had to industrialise quickly by attracting investments and entering new export markets for its manufactured goods. It had to do so quickly and did so by being different. Without Malaysia, the world would be Singapore's hinterland and the government would create the conditions for this to happen. Singapore needed the world to survive. And to do so, it made sure that the world needed it.

Newly independent states in the 1960s believed in asserting their independence by replacing imported goods with locally made ones. Foreign investment was seen as a form of economic colonisation. Multinational corporations (MNCs) were predatory asset strippers and labour exploiters. But the Singapore government boldly chose to ignore ideology and doctrine. Because Singapore's domestic market was close to non-existent, replacing imports with locally-made goods made no sense. It therefore chose to focus on exporting its manufactures. To establish an export-led economy, MNCs were seen as an important source of investment capital for building factories. They also served as conduits for technology transfer, thus building up the capability of the Singapore workforce. In doing so, Singapore broke away from the pack. By 1975, manufacturing constituted 22% of its GDP, up from 14% in 1965.

Through the 1960s and 1970s, Goh and the EDB worked tirelessly to make Singapore an attractive and viable investment destination. Jurong, earlier derided as 'Goh's Folly' became synonymous with Singapore's industrial development. In June 1968, the Jurong Town Corporation (JTC) was set up to oversee Jurong's development as a residential town and industrial estate. Over time, it became a self-sufficient town with apartment blocks, schools, markets, and cultural and recreational touches such as the Jurong Bird Park, the Chinese Gardens, *Seiwaen* (the Japanese Gardens) and the Singapore Science Centre. These soft touches were important to Goh – they showed that a good quality of life was possible for Singaporeans living in Jurong. By 1976, there were 650 factories in Jurong. And as Jurong grew, so too did the economy. Earlier, in July 1968, to finance Singapore's industralisation more effectively, Goh hived off EDB's finance portfolio to form the Development Bank of Singapore.

Just as Singapore was getting its industrialisation programme off the ground, the British government announced on 18 July 1967 that it was withdrawing its military forces east of Suez by the mid-1970s.

The British pound was then devalued in November 1967. Britain could no longer afford a global military presence nor to honour its military commitments in the Far East. Six months later, the British government brought forward the imperial retreat to 31 March 1967. The Singapore government was shell-shocked, incensed and angered by this announcement. Having just recovered its political footing, it now faced another incipient crisis that would leave it defenceless and cause a big dent in its economy. Consider the facts. British forces in Singapore provided jobs for 150,000 Singaporeans directly or indirectly and accounted for more than 20% of its GDP. They also occupied one-tenth of its land, on which sat some choice assets.

Dismayed and angry but obviously inured to crisis management by now, Lee and Goh flew to London to negotiate a deal that would advantage Singapore and cushion the impact of the withdrawal. Cool heads prevailed. They ensured that Singapore would be duly compensated and there would also be no stripping of assets. In the end, they closed a good deal – a disbursement of £50, 000, 000 was secured together with the transfer of Britain's assets in Singapore, and pledges in military assistance. In Singapore, a Bases Economic Conversion Department (BECD) was set up to oversee the conversion of military facilities such as the Sembawang Naval Base for civilian use. By the time the British left in December 1971, it was a non-event. Singapore's economic development continued apace.

Within a generation, the Singapore economy had taken off. The MNCs invested heavily in Singapore. With its open economy and pro-business agenda, Singapore had become useful and relevant in a global economy dominated by MNCs seeking skilled labour and a good business environment. Singapore had, as Lee had envisioned, become the First World oasis in the Third World that was home to high value manufacturing, financial services and petrochemical refining.

With economic growth, its gateways became more important than ever in connecting Singapore to the global economy. The networks converging at the port of Singapore became more important, more relevant and more useful than ever as the port embraced containerisation. On 23 July 1972, it opened its first container berth at Tanjong Pagar and with it came the ability to accommodate new-generation container ships and move cargo faster and more efficiently. On 30 June 1981, Singapore Airlines flight SQ28 to Frankfurt via Abu Dhabi took off from Paya Lebar Airport at 11 p.m. – it was the last civilian flight out of Paya Lebar. The next day, at 7:10 a.m., SQ101, carrying 140 passengers from Kuala Lumpur, Malaysia, touched down at Singapore Changi Airport and at 8 a.m., SQ192 took off for Penang. Changi Airport, Singapore's game changer and world beater in international aviation, was open for business.

Headwinds: The 1985 Recession

But all good times must come to an end. In 1985, Singapore's economy entered a recession, its first since independence. Twenty years of rapid growth and modernisation, driven by investment and cost advantages, had peaked. External economic conditions had also soured. This was partly cyclical and partly due to domestic factors, such as rapid wage increases, that made the economy uncompetitive. Whilst policy measures, though potentially painful for Singaporeans, could tackle with the former, solving the latter meant recognising that the existing economic model had run its course.

In March 1985, an economic committee led by Lee Hsien Loong, the Minister of State for Trade and Industry carried out a thorough and soul-searching analysis of the economy and identified new and potential growth areas. Slightly under a year later in February 1986, it delivered its recommendations. Entitled 'The Singapore Economy: New Directions,' the report addressed the immediate problems and envisioned longer-term prospects for the economy.

To cut costs and cool the economy, the committee pushed for wage cuts, tax cuts and reduced savings. To increase the use of technology, it pushed for capital formation. To enhance economic dynamism, it pushed hard for a bigger role for a bigger private sector. This was not unexpected. Earlier in January 1986, it had convened a Public Sector Divestment Committee to investigate how government-linked companies (GLCs) and suitable statutory boards could be divested and privatised. 634 GLCs and seven statutory boards were evaluated for privatisation.

Today, many of them, including Singtel and the Development Bank of Singapore, are publicly listed on the Singapore Exchange. Others, such as Keppel Corporation and Sembawang Group underwent several cycles of consolidation to become corporate conglomerates with an Asian, if not global, presence. The national shipping line, Neptune Orient Lines, however, ran aground with losses of US$ 105 million in May 2016 and was sold off to French shipping giant CMA GAM Group soon after.

In many ways, the 1986 report became both template and formula that successive governments deployed to solve economic crises. It was undoubtedly effective for it drew on the PAP's greatest strengths – its political will and its technocratic competence. One premise has remained constant – to create and maintain a conducive business environment. A small and open economy has few other choices. However, keeping up with what 'conducive' meant over time and through constantly evolving global economic trends would severely test this economic modus operandi time and again. Nevertheless, Singapore emerged from this severe recession by the end of 1987.

The Boom Years (1991 – 1996)

In the early 1990s, Singapore boomed. Consider the numbers from 1991 to 1996 – 8.7% average GDP growth, 1.8% unemployment, 2.4% inflation, 0.44 GINI coefficient, more than $40 billion in foreign direct investment, per capita GDP of US$18, 572, a six-year long real estate boom. To stay ahead of the competition, Singapore's manufacturing activities were diversified. Regionalism became the watchword as direct investment from Singapore poured into Suzhou Industrial Park in China in February 1994 and the SIJORI project, spanning Johor and the bigger Riau Islands, in December 1994. A total of S$75.8 billion was invested in China, India, Vietnam, Johor in Malaysia, and Riau in Indonesia.

In 1993, along with five of its neighbours, Singapore entered into a free-trade agreement to create the ASEAN Free Trade Area (AFTA). Singapore went on to sign more than twenty other bilateral and regional agreements to ensure that its competitive edge was not blunted by tariffs, duties, and other restrictions. Over time, these agreements formed a trading network that cemented Singapore's role in the global economy's supply chains. In 1996, the Organisation for Economic Cooperation and Development (OECD) designated Singapore a 'more advanced developing country'. It was an accolade that signalled that the goals of the 1991 Strategic Economic Plan had been achieved.

Yet even as Singapore boomed, its regional rivals were becoming more competitive and becoming an economic threat. In response, the Committee on Singapore's Competitiveness (CSC) began thoroughly reviewing the country's economic fundamentals in May 1997. Its remit was clear – to propose strategies to strengthen Singapore's economic competitiveness. But its work, long-range in its scope and focus switched to crisis management instead.

On 2 July 1997, the Thai baht went into free fall in the global currency markets. Less than a week later, Malaysia was forced to defend the ringgit. Within a month, in August 1997, the Indonesian rupiah plummeted. The Asian Financial Crisis (AFC) was unfolding. On 21 May 1998, Indonesian strongman President Suharto was toppled after thirty-two years in power. The CSC now found itself confronting a major collapse in external demand and potential erosion in Singapore's future competitiveness as its rivals' currencies devalued.

From Crisis to Crisis (1997 – 2004)

The AFC was a textbook example of how an external crisis could completely undermine the best laid long-range plans of a technocratic government. By the time the CSC published its report on 28 October 1998, Singapore had been mired in the aftershocks of the crisis for more than a year. GDP growth contracted to 1.5% in 1998 – this was spread throughout all economic sectors – and unemployment rose to 3.2% with 68,000 people unemployed. Two economic rescue packages worth $12.5 billion were introduced in 1998 to reduce business costs and contain the fallout from this recession. Although growth returned in 1999, the AFC starkly revealed how an open globalised economy was vulnerable to events beyond its control.

When the global IT investment bubble burst in 2000, the Singapore economy went into recession again, which became protracted when Al-Qaeda terrorists brought down the World Trade Centre Towers in New York on 11 September 2001. In October 2002, terrorists struck Bali and in March 2003, the Severe Acute Respiratory Syndrome (SARS) crisis hit Singapore, battering both the travel and tourism sectors badly. In seven years, the Singapore was hit by four crises, none of which were of its own making.

Even as its economy withstood these shocks well, geopolitical shifts that undermined its economic model were taking place. In December 2001, China joined the World Trade Organisation (WTO) and very quickly became the world's manufacturing workshop and Singapore's direct competitor for foreign investment. The rise of

China posed an existential threat and forced Singapore to rethink its economic game plan. Could it continue to rely on an economic model underpinned by export-led development, foreign direct investment, and extensive state involvement?

In this light, the report issued on 4 February 2003 by the Economic Review Committee (ERC) was a true watershed. Entitled "New Challenges, Fresh Goals – Towards a Dynamic Global City" it had profound implications and consequences for Singapore, both as a nation-state and economic entity. Its bold vision declared that, 'by remaking and upgrading ourselves, we will made Singapore a leading global city, a hub of talent, enterprise and innovation. Singapore will become the most open and cosmopolitan city in Asia, and one of the best places to live and work.' It aimed to be the node of nodes, a hub of hubs, a city that 'will connect China, India and Southeast Asia, and beyond.' Singapore would become a global city, on par with New York, London, and Tokyo by 2018 – within fifteen years. It would attract global capital, global wealth and global talent. The ERC report represented a complete change of course, a remake of the Singapore economy that had far-reaching political and social consequences.

Choices – Global City, City State? (2004 – 2015)

From 2005 to 2015, Singapore evolved into a global city-state and became even more affluent. The icons of a global city, tangible and intangible, began taking shape and appearing. In October 2007, the Singapore Flyer, a 165-metre tall observation wheel reminiscent of the London Eye – only bigger – was completed. In September 2008, Singapore held the world's first and only F1 night race, with race cars zipping around a challenging street circuit set against its gleaming lit-up skyline studded with skyscrapers. In 2010, the iconic Marina Bay Sands integrated resort complex, designed by Moshe Safdie, housing a casino, a museum, a luxury hotel, and a retail complex opened. In May 2012, the Marina Bay Cruise Centre welcomed its first cruise ship. By 2012, the showcase was complete with the opening of the Gardens by the Bay, designed by British landscape architects, Grant Associates.

In the meantime, a new Downtown centered around the Marina Bay Financial Centre – with a network of MRT stations, walking and cycling paths and broad boulevards – was taking shape, housing the big names of global capital – DBS, Citibank, HSBC and Standard

Chartered. An assemblage of hedge funds, private equity firms, private banks, and insurers that gathered in Singapore, which unabashedly aimed to be the "Switzerland of the East." In the mid-2000s, an exclusive and secluded residential enclave for the super-rich, complete with a marina (with six berths for mega-yachts), two golf courses, eateries, and shops, began construction on reclaimed land in Sentosa Cove. The Singapore Tourism Board (STB) even proposed, in 2006, to develop Singapore's idyllic Southern Islands into a setting reminiscent of Capri in western Italy!

On 15 September 2008, the Global Financial Crisis began when Lehman Brothers, one of the 'too big to fail' American investment banks filed for bankruptcy. It had $639 billion in assets under management (and $613 in liabilities). Around the same time, Merrill Lynch, another star in the constellation of vaunted American investment banks, sold itself to Bank of America for $50 billion. The next day, the U.S. Federal Reserve bailed out giant insurer A.I.G. to the tune of $85 billion.

Very soon, the aftershocks from this global financial meltdown reached Singapore in a very personal way. Singaporeans had invested in esoteric financial products underwritten by Lehman Brothers and marketed by the Development Bank of Singapore (and other financial institutions) – Minibond Notes, High Notes 5, Jubilee Series 3 Link Earner Notes and Pinnacle Series 8 and 10 Notes. They lost (almost) everything. Even government-linked bodies were not spared. Eight PAP town councils invested S$16 million in these products. The country's vaunted sovereign wealth funds, Temasek Holdings and the Government Investment Corporation of Singapore incurred massive losses.

Given its exposure, Singapore's economic growth entered recession once again in October 2008 – the first East Asian economy to do so. Characteristically, the government intervened with a $2.9 billion package in November 2008. In January 2009, it followed up with an additional $20.5 billion in a stimulus budget dubbed the 'Resilience Package.' By 2009, the severe but short-lived contraction was declared over.

Short-term measures aside, the government revisited its economic strategy. In January 2010, eight months after it received its mandate, the Economic Strategies Committee (ESC) released its report. It had two broad goals. The first was to 'provide for inclusive growth, with a broad-based increase in the income of our citizens' through 'skills, innovation and productivity.' The second was 'to be a vibrant and distinctive global city' but with an important caveat – it had to be 'a home that provides an outstanding quality of life for our people.' Much as it gave a nod to Singapore's economic achievements since 2003, it also recognised the breakneck GDP growth, driven by the influx of foreign manpower, could not go on indefinitely. With this, the ESC pivoted towards solving a problem that had dogged every PAP government since 1986 – productivity growth. The premise was simple: To raise productivity by 2 to 3% annually over ten years to fuel GDP growth of 3 to 5% a year. But the solution was not. Whilst low-skilled foreign labour had to be restricted, to achieve its ambition of being a global city, it had to attract 'diverse and high-quality talent from Asia and around the world.'

As such, Singaporeans were beginning to feel the pinch of living and working in a global city. Just as globalisation once transformed Singapore in the late 19th century, it did so again in the 21st century, but at a quicker pace and with greater intensity. This time, however, the consequences would hit not a transient immigration population in a colonial city but the citizens of a nation-state. Nowhere was this change quicker and more intensely felt than in its population make-up.

With the loosening of immigration policies and employment regulations, Singapore's demographics started changing. Since 1977, Singapore's birth rate had fallen below the population replacement level. Pro-natalist measures introduced in the 1990s also failed to persuade Singaporeans to have more children. The shrinking population meant a shrinking labour supply, which would hurt the economy. Immigrants were required to 'top up' a population that would otherwise start to shrink from 2025. From 2005 onwards, new citizens, permanent residents and foreign workers flowed into Singapore at an unprecedented rate.

The alphabet soup of employment passes introduced reflected this liberal policy. At its apex were the Global Investor Programme (GIP) and Foreign Investor Scheme (FIS), aimed at the super-rich who would drive Singapore's quest to become a premier wealth hub. Next were the P1 and P2 tier passes aimed at enticing professionals. The most controversial ones were the Q1 and S-Pass that admitted immigrants with a qualifying salary criterion of S$1,800 and a high school education – a decidedly low bar. A new Personalised Employment Pass was introduced in 2007 to attract foreign professionals to reside and work in Singapore. As a result, Singapore's total population swelled from 4,017,733 in 2000 to 5,353,003 in 2015. A total of 458,354 permanent residencies was granted. 189,632 new citizenships were approved.

The hard-headed economic logic driving this immigration policy was not difficult for Singaporeans to understand but its impact on a gamut of issues – jobs, national identity, social cohesion, competition, housing prices, overcrowding – discomfited Singaporeans. Two massive breakdowns on Singapore's subway system, fabled as a symbol of Singapore's reliability and efficiency, on 15 and 17 December 2011, raised concerns that the country's infrastructure was being pushed beyond its limits. The continued affordability of public housing in Singapore became a matter of deep public concern as the HDB resale price index doubled from 72.2 in Q1 2005 to 149.4 in Q2 2013. The island was getting more crowded. Population density soared from 5932 persons per square kilometre in 2005 to 7778 persons per square kilometre in 2015 – an increase of 30%.

Unsurprisingly, when the government released its Population White Paper on 29 January 2013, just six days after it lost a by-election, there was an immediate public outcry. The public latched on to one key point – the population would grow by 30% to 6.9 million by 2030. Uncharacteristically, more than four thousand Singaporeans reported rallied amidst a drizzle at the usually quiet Speaker's Corner at Hong Lim Park on 16 February 2013 in protest. No matter how sound the economic justifications were, and regardless of the reassurances that the 'Singaporean core' would always come first, Singaporeans now viewed immigration negatively.

Amidst this large-scale demographic shift, the pressures wrought by globalisation were being felt by Singaporeans. But nowhere was it more obvious that in the country's GINI coefficient – a measure of inequality. It peaked at 0.48 in 2007 but finally retreated to 0.43 in 2015. The government intervened with wage supplements and subsidies to address this growing inequality. These included the Workfare Income Supplement, GST Voucher Scheme and utilities rebates. On 1 November 2015, the government introduced Medishield Life to assuage the public worried about rising healthcare costs. Essentially a compulsory national health insurance scheme, it was kept highly affordable through a $4 billion subsidy and also covered those with pre-existing conditions that private insurers did not cover.

Pioneers of the Next Generation? (2016 – 2020)

In its 2017 report, the Committee for the Future Economy (CFE) asserted the government's central role in directing and shaping the future economy. Given the political uncertainties wrought by Britain's exit from the European Union in June 2016 and the shock outcome in the American presidential elections in November, it decided to focus on building capabilities that could be deployed nimbly, flexibly and with agility.

This was a different sort of economic restructuring. Hard targets and outcomes – being a global city and picking winners – still mattered but the CFE placed heavy emphasis on the need to be adaptable and quick-thinking in implementing and executing economic policy. Tax cuts still mattered but it was no longer an unsustainable race to the bottom; a conducive business environment was more than just low costs. Strong rule of law, robust regulatory frameworks, protection for intellectual property rights, discretion, a quality living environment – 'liveability' – all mattered to foreign investors.

But what mattered most was this – the days of cheap foreign manpower driving the economy were over. Levies were raised, and quotas cut. Fair employment practices that favoured Singaporeans were enacted. Industry Transformation Maps (ITM) were drawn up to transform small and medium enterprises. GDP growth had to be driven by productivity growth. There was no other choice. New opportunities continue to beckon, especially in the fields of technology, communication, and finance. But whether it is artificial intelligence breakthroughs or digital banks or esoteric financial products, the bottom-line remains clear – they had to deliver jobs that paid a living wage, for Singaporeans.

In 2019, in its Bicentennial year, the Singapore economy stood at a crossroads. The experience of the post-independence years showed that Singapore's economic model was a simple but complex one. Simple – because all it demanded was for Singapore to stay useful and relevant to the world, but complex – because the interaction between political vision, technocratic competence, resource management and Singaporeans' aspirations was an intricate one to execute. The challenges were no longer purely economic. A more diverse and vocal citizenry meant that hard-nosed technocratic solutions alone would not do.

Making It Possible: Housing & Education

Impressive as Singapore's economic achievements in the last fifty years are, they would not have been possible if not for its housing and education policies. Together, they have supported and augmented the state's economic agenda. Housing created social stability and provided an opportunity for social engineering to take place on a large-scale. Education instilled in the work force not only capabilities and skills but, more importantly, the values and ethos that a modern economy demanded.

Housing: From Tenants to Homeowners to Asset Holders

In what has entered the national mythos, a typical marriage proposal in Singapore begins not with the customary 'Will you marry me?' but with the rather more practical and less romantic 'Shall we apply for an HDB flat'? Public housing in Singapore, provided by the Housing and Development Board (HDB), is seen as a birth right of sorts by Singaporeans. Life in Singapore is, for many Singaporeans, life in the HDB estate where they live, study, work, and play. How did this come to be?

The achievements of Singapore's public housing programme have spoken for themselves in the last fifty years. And public housing has none of the negativity commonly associated with the term – it is not synonymous with neglect, deprivation, squalor or ghettoisation. In Singapore, living in an HDB flat in a self-contained, well-maintained, and clean HDB housing estate (also known as a 'new town' in the earlier years) with its shops, swimming pools, parks, and schools, is a way of life. Today, 80% of Singaporeans live in 1.1 million HDB flats and 90% of these flats are owner-occupied. The HDB's vision and journey which began on 1 February 1960 has been realised.

Public housing did exist in Singapore during the colonial era. In 1927, the Singapore Improvement Trust (SIT) was set up to attend to the provision of public housing. But its pace was glacial and its record dismal – it had little to show despite working hard and being severely under-resourced. From 1932 to 1959, excluding the Japanese Occupation years, the SIT built all of 2,000 houses, 50 shops and 21,000 apartment units. The one housing estate it planned for, Queenstown, started in 1952 and was only partially complete by the time of Singapore's independence. There are still pockets of SIT flats standing today. Tiong Bahru's Art Deco style SIT flats are seen nostalgically as examples of how public housing could be infused with an aesthetic flair and élan. But beautiful as they are compared to the slab blocks of the early HDB developments, not enough of these were built to house a nation, much less build a nation of homeowners.

The HDB, like many of the government agencies set up in that era, was focused on one mission: to provide low-cost public housing for a rapidly growing population. Led by Lim Kim San, its first chairman, who patriotically worked without pay, the HDB was a one-stop shop that provided end-to-end services and solutions – these ranged from urban planning to housing design and even in-house legal services. In so doing, the typical bureaucratic bottlenecks were avoided or obliterated. The HDB began with one and two-room flats and also 'emergency flats'. At the end of its first five-year building programme in 1965, the HDB had delivered 51,031 flats, far outstripping the SIT in its entire existence of thirty-two years.

On 25 April 1961, a massive blaze swept through Bukit Ho Swee. In its aftermath, the government showed both its will and capability to help the fire victims, numbering some 16,000 in all. Ten months on from the fire, everyone had been resettled, either into existing flats in neighbouring Alexandra, Queenstown and Tiong Bahru or in new flats built on the fire site. By 1967, 12,562 new flats had been built on the fire site. For the people of Bukit Ho Swee, it was an induction into the experience of high-rise living in government-built flats on a massive scale.

The government, however, did not simply want to house the people. Its ambition went further – it wanted Singaporeans to own these flats, to own their homes, to have for themselves a piece of the country, as it were. To Lee, home ownership would build rootedness and give Singaporeans a stake in the country in the form of a tangible asset. In February 1964, the Home Ownership for the People scheme was unveiled. The first step had been taken. But for home ownership to succeed, two pre-conditions must be met. The flats had to be affordable, and the people must have the means to pay for the flats. To ensure that flats were affordable, land cost, the biggest component in any housing project, had to be kept low. And to ensure that Singaporeans could pay for the flats, they needed access to a pool of funds that was regularly topped up through employment income. The government had two tools at its disposal to realise these conditions. The first was the Land Acquisition Act of 1966 and the second was the savings deposited in the Central Provident Fund.

The Land Acquisition Act took effect on 17 June 1967. It gave the government sweeping powers to acquire land for national development purposes. It also determined how landowners would be compensated if their lands were acquired. This was a landmark law that enabled the long-term transformation of Singapore's physical landscape. And this powerful law was used effectively and forcefully. By 1985, the government held 76.2% of all land in Singapore and by 2010, with the use of the law and other land transfers, the figure had risen to 90%. This was, in effect, a land nationalisation exercise writ large. This land bank gave the government the space to plan for the long-term. It used leasehold terms, ranging from thirty to ninety-nine years, to ensure that no single individual held or hoarded land in perpetuity. For the Singaporean buying an HDB flat, land acquisition made home ownership affordable.

In 1968, the government liberalised the use of CPF funds for home ownership. Singaporeans could now use their CPF savings to pay for the down-payment on their flats as well as service the monthly mortgage payments. This became a way of life in Singapore. So long as one had a job and made monthly payments into their CPF accounts, they could pay for their flats without using any cash. Singaporeans clearly took to this for by 1970, more than 60% chose to buy their flats. Today, 80% of Singaporeans own the HDB flats they live in. The home ownership vision was realised in the space of two generations.

From the 1970s onwards, as rapid economic growth gave Singaporeans rising incomes and higher expectations, the HDB shifted its focus. Bigger units such as four-room and five-room flats were built as Singaporeans demanded and could afford these larger and more expensive flats. In 1993, the building of three-room flats, once the *di rigeur* symbol of the middle-class Singaporean, was discontinued. Over the last fifty years, it has kept faith, as best as it could, with Singaporeans by ensuring that income ceilings were revised, subsidies tweaked, and grants introduced so that no one would be priced out of public housing.

The HDB's first satellite town project in Toa Payoh, with its handsome town centre, lush town park, stadium and swimming pool became the pride and showcase of the nation as it served as the

Games Village for the 7th SEAP Games held in Singapore from 1 to 8 September 1973. Earlier in 1972, Queen Elizabeth II, during a visit to Singapore, was taken to a three-room flat in Toa Payoh to see for herself what public housing was like in Singapore. In 2006, she would make a return visit to Toa Payoh. Singapore's HDB flats had clearly become a visible, tangible symbol of successful nation building. Over time, other housing estates developed all over Singapore in Ang Mo Kio, Bedok, Clementi, Tampines, Bukit Batok and Punggol – just to name a few.

For the Singaporean, the HDB flat became both a home and an asset. As HDB rules were relaxed in the 1990s, selling off one's first HDB flat for a profit and then buying a newer, bigger one, became possible. And if one had the means, private condominium apartments were plausible choices too. The race to 'upgrade' had begun. Upon retirement, the HDB flat could be sold off and owners could 'downgrade' to a smaller HDB flat and live off a combination of their CPF savings and the proceeds from the sale of their flat. This was an ideal scenario, but it was possibly problematic because it hinged on rising incomes, rising property prices and the presence of ready buyers as these owners 'downgraded' to cash in on their assets. On 24 March 2017, the National Development Minister remarked in a blog post that for HDB flats not selected for redevelopment, their leases will run out and the flats returned to the state. And as their leases ran down, 'especially towards the tail-end, the flat prices (and value) will come down correspondingly.' A new phrase 'lease decay' was coined and soon entered the national lexicon. Today, beyond providing an adequate housing supply, ensuring the HDB flat remains an asset of enduring value is the main challenge for the government as leases continue to run down in the years to come.

Education: Building People, Building the Nation

'We have a strong education system. Singapore students aim high and they achieve very good results. This is recognised around the world. We have good schools, with capable school leaders and teachers, and facilities that are amongst the best in the world.' This confident pronouncement, made on the Ministry of Education's (MOE) website reflects the success of the education system in delivering the goods.

But this was not the case in February 1978 when Lee tasked Dr. Goh Keng Swee (by then the brains behind the economy, finance and defence ministries) to form a handpicked team to 'look into the problems of the MOE'. Lee issued no specific instructions or terms of reference for he saw that 'the field was vast, the problems innumerable, the objective simple'. For Lee, the education system had to maximise a child's potential and turn him into 'a good man and a useful citizen'. This was a clear (but complex) outcome and the MOE was not delivering it. And the team assembled by Dr. Goh, comprising systems engineers from MINDEF, would uncover what exactly was preventing the MOE and the schools from doing so.

When Singapore become self-governing in 1959, it inherited an education system made up of schools from four different language streams. These were the English schools and the vernacular schools – Chinese, Malay and Tamil stream schools respectively. In this light, one of the key goals of the PAP government was to introduce the policy of bilingualism. First announced on 8 December 1959, this meant that all students had to learn English in addition to their mother tongue. By 1966, all students in English-medium schools had to learn a second language, be it Malay, Mandarin or Tamil and those from vernacular schools had to learn English as a second language. The second language was also a compulsory examination subject. But there was a problem – this system was not delivering results.

For newly independent Singapore, the schools were not just about ensuring that Singaporeans were literate, numerate and equipped with the skills and knowledge needed by a modern economy. As a small country with no natural resources, Singapore had to ensure that as many Singaporeans as possible were able to attain these outcomes. It could not afford to squander its only resource through a defective education system.

When the Goh Report was released in February 1979, it more or less excoriated the entire education system and those who led, ran and managed it. The Goh Report opened with this observation: 'It has not occurred to many Singaporeans how unnatural the present school system is'. In describing the education system as 'unnatural', the report highlighted a paradox – 'most school children are taught in two languages – English and Mandarin. Eighty-five percent of them do not speak either of these languages at home'. Terse perhaps, but entirely accurate. Worsening this paradox was the fact that more and more Chinese parents were choosing to send their children to English-stream schools. And the children, being taught in languages they did not know, were locked in a curriculum that operated on a 'one size fits all' principle. The notion that everyone might have a different learning pace was ignored. Unsurprisingly, the outcomes were not good. By 1976, 65% of a Primary One (Year One) cohort failed to complete secondary education. The big question was: How could a mass education system cater to differing learning paces and yet deliver better outcomes that benefitted more children?

The solution, which eventually became the New Education System, hinged on one key recommendation – streaming. Based on academic results at the end of Primary Three and Primary Six (or Year Three and Year Six respectively), students would be streamed into different tracks that catered to their intelligence and learning pace. There was an emphasis on English in all the tracks but one would need to study one's Mother Tongue at the level of a second language. On 30 March 1979, Parliament endorsed these recommendations. By the end of 1979, the first Primary Three (Year Three) cohort was streamed into normal, extended or monolingual tracks. At the end of 1980, the first Primary Six (Year Six) cohort was similarly streamed into special, express or normal tracks. The education rat race had begun.

In a country that prides itself as a meritocracy where a combination of hard work and ability will get you places in life, streaming disrupted all assumptions. For one, the starting line to getting somewhere in life was now a whole lot earlier – at age nine. Being in a particular stream showed everyone else how clever you were and how hardworking you were. How fast or how slow you learnt did not matter. What mattered was the crude equation that had emerged – being in the best stream meant that one was cream of the crop, clever, smart, destined to go places in life. And being in the worst stream meant the reverse. But streaming worked in terms of tangible outcomes. Attrition rates, wastage, in terms of school dropout rates, fell. Pass rates went up across the board. The recommendations worked.

But at such a cost. Though tweaks were made throughout the 1990s and 2000s to address concerns about the stress levels and self-image issues arising from streaming students from such a young age, Singaporeans never quite shook their near obsession about academic results, school rankings, enrichment classes and private tutoring. In March 2019, forty years after the Goh Report, the MOE announced that streaming in secondary schools would be done away with and 'in their place will be full subject-based banding, in which students take subjects, at a higher or lower level, based on their strengths'. By 2024, this would be extended to all secondary schools. Ong Ye Kung, the Minister for Education, reiterated his ministry's belief – 'no child's fate is fixed, and in an environment that encourages growth and development, and promotes holistic education, they will fulfil their potential to be sons and daughters of Singapore whom we are proud of'. The Goh Report's work was done.

Securing Space for the Little Red Dot – Diplomacy & Deterrence

Singapore might have become independent, but Lee and his team confronted the unchanging dictates of history and geography. It was still a small island in a strategic location, sitting at the crossroads of the world. But for the first time since the 14th century, Singapore was on its own – it was not part of something else. It stood alone. This was so anomalous that nobody thought Singapore could survive, much less prosper. It was in this context that Singapore's first Minister for Foreign Affairs, S. Rajaratnam outlined Singapore's foreign policy to Parliament on 13 December 1965. Its foreign policy had two objectives. The first was to protect Singapore's independence and sovereignty. The second was to overcome Singapore's smallness, its physical constraints and secure for itself an expanded, if not expansive, space or spaces beyond the physical. To achieve these objectives, Singapore's foreign ministers and diplomats adopted a realistic and pragmatic approach and attitude towards its international relations – Singapore's vulnerability and the fact that history is replete with small states that have failed, been conquered, or reduced to vassalage, were never far from their minds. Yet, this awareness did not cow or paralyse them. They were determined not to do what was expected of a small state – to be deferential, subordinate and maybe become a client state. Singapore's foreign ministers and diplomats would adopt an assiduous and activist approach in advocating for and protecting its national interests. And, in doing so, Singapore garnered a degree of influence that was incommensurate with its size as 'a little red dot'. This term was used pejoratively by Indonesian President B. J. Habibie in 1998, at the height of the Asian Financial Crisis, in an attempt to put Singapore in its place. The 'little red dot' has since been proudly embraced as a metaphor by a country that punches way above its weight.

Beyond its membership in the United Nations and the Commonwealth, Singapore's priorities were its neighbours. On 8 August 1967, Singapore became a founding member of the Association of Southeast Asian Nations (ASEAN) and with it, embraced regionalism as a key pillar of its foreign policy. From 1970, Singapore's relationship with Malaysia improved as the anguish of separation faded and as Singapore's independence became an irrevocable reality secured by a rapidly expanding Singapore Armed Forces (SAF). By 2010, longstanding issues such as the dispute over Pedra Banca and the KTM railway land, amongst others, had been settled, the former judicially through arbitration by the International Court of Justice and the latter in an agreement between the two countries. In 1973, Lee visited Indonesia and in an act that signalled both contrition and humility, scattered flowers at the graves of two Indonesian marines who were executed in Singapore in 1965 during the Konfrontasi. Lee also struck up a friendly and longstanding relationship with Indonesian President Suharto, one that cemented close ties between the two countries and one that lasted till 1998, when Suharto was ousted from office. In 1976, Lee visited the Peoples' Republic of China (PRC), only doing so after Malaysia, the Philippines and Thailand had begun their own rapprochement with the PRC. Singapore would only establish formal diplomatic ties with the PRC in 1990, the last country in ASEAN to do so.

Singapore's foreign policy took a decided slant towards the United States of America (USA) when Lee called on President Lyndon Baines Johnson in October 1967. Part of this was driven by economics, to draw American MNCs to invest in Singapore. It was also driven by realism for Lee believed that it was critical to keep the US engaged in the region. Over time, the two countries drew closer. Lee became valued by American presidents for his insights into the region and his counsel. In October 1985, Lee addressed a joint session of the US Congress, an honour for Singapore and for Lee, and a reflection of the close ties between the two countries. In 1991, as the US withdrew from its bases in the Philippines, Singapore concluded a Memorandum of Understanding (MoU) that enabled it to access Singapore's Paya Lebar Airbase and Sembawang Wharves. In 2001, Singapore's Changi Naval Base opened; it was large enough to accommodate a US Navy aircraft carrier. A bilateral free trade agreement signed in 2003 and a further agreement on security cooperation signed in 2005 reflected the deep partnership between the two countries.

Singapore played an activist role when it saw developments inimical to its interests. On 12 January 1979, after Vietnam invaded Cambodia, it initiated, led and coordinated ASEAN's response and eventual condemnation of Vietnam. As a littoral state that depended on access to open shipping routes and in ensuring that these routes stayed open, it played a leading role in the United Nations Convention on the Law of the Sea. It was similarly activist when it came to advancing its interests, for example, in pushing for greater economic integration in ASEAN and in participating in international organisations such as the World Trade Organisation. On 1 January 2001, Singapore took up its seat as a two-year non-permanent member of the United Nations Security Council (UNSC). The little red dot was big on the global stage.

Singapore's foreign policy continues to be guided by the objectives laid down when it became an independent nation. It derives influence from its usefulness to the rest of the world; it is this usefulness, which depends on its economic roles, that is its value-proposition. In this sense, Singapore's raison d'etre has not changed. The world will take an interest in it so long as it can supply what they want. And so long as Singapore can supply what they want, it will be relevant to them. The rise of China and its increasingly assertive stance in the South China Sea since 2009, coupled with an increasingly insular and isolationist USA since 2017, pose a delicate challenge for Singapore in its balancing act as a friend to all, but an enemy to none. Closer to home in Malaysia, the shock defeat of UMNO and the election of the Pakatan Harapan government in May 2018, together with the resurrection of Dr. Mahathir Mohamed as Prime Minister, has heralded a more abrasive and provocative relationship. Singapore's nimbleness and agility in maintaining its foreign policy objectives will be tested thoroughly as the 21st century unfolds further.

In so far as Singapore's foreign policy has been effective, it is only so because of the deterrent posture it exercises through its military capabilities. Singapore's defence policy, much like its foreign policy, is driven by a deep and innate sense of vulnerability and its geostrategic constraints – Singapore cannot choose its neighbours and while it can do its best to engender good relations, things can and do wrong. *Konfrontasi*, the low-level insurgency against Malaysia from 1963 to 1966 is a case in point. Neither can Singapore ignore the lessons of history that have shown that the island can be overrun in a matter of days, that the island on its own has no strategic depth, no space to withdraw to, to regroup and hit back. Nor can it depend on others for its defence. The British surrender to the Japanese left a civilian population helpless and at the mercy of the invader. And treaty obligations are anything but permanent. The British decision to accelerate its withdrawal from Singapore is a case in point. History had taught Singapore leaders that 'we must ourselves defend Singapore'.

In 1967, Parliament passed an amendment to the National Service Act and the first batch of recruits, numbering nine hundred, was enlisted in July that year. But the Singapore Armed Forces (SAF) had neither the capability nor the capacity to take more then. It was not until 1970, with the passage of the Enlistment Act, that National Service (NS) – two years full-time and annual in-camp training (ICT), came into being. One could serve NS not just in the SAF but also in the Singapore Police Force or in the Singapore Civil Defence Force.

The SAF, comprising the Army, the Republic of Singapore Navy (RSN) and the Republic of Singapore Air Force (RSAF) uses metaphors to describe Singapore's defence posture and the thinking behind its doctrines and decisions. To describe the growth, evolution and development from metaphor to metaphor, the SAF likes to think in terms of generations. But before the first-generation SAF could begin its work, the building blocks had to be put in place. On 14 February 1966, months after independence, the Singapore Armed Forces Training Institute (SAFTI) was established to train officers and non-commissioned officers (NCOs) to form the leadership nucleus of a conscript based SAF. SAFTI commissioned its first batch of officers on 16 July 1967, just in time for the first intake of National Servicemen. This first batch of officers are close to legend in the SAF's annals and part of this mystique is drawn from the fact that they were trained by Israeli advisors who took them through the paces of leading men and commanding an army. The government referred to them as 'Mexicans' in a weak attempt to disguise their nationality for fear of upsetting Singapore's neighbours. These 'Mexicans' taught Singapore's soldiers how to fight, where to fight and when to fight. They taught Singapore's soldiers to translate these lessons into training manuals to be used by a citizen army. In May 1967, the Singapore Maritime Command, which became the RSN in 1975, was established. Shortly after, on 1 September 1968, the Singapore Air Defence Command, which became the RSAF in 1975, took wing.

Arms purchases soon followed as the defence budget was expanded. On 9 August 1969, Singapore's AMX-13 tanks, purchased second-hand from the Israelis, went on parade and rolled impressively past the reviewing dais. Razak, Malaysia's Deputy Prime Minister and Defence Minister, an invited guest, watched in shock as the tanks trundled past. At that point, the Malaysian Armed Forces had not a single tank in its arsenal. Speaking to Dr. Goh after the parade, Razak sought reassurances that Singapore had no hostile intentions towards Singapore! It was a not so subtle message from Singapore about its military capabilities.

Singapore's military build-up continued. In 1968, it began building up its naval capability with an order for German missile gunboats – the RSS Sea Wolf class. In 1969, its first patrol craft, RSS Independence, was delivered. In 1971, its air force capabilities were boosted when its first fighter aircraft, the Hawker Hunter, arrived. Upon Britain's withdrawal announcement, Singapore took over the Bloodhound surface-to-air missile batteries. In 1971, the Five Power Defence Arrangement (FPDA), a consultative body comprising Australia, New Zealand, Britain, Singapore and Malaysia, kicked in. The building blocks of Singapore's defence were finally in place.

Metaphorically, the first-generation SAF saw itself as a 'poisonous shrimp'. It was a choice that described Singapore's defence posture aptly throughout the 1970s. By the late 1970s, the SAF mustered 40,000 active personnel and had 130,000 in reserves. In 1976, it fielded its first division - the 3rd Singapore Infantry Division. By the 1980s, the second-generation SAF no longer saw itself as a 'poisonous shrimp' but as a 'porcupine', small but able to defend itself against threats by curling itself up into a spiky ball. The SAF was now able to strike back and any aggressor would, as Lee Hsien Loong put it: 'have to pay a high price for trying to subdue me and you may still not succeed.' While building up this capability, the SAF began to grapple with the consequence of a falling birth rate. Singapore's divisions, brigades and battalions, though reduced to become smaller in size and headcount, were no less capable. In 1991, the 3rd Singapore Infantry Division was now the 3rd Singapore Division, a combined arms formation deploying infantry, armour, artillery, engineers and signals as an integrated force. Equipment upgrades continued apace. The RSAF acquired more advanced fighters, first the F-5E Tiger IIs and then the F-16 Fighting Falcons, E-2C Hawkeye early warning aircraft and KC-135 air-to-air refuelling tankers. Ironically for an island nation, the RSN was a Cinderella service for most of the 1970s. In the 1980s, its capabilities were upgraded to better defend Singapore's maritime interests. Missile corvettes boosted its offensive capabilities as did the deployment of Harpoon anti-ship missiles. Its amphibious capabilities were enhanced with new locally designed and built landing platform dock ships in the late 1990s. Submarines, second-hand ones, were acquired in the mid-1990s to build and develop an underwater warfare capability. As the 2000s approached, the SAF transformed into a third-generation force, this time seeing itself as a 'dolphin', at ease and secure in swimming with the sharks but also intelligent enough to deal with aggressors. The SAF continued to upgrade its weaponry but its focus had expanded. It was no longer about having weapons but having weapons operate as a system on the battlefield that would envelop and overcome the enemy. With this integration, it would win by relying on information superiority to remove what Carl von Clausewitz, the German military thinker, termed 'the fog of war'. Just how advanced is the SAF? In terms of its hardware, with its Leopard 2SG main battle tanks, the RSS Formidable frigates and F-15SG fighter-bombers, the SAF is cutting edge. But what matters most to any military is its ability to deploy force effectively. In this light, the Chief of Defence Force, Lieutenant-General Ng Chee Meng, pronounced in 2014 that the SAF was able to 'bring lethal firepower at a very short time to hit moving targets – one shot, one kill…we have the capabilities to ensure we fulfil the mission to protect Singapore'. The fourth generation SAF had arrived.

CONCLUSION

In 1969, at Singapore's sesquicentennial celebrations of its founding in 1819, the focus was rooted firmly in remembering, if not actually commemorating Singapore's colonial legacy. At that time, it was felt that for a new independent nation still coming to terms with communal violence and racial riots, it was prudent not to address the pre-colonial era with its possible emotional overtones. Perhaps it was even a matter of academic interest only.

On 9 August 2015, Singapore celebrated its Golden Jubilee with an impressive parade at the Padang. Prior to that, in June 2015, it showcased its creativity and organisational prowess by successfully hosting the 28th Southeast Asian (SEA) Games. Together with the passing of the founding PM Lee Kuan Yew on 23 March 2015, the Singapore people pulled together as a nation, as Singaporeans, experiencing a common emotional experience that at once spanned and transcended joy, pride, grief and sadness.

Four years later in January 2019, Singapore kicked off the Bicentennial of its founding in a low-key, almost muted fashion. But unlike the sesquicentennial celebrations in 1969, in which the past took a back seat, the Bicentennial wholeheartedly embraced Singapore's early modern, precolonial past. Its 700 years are now a source of pride, an inspiration for a nation-state quietly confident of its people having become Singaporeans, who have overcome the emotional heartstrings that tugged at and divided them in the distant past.

Underscoring both these events was an abiding sense that as a small nation-state, Singapore remains vulnerable both to internal fissures and external developments. And this 'truth' or stricture has informed, shaped and influenced its development, over the past 700 years. Colonial Singapore grappled with the problems of managing a fast-growing port city populated by a people it admittedly did not know much about. It agonised over fiscal and financial matters: how it would pay for all the expenses that came with running a staple port, developing a naval base and mustering the defence for Imperial interests in the Far East. For Lee and his team of lieutenants, coming to terms with Singapore's deep vulnerability and overcoming its existential threats and dangers meant that it had to build a strong, cohesive, disciplined and exceptional state. Over the last fifty years or so, this meant stunning levels of economic growth, world-beating achievements in its infrastructure, deep defence capabilities, a world-leading education system, a tightly-managed political system and a people who have tacitly accepted the uneasy trade-off between a good material life and individual liberties.

Looking forward to the next fifty years to 2065 or perhaps even to its tercentennial in 2119, it is fitting to ask this question once again: Will Singapore survive? Will there be Singaporeans? Undoubtedly, as history has shown, Singapore the island will survive, barring the vagaries of global climate change. But as history has also shown, Singapore's existence in the last 700 years waxed and waned in response to regional and global developments that were mostly beyond its control. Whereas a government can indulge in long-term planning and projections, it is not realistic to expect all disruptive forces and elements to be fully anticipated. The people of Temasek did not anticipate the rise of Melaka. The British did not expect a militaristic Japan to threaten its Far Eastern interests. Merger with Malaysia failed due to communal tensions. In sum, governing Singapore is a balancing act that calls for nimbleness, agility and an element of luck.

In this account of Singapore history, the reader has been presented with narratives that at times seem complex, disparate and non-linear. This complexity that so characterises Singapore's past is one that will persist and continue to plague governments and policy-makers well into the distant future. Will Singapore be able to keep up with the seismic realignment and shifts in the global order - what if it is forced to take sides? How will it hold its people together? Will they be fractured along the lines of race, religion and inequality accelerated by the unfettered speed and virality of news on social media? Truly, only time will tell.

Bibliography

BOOKS

Ahmad, Abdullah. *Conversations with Tunku Abdul Rahman*. Marshall Cavendish Editions, 2016.

Alfanso @ G. Alphonso, and Albert Lau. *The Causeway.* National Archives of Malaysia and National Archives of Singapore, 2011.

Andaya, Barbara Watson, and Leonard Y. Andaya. *A History of Early Modern Southeast Asia: 1400 – 1800*. Cambridge University Press, 2015.

Barr, Michael D., and Carl A. Trocki. *Paths Not Taken Political Pluralism in Post-war Singapore*. NUS Press, 2008.

Barr, Michael D. *Singapore: A Modern History*. I.B. Tauris, 2019.

Bastin, John and Lim Chen Sian. *The founding of Singapore 1819: based on the private letters of Sir Stamford Raffles to the Governor-General and Commander-in-Chief in India, the Marquess of Hastings, preserved in the Bute Collection at Mount Stuart, Isle of Bute, Scotland / John Bastin ; together with a description of the earliest landward map of Singapore preserved in the Bute Collection at Mount Stewart, Isle of Bute, Scotland / Lim Chen Sian.* National Library Board, 2012.

Bastin, John. *Raffles and Hastings: Private Exchanges behind the Founding of Singapore*. Marshall Cavendish Editions, 2014.

Bastin, John. *Sir Stamford Raffles and Some of His Friends and Contemporaries: A Memoir of the Founder of Singapore*. World Scientific, 2019.

Bloodworth, Dennis. *The Tiger and the Trojan Horse*. Marshall Cavendish Editions, 2011.

Borschberg, Peter. *Jacques De Coutre's Singapore and Johor 1594 – c.1625*. NUS Press, 2015.

Borschberg, Peter. *Admiral Matelieff's Singapore and Johor, 1606 – 1616*. NUS Press, 2016.

Braddell, Roland St. John. *The Lights of Singapore*. Methuen & Co., 1934.

Braddell, Roland St. John. *The Law of the Straits Settlements: A Commentary*. Oxford University Press, 1982.

Buruma, Ian. *Year Zero*. Atlantic Books, 2013.

Cheah, Boon Kheng. *Red Star over Malaya: Resistance and Social Conflict during and after the Japanese Occupation of Malaya, 1941 – 46*. NUS Press, 2012.

Cheong, Koon Hean. *Singapore Chronicles: Public Housing*. Straits Times Press and Institute of Policy Studies, 2018.

Chew, Ernest, and Edwin Lee. *A History of Singapore*. Oxford University Press, 1991.

Chew, Melanie. *Leaders of Singapore*. World Scientific, 1996.

Chong, Terence. *Management of Success: Singapore Revisited*. ISEAS, 2010.

Chua, Beng Huat. *Liberalism Disavowed Communitarianism and State Capitalism in Singapore*. NUS Press, 2018.

Chung, May Khuen, Ong May Anne, Sim Wan Hui, Tamilselvi Siva, Jason Toh and Wong Hong Suen. *Vintage Singapore: Souvenirs from the recent past*. Editions Didier Millet, 2006.

Collingham, Elizabeth M. *The Hungry Empire: How Britain's Quest for Food Shaped the Modern World*. Vintage, 2018.

Comber, Leon. *Singapore Chronicles: Japanese Occupation*. Straits Times Press and Institute of Policy Studies, 2017.

Da Cunha, Derek. *Singapore Places its Bets: Casinos, Foreign Talent & Remaking a City State*. Straits Times Press Reference, 2010.

D'Silva, Judith, and Goh Eck Kheng. *Giving Strength to Our Nation: The SAF and Its People*. Ministry of Defence, 2015.

Dobbs, Stephen. *The Singapore River: A Social History, 1819 – 2002*. Singapore University Press, National University of Singapore, 2003.

Drysdale, John. *Singapore, Struggle for Success*. Times Books International, 1984.

Frei, Henry. *Guns of February: Ordinary Japanese Soldiers' Views of the Malayan Campaign and the Fall of Singapore 1941 – 42.* Singapore University Press, 2004.

Glendinning, Victoria. *Raffles and the Golden Opportunity 1781 – 1826*. Profile Books, 2018.

Goh, Evelyn, and Daniel Chua. *Singapore Chronicles: Diplomacy*. Straits Times Press and Institute of Policy Studies, 2015.

Goh, Keng Swee. *Report on the Ministry of Education, 1978*. Singapore National Printers, 1979.

Goh, Yong Kiat. *Where Lions Fly: 100 Years of Aviation in Singapore, 1911-2011*. Straits Times Press, 2012.

Gopinathan, Saravanan. *Singapore Chronicles: Education*. Straits Times Press and Institute of Policy Studies, 2015.

Hack, Karl. *Singapore from Temasek to the 21st Century: Reinventing the Global City*. NUS Press, 2010.

Heng, Chye Kiang, and Yeo Su-Jan. *Singapore Chronicles: Urban Planning*. Straits Times Press and Institute of Policy Studies, 2017.

Heng, Derek Thiam Soon., and Syed Muhd. Khairudin Aljunied. *Singapore in Global History*. Amsterdam University Press, 2011.

Ho, Chi Tim, and Ann Wee. *Singapore Chronicles: Social Services.* Straits Times Press and Institute of Policy Studies, 2016.

Ho, Peter. *Singapore Chronicles: Governance*. Straits Times Press and Institute of Policy Studies, 2016.

Ho, Peter. *The Challenges of Governance in a Complex World.* World Scientific, 2018.

Ho, Shu Huang, and Samuel Chan Ling Wei. *Singapore Chronicles: Defence*. Straits Times Press and Institute of Policy Studies, 2015.

Ho, Shu Huang, Graham Gerard Ong, and Morton Feldman. *National Service in Singapore*. World Scientific, 2019.

Hong, Lysa, and Huang Jianli. *Scripting of a National History: Singapore and its Pasts*. Hong Kong University Press, HKU, 2008.

Huang, Abigail, Veronica Chee, Joycelyn Lau, Justin Zhuang, and Sheere Ng. *50 Records from History: Highlights from the National Archives of Singapore.* National Archives of Singapore, National Library Board, 2019.

Huff, W. G. *The Economic Growth of Singapore: Trade and Development in the Twentieth Century*. Cambridge University Press, 2010.

Hunt, Tristram. *Ten Cities that made an Empire*. Penguin Books, 2015.

Hussin, Nordin. *Trade and Society in the Straits of Melaka: Dutch Melaka and English Penang, 1780 – 1830*. NUS Press, 2009.

Ibrahim, Zuraidah. *Singapore Chronicles: Opposition*. Straits Times Press and Institute of Policy Studies, 2016.

Kenley, David L. *New Culture in a New World: The May Fourth Movement and the Chinese Diaspora in Singapore, 1919-1932*. Routledge, 2013.

Koh, Gillian. *Singapore Chronicles: Civil Society*. Straits Times Press & Institute of Policy Studies, 2016.

Koh, Tommy, Timothy Auger, Jimmy Yap and Ng Wei Chian, (Eds.) *Singapore: The Encyclopedia*. National Heritage Board and Editions Didier Millet, 2012.

Koh, Tommy T. B., and Scott Wightman. *200 Years of Singapore and the United Kingdom*. Straits Times Press, 2019.

Kwa, Chong Guan. *Singapore Chronicles: Pre-colonial Singapore*. Straits Times Press and Institute of Policy Studies, 2017.

Kwa, Chong Guan, Peter Borschberg, Benjamin Khoo, and Xu Shengwei. *Studying Singapore before 1800*. NUS Press, 2018.

Kwa, Chong Guan, Derek Heng, Peter Borschberg, Tan Tai Yong. *Seven Hundred Years: A History of Singapore.* National Library Board and Marshall Cavendish Editions, 2019.

Kwok, Kian-Woon, and Teng Siao See. *Singapore Chronicles: Chinese*. Straits Times Press and Institute of Policy Studies, 2018.

Latif, Asad-ul Iqbal. *Lim Kim San: A builder of Singapore*. Institute of Southeast Asian Studies, 2009.

Lal, Brij V., Peter Reeves, and Rajesh Rai. *The Encyclopaedia of the Indian Diaspora*. Editions Didier Millet and National University of Singapore, 2006.

Lau, Albert. *The Malayan Union Controversy: 1942 – 1948.* Oxford University Press, 1991.

Lau, Albert. *A Moment of Anguish: Singapore in Malaysia and the Politics of Disengagement*. Times Academic Press, 1998.

Lee, Edwin. *Singapore: The Unexpected Nation*. Institute of Southeast Asian Studies, 2008.

Lee, Geok Boi. *The Syonan Years: Singapore under Japanese rule (1942 – 1945)*. National Heritage Books and Epigram, 2005.

Lee, Kuan Yew. *The Singapore Story: Memoirs of Lee Kuan Yew.* Times Editions, 1998.

Lee, Kuan Yew. *From Third World to First: The Singapore Story (1965 – 2000).* Times Editions, 2000.

Lee, Kuan Yew. *The Battle for Merger*. National Archives of Singapore, 2014.

Lee, Kuan Yew, Goh Chok Tong, and Lee Hsien Loong. *National Day Rally Speeches: 50 Years of Nationhood in Singapore, 1966-2015*. National Archives of Singapore and Cengage, 2017.

Lee, Kuan Yew, and Han Fook Kwang. *Lee Kuan Yew: The Man and His Ideas*. Times Editions, 1998.

Lee, Soo Ann. *Singapore Chronicles: Economy*. Straits Times Press & Institute of Policy Studies, 2018.

Lee, Terence, and Kevin Tan. *Change in Voting: Singapore's 2015 General Election*. Ethos Books, 2016.

Lim, Linda. *Business, Government & Labour: Essays on Economic Development in Singapore and Southeast Asia*. World Scientific, 2017.

Lim, Linda (Ed.) *Singapore's Economic Development: Retrospection & Reflections*. World Scientific, 2016.

Lim, Siong Guan. *Can Singapore Fall? Making the Future for Singapore*. World Scientific, 2018.

Liu, Gretchen. *In Granite and Chunam: The National Monuments of Singapore*. Landmark Books, 1996.

Liu, Gretchen. *Singapore: A Pictorial History*. Archipelago Press and National Heritage Board, 1999.

Loh, Kah Seng. *Squatters into Citizens: The 1961 Bukit Ho Swee Fire and the Making of Modern Singapore.* NIAS Press, 2013.

Loke, Hoe Yeong. *Let the People Have Him: Chiam See Tong: The Early Years*. Epigram Books, 2014.

Makepeace, Walter Gilbert E. Brooke and Roland St. J. Braddell. *One Hundred Years of Singapore: Being Some Account of the Capital of the Straits Settlements from Its Foundation by Sir Stamford Raffles in 6th Feb 1819 to 6th Feb 1919*. Murray, 1921.

Maritime Museum (Singapore). *Singapore Port History*. Port of Singapore Authority,1982.

Mauzy, Diane K., and R. S. Milne. *Singapore Politics under the People's Action Party*. Routledge, 2002.

Merriman, John M. *A History of Modern Europe*. W.W. Norton, 1996.

Miksic, John N., and Low Mei Gek Cheryl-Ann. *Early Singapore, 1300s-1819. Evidence in Maps, Text, and Artefacts*. Singapore History Museum, 2005.

Moore, Donald, and Joanna Moore. *The First 150 Years of Singapore*. Donald Moore Press, 1969.

Murfett, Malcolm. *Between Two Oceans: A Military History of Singapore from 1275 to 1971*. Marshall Cavendish Editions, 2011.

Ngiam, Tong Dow. *Dynamics of the Singapore Success Story*. Cengage Learning Asia, 2011.

Ooi, Kee Beng. *The Reluctant Politician: Tun Dr Ismail and His Time*. Institute of Southeast Asian Studies, 2007.

Ooi, Kee Beng. *In Lieu of Ideology: The Intellectual Biography of Goh Keng Swee*. Institute of Southeast Asian Studies, 2010.

Osterhammel, Jürgen. *The Transformation of the World: A Global History of the Nineteenth Century*. Princeton University Press, 2015.

Pan, Lynn. *The Encyclopedia of the Chinese Overseas*. Editions Didier Millet, 2006.

Peh, Shing Huei. *Tall Order: The Goh Chok Tong Story*. World Scientific. 2019.

Poh, Soo Kai, Chen Guofang, and Lysa Hong. *The 1963 Operation Coldstore in Singapore: Commemorating 50 Years*. Strategic Information and Research Development Centre, 2013.

Pruessen, Ronald W., Tan Tai Yong, and Marc Frey. *The Transformation of Southeast Asia: International Perspectives on Decolonization*. Sharpe, 2003.

Reid, Anthony. *A History of Southeast Asia: Critical Crossroads*. Wiley Blackwell, 2015.

Roff, William R. *The Origins of Malay Nationalism*. Oxford University Press, 1995.

Saw Swee Hock, *The Population of Singapore (3rd Edition)*. ISEAS, 2012.

Saw, Swee Hock. *Population Polices and Programmes in Singapore (2nd Edition)*. ISEAS, 2016.

Shashi Jayakumar, *A History of the People's Action Party, 1985-2021*, NUS Press, 2021.

Shennan, Margaret. *Out in the Midday Sun - the British in Malaya 1880-1960*. Monsoon Books, 2016.

Singh, Daljit. *Singapore: An Illustrated History*. Ministry of Culture, 1984.

Singh, Daljit (Ed.) *Southeast Asian Affairs 2004*. ISEAS, 2012.

Soon, Carol & Gillian Koh. *Civil Society & the State in Singapore*. Institute of Policy Studies, 2017.

Song Ong Siang. *One Hundred Years' History of the Chinese in Singapore*. Oxford University Press, 1984.

Takeuchi, Yoshimi, and Richard Callchman. *What Is Modernity? Writings of Takeuchi Yoshimi*. Columbia University Press, 2005.

Tan, Aileen, Laure Lau, and Joseph Grimberg. *Maritime Heritage of Singapore*. Suntree Media, 2005.

Tan, Jing Quee, Jomo K. S., and Poh Soo Kai. *Comet in Our Sky: Lim Chin Siong in History*. Strategic Information and Research Development Centre, 2015.

Tan, Kevin. *Marshall of Singapore: A Biography*. Institute of Southeast Asian Studies, 2009.

Tan, Kevin. *International Law, History & Policy: Singapore in the Early Years*. National University of Singapore – Centre for International Law, 2011.

Tan, Kevin. *An Introduction to Singapore's Constitution*. Talisman Publishing, 2014.

Tan, Kevin, and Lam Peng Er. *Lee's Lieutenants: Singapore's Old Guard*. Straits Times Press, 2018.

Tan, Kevin, and Lim Chen Sian. *Raffles' Letters: Intrigues behind the Founding of Singapore*. National Library Board, 2012.

Tan, Kevin, and Terence Lee. *Voting in Change: Politics of Singapore's 2011 General Election*. Ethos Books, 2011.

Tan, Kevin and Thio Li-Ann. *Singapore: 50 Constitutional Moments That Defined a Nation*. Marshall Cavendish Editions, 2015.

Tan, Siok Sun. *Goh Keng Swee: A Portrait*. Editions Didier Millet, 2015.

Tan, Tai Yong. *Creating Greater Malaysia: Decolonization and the Politics of Merger*. Institute of Southeast Asian Studies, 2008.

Tarling, Nicholas. *Singapore Chronicles: Colonial Singapore*. Straits Times Press and Institute of Policy Studies, 2015.

Ting, Kennie. *Singapore 1819: A Living Legacy*. Talisman Publishing, 2019.

Trocki, Carl A. *Prince of Pirates: The Temenggongs and the Development of Johor and Singapore, 1784-1885*. NUS Press, 2012.

Turnbull, Constance Mary. *The Straits Settlements, 1826 – 67: Indian Presidency to Crown Colony*. Athlone Press, 1973.

Turnbull, Constance Mary. *A History of Singapore 1819 – 1988*. Oxford University Press, 1989.

Turnbull, Constance Mary. *A History of Modern Singapore 1819 – 2005*. NUS Press, 2009.

Visscher, Sikko. *The Business of Politics and Ethnicity: A History of the Singapore Chinese Chamber of Commerce and Industry*. NUS Press, 2007.

Welsh, Bridget, James Chin, Arun Mahizhnan and Tan Tarn How (Eds.) *Impressions of the Goh Chok Tong Years in Singapore*. NUS Press, 2009.

Wheatley, Paul. *The Golden Khersonese*. University of Malaya Press, 2010.

Wright, Arnold, and H. A. Cartwright. *Twentieth Century Impressions of British Malaya: Its History, People, Commerce, Industries, and Resources*. Lloyd's Greater Britain Pub., 1908.

Wright, Nadia H. *William Farquhar and Singapore: Stepping out from Raffles' Shadow*. Entrepot Publishing, 2019.

Yap, Sonny, Richard Lim, and Weng Kam Leong. *Men in White: The Untold Story of Singapore's Ruling Political Party*. Singapore Press Holdings, 2010.

Yen, Ching-hwang. *A Social History of the Chinese in Singapore and Malaya, 1800 – 1911*. Oxford University Press, 1987.

Yeoh, Brenda S. A., and Theresa Wong. *Over Singapore 50 Years Ago an Aerial View in the 1950s*. Editions Didier Millet and National Archives of Singapore, 2007.

Yong, Ching Fatt. *Chinese Leadership and Power in Colonial Singapore*. Times Academic Press, 1994.

Yong, Ching Fatt. *The Origins of Malayan Communism*. South Seas Society, 1997.

Yong, Ching Fatt. *Tan Kah Kee: The Making of an Overseas Chinese Legend*. World Scientific, 2014.

Yong, Ching Fatt, and R. B. McKenna. *The Kuomintang Movement in British Malaya 1912-1949*. Singapore University Press, 1990.

Zaccheus, Faith Melody, and Sally Lam. *Monumental Treasures: Singapore's Heritage Icons*. Straits Times Press, 2018.

A Short History of the Port of Singapore: With Particular Reference to the Undertakings of the Singapore Harbour Board. Fraser & Neave, 1922.

Papers Presented: Seminar on Planning for Recreation. Singapore Planning and Urban Research Group, 1970.

Seminar on the Planning & Development of New Urban Centres. Singapore Planning and Urban Research Group 1969.

SPUR 65 – 67. Singapore Planning & Urban Research Group, 1967.

SPUR 68 – 71. Singapore Planning & Urban Research Group, 1971.

JOURNAL ARTICLES & PAPERS

Ball, S. J. 'Selkirk in Singapore.' *Twentieth Century British History* 10, no. 2 (January 1999): 162-91.

Borschberg, Peter. Jacques de Coutre as a Source for the Early Seventeenth-Century History of Singapore, the Johor River, and the Straits. *Journal of the Malaysian Branch of the Royal Asiatic Society* 81, no. 2 (December 2008): 71-97.

Borschberg, Peter. 'The Singapore Straits in the Latter Middle Ages and Early Modern Period (c. 13th to 17th Centuries) Facts, Fancy and Historiographical Challenges.' *Journal of Asian History* 46, no. 2 (2012): 193-224

Borschberg, Peter. 'The Dark Space of Singapore History, c.1500-1800.' *Passage* (2015).

Borschberg, Peter. 'Three Questions about Maritime Singapore, 16th – 17th Centuries.' *Ler História* 72, no. 6 (2018): 31-54.

Ching-Hwang, Yen. 'Overseas Chinese Nationalism in Singapore and Malaya 1877–1912.' *Modern Asian Studies* 16, no. 3 (July 1982): 397-425.

Chung, Ong Chit. 'The 1959 Singapore General Election.' *Journal of Southeast Asian Studies* 6, no. 1 (March 1975): 61-86.

Ee, Joyce. 'Chinese Migration to Singapore, 1896 – 1941.' *Journal of Southeast Asian History* 2, no. 1 (March 1961): 33-51.

Hayashi, Hirofumi. 'The Battle of Singapore, the Massacre of Chinese and Understanding of the Issue in Postwar Japan'. *The Asia-Pacific Journal* 7, no. 3 (July 2009).

Hussin, Nordin. 'Trading Networks of Malay Merchants and Traders in the Straits of Melaka from 1780 to 1830.' *Asian Journal of Social Science* 40, no. 1 (2012): 51-82.

Jones, Matthew. 'Creating Malaysia: Singapore Security, the Borneo Territories, and the Contours of British Policy, 1961 – 1963.' *The Journal of Imperial and Commonwealth History* 28, no. 2 (May 2000): 85-109.

Lee, Terence and Cornelius Kan. '*Blogospheric pressures in Singapore: Internet discourses and the 2006 general election.* Continuum, 23, no. 6 (2009): pp. 871-886.

Phang, Sock Yong. 'Singapore's Housing Policies: Responding to the Challenges of Economic Transitions.' *Singapore Economic Review* 60, no. 3 (2015): 1 – 25.

Miller, W. G. 'English Country Traders and Their Relations with Malay Rulers in the Late Eighteenth Century.' *Journal of the Malaysian Branch of the Royal Asiatic Society* 84, no. 1 (2011): 23-45.

Saw, Swee-Hock. 'Population Trends in Singapore, 1819–1967.' *Journal of Southeast Asian History* 10, no. 1 (January 1969): 36-49.

Tan, Ee Leong. 'The Chinese banks incorporated in Singapore & the Federation of Malaya.' *Journal of the Malayan Branch of the Royal Asiatic Society* 6, no. 1 (1928):113-139.

Tan, Kevin. 'The Evolution of Singapore's Modern Constitution: Developments from 1945 to the present-day.' *Singapore Academy of Law Journal*, (1989).

Tan, Shin Bin and Leong Ching. 'The Evolution of Public Transport Policies in Singapore.' *Lee Kuan Yew School of Public Policy* (2013).

Tan, Shin Bin and Leong Ching. 'Public Housing in Singapore: Examining Fundamental Shifts.' *Lee Kuan Yew School of Public Policy* (2014).

Wahid Jumblatt Abdullah. 'New Normal' no more: Democratic Backsliding in Singapore after 2015.' *Democratization* 27, no. 7 (2020): 1123 – 1141.

Winstedt, R.O. 'A History of Johore (1365—1895 A.D.)' *Journal of the Malayan Branch of the Royal Asiatic Society* 10, no. 3 (December 1932): 1-167.

Yong, Ching Fatt. 'Leadership and Power in the Chinese Community of Singapore during the 1930s.' *Journal of Southeast Asian Studies* 8, no. 2 (September 1977): 195-209.

Yoong, Ng Siew. 'The Chinese Protectorate in Singapore, 1877 – 1900.' *Journal of Southeast Asian History* 2, no. 1 (March 1961): 76-99.

BIBLIOGRAPHY: UNPUBLISHED WORK

Han, Ming Guang. *Collaboration during the Japanese Occupation: issues and problems focusing on the Chinese community.* Academic Exercise – Department of History, Faculty of Arts & Social Sciences, National University of Singapore, 2010.

Schenk, Ingrid J. *The State and Economic Growth in a Changing Global Political Economy: A Case Study of Singapore.* Thesis (M.A.), University of Guelph, 1995.

Stowell, Margaret. *The Port of Singapore*. Thesis (M.Sc.), University of Chicago, 1939.

Tan, Peng Hong. *Reaching a Compromise: The Deliberations of the Singapore Internal Security Council (1962 – 1963),* Academic Exercise – Department of History, Faculty of Arts & Social Sciences, National University of Singapore, 1998.

Tsai, Simon Yang-Chien. *Trading for Tea: A Study of the English East India Company's Tea Trade with China and the Related Financial Issues (1760-1833).* Doctoral thesis – School of Historical Studies, University of Leicester, 2003.

Wee, Samuel Tien Wang. *British Strategic Interests in the Straits of Malacca (1786 – 1819).* Thesis (M.A.) – Department of History, Simon Fraser University, 1992.

OFFICIAL REPORTS

Committee of the Future Economy (2017).

Committee on Singapore's Competitiveness (1998).

Report of the Economic Committee (1986).

Report of the Economic Review Committee (2003).

Report of the Economic Strategies Committee (2010.)

Report of the Public Sector Divestment Committee (February 1987).

The Strategic Economic Plan: Towards a Developed Nation (1991).

ONLINE SOURCES

Singapore Infopedia
- 1955 Legislative Assembly Singapore Election
- Albert Winsemius
- Anson Road
- Anti-Catholic Riots (1851)
- Arthur E. Percival
- Beach Road Camp
- Bilingual Policy
- Bukit Timah Railway Station
- Capitol Building
- Capitol Theatre
- Cecil Clementi
- Central Fire Station
- Chinese Post Office Riots
- Clifford Pier
- Communal riots of 1964
- Communist Party of Malaya
- Former Custom House building
- Former Kallang Airport building
- Frank Dorrington Ward
- Frank Swettenham
- Franklin Charles Gimson
- Fraser & Neave
- Fullerton Building
- Gillman Barracks
- Goh Chok Tong
- Grow More Food Campaign
- Guthrie & Co.
- Haji Ambo Sooloh
- History of urban planning in Singapore
- History of general elections in Singapore
- History of Singapore currency
- Hokkien Teochew Riots
- Iskandar Shah
- Japanese surrender
- Jek Yeun Thong
- John Fearnes Nicoll
- Joshua Benjamin Jeyaratnam
- Jurong
- Khoo Seok Wan
- King Edward VII College of Medicine
- Kreta Ayer Incident (1927)
- Laurence Nunns Guillemard
- Lee Kong Chian
- Lee Siew Choh
- Lim Boon Keng
- Lim Chin Siong
- Lim Nee Soon
- Lim Yew Hock
- Mamoru Shinozaki
- Merdeka Talks
- Merger with Malaysia
- Metrication in Singapore
- Ministry of Education
- National Loyalty Week
- Nanyang Siang Pau
- New Education System
- Operation Sook Ching
- Opium and its history in Singapore
- Paya Lebar Airport
- People's Action Party: Pre-independence years
- Peranakan (Straits Chinese) community
- Pineapple
- Port of Singapore
- Port of Singapore Authority (PSA)
- Public housing in Singapore
- Pulau Brani
- Pulau Bukom
- Raffles College
- Raffles Library and Museum (1942 – 1945)
- Railway in Singapore
- Referendum on merger with Malaysia
- Rendel Commission
- Sang Nila Utama
- Seah Liang Seah
- Sejarah Melayu (Malay Annals)
- Sembawang Naval Base
- Singapore Armed Forces Training Institute (SAFTI)
- Singapore Harbour Board (1913 – 1964)
- Singapore Improvement Trust
- Singapore Progressive Party
- Sir Robert Black
- Song Ong Siang
- Speak Mandarin Campaign
- State Development Plan
- Straits Chinese British Association
- Straits Settlements Association
- Tan Hiok Nee (Tan Yeok Nee)
- Tan Kah Kee
- Tan Sri Abdul Samad Ismail
- Tanjong Pagar
- Tanjong Pagar Railway Station
- The Chinese Protectorate
- The Straits Times
- Tiong Bahru
- Toa Payoh New Town
- Tomoyuki Yamashita
- Trams
- Urban Redevelopment Authority
- Utusan Melayu
- Vernacular education
- William A.C. Goode
- William A. Pickering
- William Farquhar

HistorySG
- 1958 State of Singapore Constitution is adopted
- 1959 Legislative Assembly General Election
- 2006 Parliamentary General Election
- Admiral Cornelis Matelieff de Jonge
- Arthur Young starts his term as Governor
- British Military Administration is established
- Chinese Immigrants Ordinance 1877 is passed

Economic Development Board is formed
Final report of the Commission of Inquiry into Education
First Parliament of the Republic of Singapore convenes
Formation of ASEAN
Gifted Education Programme is introduced
Gunseikanbu assigned to manage Japanese-occupied Singapore
Immigration Restriction Ordinance is passed
Interim report on the six-day school week is submitted
J.B. Jeyaratnam wins Anson by-election
Jacques de Coutre's memorial for fortresses in Singapore
Juan de Silva arrives in the Singapore Strait
Land Acquisition Act is enforced
Laurence Guillemard arrives in Singapore to become governor
Lee Kuan Yew declares de facto independence for Singapore
Lee Kuan Yew delivers radio talks in the battle for merger
Lim Kim San is appointed chairman of the HDB
Malayan Union is inaugurated
Malaysian Solidarity Convention is formed
Merdeka Talks – First All-Party Mission to London is Held
Merdeka Talks – Second All-Party Mission to London is Held
Merdeka Talks –Third All-Party Mission to London is Held
Ministry of Education is established
National Loyalty Week is held
New Education System (NES) is introduced
Remaking Singapore Committee is formed
Report on the Ministry of Education (Goh Report)
Shahbandar of Singapore
Singapore 21: Together we make the difference is launched
Singapore Citizenship Ordinance is passed
Singapore experiences its first post-independence recession
Singapore Harbour Board is established
Singapore in Johann Heinrich Zedler's Universal-Lexico
Singapore joins the United Nations
Singapore Labour Front is formed
Singapore's first national day
Singapore as 'Falsa Demora'
Societies Ordinance comes into force
Special Branch mounts Operation Coldstore
Sri Vijaya-Malayu
State of Singapore Act is passed
The 1603 Naval Battle of Changi
The Housing and Development Board is established
The Singapore Army is established
The Sri Bija Diraja is entrusted overlordship of Singapura
The Yuan in the Straits of Malacca
Toa Payoh is chosen as Games Village of the 7th SEAP Games
Tokubetsu Shi is set up in Japanese-occupied Singapore
Tunku announces proposal for merger
Wang Dayuan

PRESS REPORTS

'2008: Lehman collapse sparks global financial crisis.' *The Business Times*. 22 August 2016.

'A deep, dark, secret love affair.' 16 July 2004. https://www.haaretz.com/1.4758973.

'A primer on national conversations. We take a look back at the three reviews we have had before: The Next Lap in 1991, Singapore 21 in 1999, and Remaking Singapore in 2002.' *The Straits Times*, 23 August 2012.

'A strong and silent keeper of the peace.' *The Straits Times*, 1 July 2008.

'After polls come post-mortems: What went right? What went wrong? *The Straits Times*, 13 May 2006.

'Ailment in the body politic.' *The Straits Times*, 30 December 1984.

'Average workers and the productivity puzzle.' *The Straits Times*, 22 May 2015.

'Ask DPM Tharman Special.' *The Straits Times*, 23 April 2013.

'Behind the scenes at the state funeral.' *The Straits Times*, 16 May 2015.

'Beware the pitfalls of another national conversation.' 4 June 2018. https://www.todayonline.com/commentary/beware-pitfalls-another-national-conversation

'Bouncing of Tharman's trampoline.' *The Business Times*, 23 May 2015.

'C-in-Cs issue order of the day.' *The Straits Times*, 8 December 1941.

'Death of Lee Kuan Yew was most iconic Twitter moment in Singapore over past decade.' *The Straits Times*, 21 March 2016.

'Did PM help or hinder?' *The Straits Times*, 31 December 1984.

'Dr. Lee Wei Ling's eulogy to her father Lee Kuan Yew at Mandai Crematorium.' *The Straits Times*, 29 March 2015.

'Elite told: Guard the social order.' *The Straits Times*, 19 May 1971.

'Emerging Stronger Conversations: Bringing together voices to build a more resilient society.' *The Straits Times*, 28 September 2020.

'Features of Singapore base.' *The Straits Times*, 4 December 1940.

'Five-year PAP plan for Singapore.' *The Straits Times*, 26 April 1959.

'Former Singapore PM Lee Kuan Yew in hospital for severe pneumonia, now stable.' *The Straits Times*, 21 February 2017.

'Full text: five principles of Singapore's foreign policy.' *The Straits Times*, 17 July 2017.

'Future fraught with more danger.' *The Straits Times*, 15 December 1965.

'GE2015: PAP vote share increases to 69.9%, party wins 83 of 89 seats including WP-held Punggol East.' *The Straits Times*, 12 September 2011.

'Giving a lift to the upgrading debate.' *The Straits Times*, 4 May 2006.

'Henry Kissinger: The world will miss Lee Kuan Yew.' *The Washington Post*, 23 March 2015.

'In Singapore's election, the protest vote grows louder.' *The New York Times*, 7 May 2006.

'Invitations to reply to Lee on the air.' *The Straits Times*, 11 October 1961.

'Israel and Singapore: The ties that bind.' *The Jerusalem Post*, 5 January 2016.

'Japan strikes against Britain and U.S.' *The Straits Times*, 8 December 1941.

'Know your Singapore' show at Esplanade.' *The Straits Times*, 8 July 1968.

'Lee hopes for 'new quid pro quo' relationship.' *The Straits Times*, 15 December 1965.

'Lee Kuan Yew: Huge queue to view founder lying in state.' *The Straits Times*, 25 March 2015.

'Lib Socs join anti-PAP alliance.' *The Straits Times*, 7 April 1959.

'Lord Moyne's message to Singapore.' *The Straits Times*, 15 February 1942.

'Net was abuzz with politics during poll period.' *The Straits Times.* 9 May 2006.

'No escape if PAP are voted in.' *The Straits Times*, 8 May 1959.

'No more streaming for students.' *The Straits Times*, 5 March 2019.

'No Opposition – so a pledge to put everything fairly before the House.' *The Straits Times*, 15 December 1965.

'Opposition MPs boycott Singapore's first House session.' *The Straits Times*, 6 December 2015.

'PAP is trying to confuse.' *The Straits Times*, 22 December 1958.

'PAP warns Federation leaders on elections.' *The Straits Times*, 16 February 1959.

'PAP wins all but two.' *The Straits Times*, 23 December 1984.

'PM: What the results mean.' *The Straits Times*, 23 December 1984.

'Probe team told to license 'pirates.' *The Straits Times*, 6 May 1966.

'Public projects: A chance to see and comment.' *The Straits Times*, 12 August 1967.

'Ready in the Far East: Churchill avers.' *The Straits Times*, 9 December 1941.

'Regulations for guidance of Chinese Advisory Board.' *The Straits Times*, 23 December 1889.

'Remembering Lee Kuan Yew.' *The Straits Times*, 29 March 2015.

'Safety net? More like a trampoline: DPM Tharman.' *The Straits Times*, 20 May 2015.

'Singapore makes a pitch to draw the wealthy.' *The New York Times*, 26 April 2007.

'Singapore 'set to be No. 2 wealth centre in the world.' *The Straits Times*, 12 March 2013.

'Singapore Together: Redefining the national conversation.' *The Straits Times*, 14 July 2019.

'Southern Islands may be next big tourist destination.' *The Straits Times*, 28 November 2006.

'Southern Islands could be premium resort: STB.' *The Business Times*, 29 November 2006.

'Southern shores of Singapore.' *The New Paper*, 31 March 2004.

'Speaking their minds out loud.' *The Straits Times*, 1 January 1985.

'Special Branch arrest fifty people.' *The Straits Times*, 17 December 1962.

'Split vote talks fail.' *The Straits Times*, 29 May 1959.

'SPUR keeps a watching brief on things.' *The New Nation*, 24 January 1972.

'SPUR to progress.' *The Straits Times*, 6 March 1971.

'Strong Jap pressure.' *The Straits Times*, 15 February 1942.

'The Assembly is dissolved.' *The Straits Times*, 1 April 1959

'Thousands flock to N-Day celebrations.' *The Straits Times*, 4 June 1961.

'The Battle of Singapore.' *The Straits Times*, 27 February 1948.

'The future of wages in S'pore.' The Straits Times, 5 February 2013.

'The Meaning of Syonan.' *The Syonan Shimbun*, 21 February 1942.

'The missing Opposition.' *The Straits Times*, 9 December 1965.

'The Kings of Singapore.' *The Straits Times*, 26 February 1948.

'Travelling display of S'pore environment.' *The Straits Times*, 27 May 1968.

'Two main reasons for loss of support.' *The Straits Times*, 10 April 1985.

'Urban development plans by experts.' *The Straits Times*, 15 August 1967.

'Urgent Canberra plea for planes.' *The Straits Times*, 24 January 1942.

'Views on why PAP lost in Anson by-election and its lessons.' *The Straits Times*, 22 November 1981.

'What went wrong for PAP.' *The Straits Times*, 29 December 1984.

'We are all together in this war, says Governor.' *The Straits Times*, 24 January 1942.

'We're bound to win, say both Lee and Lim.' *The Straits Times*, 12 February 1959.

'Why Pang was the wrong man for the job.' *The Straits Times*, 9 November 1981.

'Why they proposed streaming in schools 40 years ago.' *The Straits Times*, 17 March 2019.

SPEECHES

'Speech by the Chief Minister, Mr. Lim Yew Hock, winding up the debate in the Legislative Assembly on Thursday, April 24, 1958.' *Singapore Government Press Statement*, JK/INFS.AP.63/58.

'Speech by the Chief Minister, Mr. Lim Yew Hock, in the Legislative Assembly on Wednesday, July 16, 1958.' INFS.JL.48/58.

'Text of speech by the Prime Minister, Mr. Lee Kuan Yew, on the merger motion at the sitting of the Legislative Assembly, on Friday, November 24, 1961.' *Singapore Government Press Statement*, MC No. 95/61.

'Text of speech by the Prime Minister, Mr. Lee Kuan Yew, at Malaysia Solidarity Day Mass Rally and March Past on the Padang on Saturday, August 31, 1963.' *Singapore Government Press Statement*, MU No. 59/63 (PM).

'Speech by Singapore's Prime Minister, Mr. Lee Kuan Yew, during the debate in the Federal Parliament on 27th May 1965, on the motion of thanks to the *Yang Di-Pertuan Agong* for his speech from the throne.'

'Speech by BG (RES) George Yong-Boon Yeo, Acting Minister for Information and the Arts, and Senior Minister of State for Foreign Affairs, at the NUSS Society Inaugural Lecture 1991 at the World Trade Centre Auditorium on Thursday, 20 June 1991 at 8 p.m. – Civil society: Between the family and the state.' *Singapore Government Press Release*, 15/JUN/03-1/91/06/20

Acknowledgements

I would like to thank Kevin Tan, my long-time mentor and friend, for challenging me to write this book and for his extensive support as editor and critic. Together with his wife Meng Lang who proof-read my drafts, he made this book possible. Their unconditional friendship reminded me of the goodness of human nature during the course of writing this book.

Kwok Kian-Woon, my other long-time mentor and friend, continues to inspire me in his own quiet manner. Years ago, he introduced the Gramscian tenet of 'pessimism of the intellect, optimism of the will' to me. To this day, it keeps me going as a writer and as a human being.

This book is the distillation of years of reading and thinking about the issues that frame Singapore's complex and textured history. In this, I have been fortunate to have been mentored by exemplary professors and historians – Albert Lau, Peter Borschberg, Kwa Chong Guan and Kevin Blackburn. Their intellectual engagement did much to hone my instincts in reading and writing history.

Thanks also goes to my publisher, Ian Pringle of Talisman Publishing, for seeing the possibilities behind this book. Janice Ng, Stephy Chee and Wong Sze Wey were a fantastic design team who translated my ideas into reality. My thanks goes to them as well.

My late teacher, Mim, was the first person to take me to task for lazy thinking, sloppy writing, and to expose me to the power of words. This book is dedicated to her memory.

Lastly, to my family and friends, thank you for being there for me. This book is yours as much as it is mine.

Image Credit

All images used in this publication are in the public domain with the exception of those listed below:

Map of Singapore: Reproduced from Dr Frédéric Durand and Dato' Richard Curtis. *Maps of Malaya and Borneo: Discovery, Statehood and Progress.* EDM, 2013.

Photograph of Tan Kah Kee. Retrieved from https://www.tkkfoundation.org.sg/biography Courtesy of the Tan Kah Kee Foundation.

Photograph of Chief Minister David Marshall: Ministry of Information and the Arts Collection, courtesy of National Archives of Singapore.

Group photograph of the visit by the Secretary of State for the Colonies, Alan Lennox-Boyd in August 1955: Ministry of Information and the Arts Collection, courtesy of the National Archives of Singapore.

President Yusof Ishak inspecting the Guard of Honour: Yusof Ishak Collection, courtesy of National Archives of Singapore.

Singapore's AMX-13 tanks at the 1969 National Day Parade: Yusof Ishak Collection, courtesy of the National Archives of Singapore.

Joshua Benjamin Jeyaratnam at the National Day Reception: Ministry of Information and the Arts Collection, courtesy of the National Archives of Singapore.